Communications in Computer and Information Science 1044

Commenced Publication in 2007
Founding and Former Series Editors:
Phoebe Chen, Alfredo Cuzzocrea, Xiaoyong Du, Orhun Kara, Ting Liu,
Krishna M. Sivalingam, Dominik Ślęzak, Takashi Washio, and Xiaokang Yang

More information about this series at http://www.springer.com/series/7899

Dennis Beck · Anasol Peña-Rios ·
Todd Ogle · Daphne Economou ·
Markos Mentzelopoulos ·
Leonel Morgado · Christian Eckhardt ·
Johanna Pirker · Roxane Koitz-Hristov ·
Jonathon Richter · Christian Gütl ·
Michael Gardner (Eds.)

Immersive Learning Research Network

5th International Conference, iLRN 2019
London, UK, June 23–27, 2019
Proceedings

 Springer

Editors
Dennis Beck
University of Arkansas
Fayetteville, AR, USA

Todd Ogle
University Libraries
Virginia Tech
Blacksburg, VA, USA

Markos Mentzelopoulos
Computer Science
University of Westminster
London, UK

Christian Eckhardt
California Polytechnic State University
San Luis Obispo, CA, USA

Roxane Koitz-Hristov
Institute for Software Technology
Graz University of Technology
Graz, Steiermark, Austria

Christian Gütl
Institute for Information Systems
and Computer Media
Graz University of Technology
Graz, Steiermark, Austria

Anasol Peña-Rios
British Telecom Research Labs
Ipswich, UK

Daphne Economou
University of Westminster
London, UK

Leonel Morgado
Universidade Aberta
Coimbra, Portugal

Johanna Pirker
Institute for Information Systems
and Computer Media
Graz University of Technology
Graz, Steiermark, Austria

Jonathon Richter
Salish Kootenai College
Pablo, MT, USA

Michael Gardner
University of Essex
Colchester, UK

ISSN 1865-0929   ISSN 1865-0937   (electronic)
Communications in Computer and Information Science
ISBN 978-3-030-23088-3   ISBN 978-3-030-23089-0   (eBook)
https://doi.org/10.1007/978-3-030-23089-0

This Springer imprint is published by the registered company Springer Nature Switzerland AG
The registered company address is: Gewerbestrasse 11, 6330 Cham, Switzerland

iLRN 2019 Preface

These are the curated works of the 5th Annual Immersive Learning Research Network, or iLRN – an international network of developers, educators, and research professionals developing and sharing the scientific, technical, and applied potential of immersive learning. iLRN seeks out, innovates, and shares the evidence for high-quality immersive learning across the disciplines. Research demonstrates that effective immersive learning experiences – those where the learner feels "situated" within an ecologically rich, digitally enhanced space requires applied fundamental knowledge in three connected bodies of expertise: computer science, game studies, and the learning sciences. This is the "fundamental DNA of every good immersive learning experience." Of course, there are myriad techniques within a host of different media and every conceivable area for application of these immersive experiences, thus, employing a wealth of knowledge that spans virtually every discipline. The Immersive Learning Research Network vision is to create a productive dialogue and co-design opportunities for computer, gaming, and learning scientists to collaborate and meaningfully connect with teachers, industry, and everyone to create and practice the use of immersive experiences of the highest quality.

One way of doing this is by hosting annual meetings of scholar-designers from across the disciplines by immersing for a week within a unique host city. Beginning in 2015 in Prague, Czech Republic, iLRN has convened in North America and Europe in respective years. These conferences support and create opportunities for iLRN members to meet and collaborate in collaborative contexts, build professional immersive learning research and development capacity, and share experiences in various practice-based and scientific tracks in a variety of formats. More than this, iLRN has become an incubator where members collaboratively develop a comprehensive research and outreach agenda encompassing the breadth and scope of learning possibilities, emerging technology capabilities, and addressing the challenges using immersive learning environments. We have an official podcast, a growing knowledge base, and ever-new network services to assist scholars and designers at various stages of their career to create and share new knowledge in this exciting, innovative, and powerful experiential learning arena.

This year, 2019, marked the 5th Annual iLRN conference, hosted at the University of Westminster in London, UK. Appropriately, this year's iLRN special call/theme was: "The Immersive City." Founded by the Romans in 43 AD along the River Thames, London is among the oldest of the world's great cities—its history spanning nearly two millennia—and one of the most cosmopolitan. By far Britain's largest metropolis, London is also the country's economic, transportation, and cultural center. The immersive learning landscape of London includes small, agile entrepreneurs as well as long-standing giants in a densely packed, information-rich concrete, digital, commerce, and arts playground and marketplace.

iLRN 2019 in London, UK, was a unique opportunity for the iLRN community to encompass the views of architects, urban planners, sustainability experts, and others focused on life and learning in the city to discuss and share the use of immersive learning environments for improving cities and people's lives. Sustainable urban living, civic engagement, generative growth, city simulations and forecasts, transportation, food, water, energy, pollution, and waste systems, sensor networks, algorithmic design, and the intersection of virtually every other technological and socioeconomic trend on the planet with respect to urban environments intertwined at iLRN 2019. Imagine if cities were designed with augmented reality, virtual reality, and cross reality in mind. Consider how immersive digital environments may be used to help people better understand and create urban spaces. Attendees of iLRN 2019 helped establish the emerging community within our network focusing on urban environments for a better tomorrow.

Like all iLRN conferences, iLRN 2019 was an important forum for immersive learning research. The call for papers resulted in over 60 research submissions from around the world. Every submission underwent a rigorous review by at least three members of the Program Committee to maintain high scientific and quality standards. The editorial board decided, based on the reviewers' comments, to accept nine full and eight long papers for the Springer proceedings, which is an acceptance rate of 28.3%. The papers are arranged into two parts of the proceedings, the main track and the special tracks. The accepted papers' authors are from Brazil, Cyprus, England (Brighton, Durham, Essex [2], London, Reading), Germany, Scotland (2) and the USA (Arkansas, California [3], Florida, Missouri, Ohio).

We would like to thank all who contributed to the success of this conference, in particular the members of the iLRN committee (and the additional reviewers) for carefully reviewing the contributions and selecting a high-quality program. Our general chair, Michael Gardner, and scientific chair, Christian Gütl did a wonderful job in organizing and coordinating the conference details. Leonel Morgado and Christian Eckhardt performed admirably as program co-chairs, handling the development of a rigorous program, and Johanna Pirker and Roxane Koitz-Hristov did the same for the special tracks. Dennis Beck, Anasol Peña-Rios, and Todd Ogle prepared this volume with care and professionalism. And of course, we would like to especially thank Daphne Economou and Markos Mentzelopoulos, iLRN 2019 local co-chairs, for taking care of the local arrangements and many other aspects in the organization of the conference.

We also need to thank the following people for their excellent work as special track co-chairs:

- Johanna Pirker, Foaad Khosmood, Kai Erenli, and Roxane Koitz-Hristov – Immersive and Engaging Educational Experiences Special Track
- Nabil Zary, Fernando Bello, and Pascal Staccini – Immersive Medical Education Special Track
- Giuliana Dettori – Self-Regulated Learning in Immersive Environments
- Catherine Cassidy, Jonathon Richter, and Alan Miller – Platforms for Digital Heritage and Preservation Special Track
- Patricia Charlton and George Magoulas – Reshaping Learning for All in Immersive Learning Environments Through Creative Learning Special Track

- Vic Callaghan, Jennifer O'Connor, Michael Gardner, Tiina Kymäläinen, Simon Egerton, Anasol Peña-Rios, Angélica Reyes, Jonathon Richter, Minjuan Wang, Jen Wu, Victor Zamudio, Shumei Zhang, and Ping Zhang – The Future of Education Special Track

We hope that you enjoy reading the content of these proceedings. We encourage you to browse the papers, reflect on the interdisciplinary connections and applications, contact the authors to continue discussions, and immerse yourself in the city – the future of urban learning with immersive technologies.

Jonathon Richter
Michael Gardner
Christian Gütl
Dennis Beck
Anasol Peña-Rios
Todd Ogle

iLRN 2019 Main Conference Preface

ILRN 2019 was the fifth annual international conference of the Immersive Learning Research Network (iLRN). It followed on from the previous edition held in Missoula in June 2018. The topic is becoming increasingly relevant as the power and affordability of suitable computers, mobile devices, network connectivity, and interface technologies have made virtual and augmented reality environments more accessible than ever before. The vision of the iLRN is to develop a comprehensive research and outreach agenda that encompasses the breadth and scope of learning potentialities, affordances, and challenges of immersive learning environments. To achieve this, the iLRN mission is to invite and organize scientists, practitioners, organizations, and innovators across the disciplines to explore, describe, and apply the optimal use of immersive worlds and environments for educational purposes. Further, the conference, meetings, and virtual symposia aim to build capacity to explain and demonstrate how these immersive learning environments best work using a variety of rigorous, systematic, and meaningful research methods and outreach strategies. To achieve this, ILRN has invited scientists, practitioners, organizations, and innovators across all disciplines to report on their research in the ILRN 2019 international conference. We received 63 papers for this event and after a rigorous reviewing process 18 were selected as full papers for this Springer publication (30% acceptance rate). The authors of these papers hail from Austria, Australia, Cyprus, England, Germany, Portugal, Saudi Arabia, Scotland, and in the United States, Arkansas, California, Florida, Ohio, and Pennsylvania.

Papers in the main conference report on the use of immersive learning environments to address a variety of educational challenges.

Jambi et al. exhibit the effects of an interactive role-play learning activity, supported within a multi-user virtual environment, on the learning process. Chehimi et al. introduce a new method that is user-driven, not researcher-driven, which adapts to the varying cognitive and physical states people go through in MR, and utilize empathy maps to capture feelings, thoughts, actions and verbal expressions from a first-person perspective. On the basis of the Educational Framework for Immersive Learning, Dengel et al. developed a research model including the factors presence, immersion, cognitive abilities, motivation, and emotion. Rhodes et al. explore the development and reception of the Virtual Time Binoculars platform – a system for delivering virtual reality (VR) heritage apps suitable for use on most smartphones, and outline the historical and technical challenges of modelling Edinburgh's sixteenth-century cityscape. Cassidy et al. review a VR framework implemented into an exhibit in three cultural heritage centers. By taking advantage of existing visitor digital literacies, the exhibit provided accessible immersive exploratory experiences for inter-generational audiences. To gain a better understanding on the role of immersive learning in regard to one's intuition on the order of magnitude and scale, Brown et al. developed a semi-tangible VR application that serves as virtual learning environment (VLE). Webb et al. investigated whether the addition of haptics (virtual touch) to a 3D VR simulation promotes understanding of key nanoscale concepts in membrane systems for students aged 12–13 by developing a virtual model of a section of the cell membrane and a haptic enabled interface that enables students to interact with the model and to manipulate objects in the model. Hadwen-Bennett et al. present an Adaptive Hypermedia Driven Serious Game based around Pask's holist-serialist dimension of cognitive style to explore the potential value of adaptive hypermedia and game-based learning. Chu et al. developed and evaluated an interactive, real-time, and real-scale VR application used to understand the theory of special relativity by conducting a user study to find correlations between their perceived immersion during and after the simulation and their acquisition of special relativity theory. Schmidt et al. present the formative design and evaluation of Virtuoso, an immersive learning intervention for adults significantly impacted by autism, consisting of two components: a spherical, video-based VR intervention, and a headset-based VR intervention. To investigate the usability of prototypes from the perspective of the end-users and their activities, Doumanis et al. describe their experiences in using a single-perspective method for gathering user requirements in the Real and Virtual Engagement In Realistic Immersive Environment project. To enrich geoscience education, Klippel et al. developed and evaluated an immersive virtual field trip in previous small-scale studies, in order to make it accessible to larger audiences. Samaroudi et al. investigated digitally fabricated replicas and how these contribute as novel interpretative means to support visitor experiences in cultural heritage contexts by evaluate the experience that visually impaired users had with a 3D printed relief of a Victorian environmental display, or diorama, from the Booth Museum of Natural History in Brighton (UK) along with a pervasive audio mobile application. Alsaqqaf et al. aim to provide a conceptual framework to facilitate the designing of virtual field trip games, since there is a need for an alternative way to provide learners with rich field trip and fieldwork experience. Extending prior research in game-based learning, Georgiou et al. investigated children's immersion in a high-embodied digital learning game integrated in an authentic school classroom, in comparison with a low-embodied digital version of the game. Longford et al. outline the results of a Modified System for the Multiple Level Observation of Groups analysis for group formation, structure and interactions by discussing why groups can be beneficial to student learning in education, but also how misusing groups has negative effects. Osking et al. state and evaluate the hypothesis, that dialogue control systems used in VR experiences are often adapted from older media, therefore a voice control dialogue system may preserve this illusion and thereby enhance the emotional impact of narrative experiences.

We hope you will find this collection of papers informative and engaging. We encourage you to join ILRN and participate in future events.

Leonel Morgado
Christian Eckhardt
iLRN 2019 Main Conference Programme Co-chairs

Special Tracks Preface

Immersive digital learning is a continuously growing research area that has made a considerable impact during the past few years. Yet, a grand challenge and opportunity of this complex and expanding research area lie in the topic's interdisciplinary and expansive nature. Immersive learning comprises various disciplines per se and hence fosters collaboration between specialists from different fields and areas of expertise. After our successful experiences at iLRN 2015, we have continued to organize special tracks as a way to unite experts from numerous disciplines to exchange ideas and research insights in focused areas.

This year, we again invited scientist and practitioners from various research fields to submit tracks on different areas of immersive learning. iLRN 2019 hosted two special tracks covering the following topics:

- The track "Platforms for Digital Heritage and Preservation" chaired by Catherine Cassidy from the University of St. Andrews, Jonathon Richter from Salish Kootenai College, as well as Alan Miller from Smart History aimed at technology, such as platforms or frameworks, that enables current and future opportunities in digital heritage.
- In the track "Immersive and Engaging Educational Experiences," the track chairs, Johanna Pirker from Graz University of Technology, Foaad Khosmood from California Polytechnic State University, Kai Erenli from University of Applied Science BFI Vienna and Roxane Koitz-Hristov, Graz University of Technology, invited participants to discuss the potential of immersive and engaging learning environments as teaching and training tools.

For the special tracks, 16 submissions were received, of which six were chosen as full papers to be published in the Springer proceedings, for an overall acceptance rate of 37.5%.

We would like express our sincere thanks to all special track chairs and reviewers for their commitment; the high-quality research and presentations of the special tracks on different research topics in immersive learning are a vital part of the conference. Hence, we thank each individual who worked toward making the special tracks this integral part of the main conference.

Johanna Pirker
Roxane Koitz-Hristov

Organization

General Chair

Michael Gardner   University of Essex, UK

Scientific Chair

Christian Gütl   Graz University of Technology, Austria

Engagement Chair

Jonathon Richter   Salish Kootenai College, USA

Program Co-chairs

Leonel Caseiro Morgado   Universidade Aberta, Portugal
Christian Eckhardt   California Polytechnic State University, USA

Special Track Co-chairs

Johanna Pirker   Graz University of Technology, Austria
Roxane Koitz-Hristov   Graz University of Technology, Austria

Workshops Co-chairs

Foaad Khosmood   California Polytechnic State University, USA
Christian Eckhardt   California Polytechnic State University, USA

Poster and Demo Track Chair

Drew Cattanach   University of Westminster, UK

Industry Track Chair

Jeffrey Ferguson   University of Westminster, UK

Partnerships, Sponsorships and Outreach Chair

Mark J. W. Lee   Charles Sturt University, Australia

Finance Director

Patrick O'Shea   Appalachian State University, USA

Publicity and Public Relations Co-directors

Anasol Peña-Rios   British Telecom, UK
Katya Alvarez-Molina   Universität Bremen, Germany

Publications Co-chairs

Dennis Beck   University of Arkansas, USA
Anasol Peña-Rios   British Telecom, UK
Todd Ogle   Virginia Tech, USA

Conference Registration Chair

Matthew Hollick   University of Westminster, UK

Submission Systems Director

Johanna Pirker   Graz University of Technology, Austria

Website Director

Anasol Peña-Rios   British Telecom, UK

Local Co-chairs

Daphne Economou   University of Westminster, UK
Markos Mentzelopoulos   University of Westminster, UK

North America Co-chairs

Krzysztof Pietroszek   American University Washington DC, USA
Chris Dede   Harvard University, USA
Minjuan Wang   San Diego State University, USA
Kurt Squire   UC-Irvine, USA
Mina Johnson-Glenberg   Arizona State University, USA

Latin America Chair

Victor Manuel Zamudio   Instituto Tecnológico de León, Mexico
   Rodríguez

South America Co-chairs

Andreas Pester   Carinthia University of Applied Sciences, Austria
Roger Tavares   UFRN, Brazil
Eliane Schlemmer   UNISINOS, Brazil

Asia Pacific Co-chairs

Yiyu Cai   Nanyang Technological University, Singapore
Mark J. W. Lee   Charles Sturt University, Australia

Europe Co-chairs

Ralf Klamma   RWTH Aachen University, Germany
Fotis Liarokapis   Masaryk University, Czech Republic

Middle East Co-chairs

Mohammad Al-Smadi   Jordan University of Science and Technology, Irbid,
                          Jordan
Samir Abou El-Seoud   The British University in Egypt
Hanan Gazit   Juloot Interactive and IDC Herzliya, Israel

Program Committee

Alexander Nussbaumer   Graz University of Technology, Austria
Alexandra Gago Da Câmara   Universidade Aberta, Portugal
Allan Fowler   Kennesaw State University, USA
Alok Mishra   Atilim University, Turkey
Ana Isabel Veloso   University of Aveiro, Portugal
Anasol Peña-Rios   British Telecom, UK
Andreas Pester   Carinthia University of Applied Sciences, Austria
Andreas Schmeil   University of Lugano, Switzerland
Angela Fessl   Know-Center Graz, Austria
António Coelho   University of Porto, Portugal
Brenda Bannan   George Mason University, USA
Britte Cheng   Menlo Education Research, USA
Bruno Joho   Lucerne University of Applied Science and Arts,
                              Switzerland
Bushra Zaineb   San Diego State University, USA
Chris Dede   Harvard, USA
Christian Eckhardt   California Polytechnic State University, USA
Christian Gütl   Graz University of Technology, Austria
Claudio Brito   COPEC, Brazil
Colin Allison   University of St. Andrews, UK
Dai Griffiths   University of Bolton, UK

Max North	Southern Polytechnic State University, USA
Michael Gardner	University of Essex, UK
Michael Kickmeier-Rust	Graz University of Technology, Austria
Michael Thomas	University of Central Lancashire, UK
Mikhail Fominykh	Independent researcher
Mina Johnson-Glenberg	Mina Arizona State University, USA
Minjuan Wang	San Diego State University, USA
Mohammad Al-Smadi	Jordan University of Science and Technology, Jordan
Monique Janneck	Fachhochschule Lübeck, Germany
Patrick O'Shea	Appalachian State University, USA
Pedro Santos	University of Lisbon, Portugal
Pedro Veiga	Universidad de Aberta, Portugal
Puneet Sharma	Arctic University of Norway, Norway
Ralf Klamma	RWTH Aachen University, Germany
Riccardo Berta	Università degli Studi di Genova, Italy
Roger Tavares	Federal University of Rio Grande do Norte, Brazil
Roland Klemke	Open University of the Netherlands, The Netherlands
Roxane Koitz-Hristov	Graz University of Technology, Austria
Ryan Locke	Abertay University, UK
Samir Abou El-Seoud	The British University in Egypt
Sean Hauze	San Diego State University, USA
Stephanie Linek	ZBW Leibniz Information Centre for Economics, Germany
Styliani Kleanthous	University of Cyprus, Cyprus
Stylianos Mystakidis	University of Patras, Greece
Todd Ogle	Virginia Tech, USA
Victor Manuel Zamudio Rodríguez	Instituto Tecnológico de León, Mexico
Volker Settgast	Fraunhofer Austria Research GmbH, Austria
Wafa Bourkhis	University of Artois, France and University of Tunis, Tunisia
Yiyu Cai	Nanyang Technological University, Singapore

Special Track on Platforms for Digital Heritage and Preservation

Special Track Chairs

Catherine Cassidy	University of St. Andrews, UK
Jonathon Richter	Salish Kootenai College, USA
Alan Miller	Smart History

Program Committee

Christian Echhardt	California Polytechnic State University, USA
Catherine Cassidy	University of St. Andrews, UK
Suzanne Francis-Brown	University of the West Indies (UWI) Museum, Jamaica
Johanna Pirker	Graz University of Technology, Austria
Alissandra Cummins	Barbados Museum and Historical Society, Barbados
Natalie McGuire	Barbados Museum and Historical Society, Barbados
Niall McShane	Ulster University, Ireland
Leonel Morgado	Universidade Aberta, Portugal
Anna Vermehren	Museum Nord, Norway
Jo Vergunst	University of Aberdeen, UK
Craig Vezina	Z School, UK
Nicole Meehan	University of St. Andrews, UK
David Strachan	Perth and Kinross Heritage Trust, UK
Jonathon Richter	Salish Kootenai College, USA
Karin Weil	Universidad Austral de Chile, Chile
Liz Falconer	Bournemouth University, UK
David Caldwell	Diebold Nixdorf
Alan Miller	University of St. Andrews, UK

Special Track on Immersive and Engaging Educational Experiences

Special Track Chairs

Johanna Pirker	Graz University of Technology, Austria
Foaad Khosmood	California Polytechnic State University, USA
Kai Erenli	University of Applied Science BFI Vienna, Austria
Roxane Koitz-Hristov	Graz University of Technology, Austria

Program Committee

Allan Fowler	Kennesaw State University, USA
Brian Mcdonald	Glasgow Caledonian University, UK
Dominic Kao	Massachusetts Institute of Technology, USA
Ryan Locke	Abertay University, UK
Volker Settgast	Fraunhofer Austria, Austria
Kai Erenli	University of Applied Sciences BFI Vienna, Austria
Zoë J. Wood	California Polytechnic State University, USA
Britte H. Cheng	SRI International, USA
Helen Wauck	University of Illinois Urbana-Champaign, USA
Guenter Wallner	University of Applied Arts Vienna, Austria

Special Session on Research in Progress

Special Session Chairs

Michael Gardner	University of Essex, UK
Daphne Economou	University of Westminster, UK

Sponsor

Graz University of Technology, Institute for Information Systems and Computer Media

Contents

Pedagogical Strategies

Immersion and Presence

Science, Technology, Engineering, and Mathematics (STEM)

Immersive Learning in the Wild: A Progress Report

Alexander Klippel[1]([✉]), Danielle Oprean[2], Jiayan Zhao[1], Jan Oliver Wallgrün[1],
Peter LaFemina[3], Kathy Jackson[4], and Elise Gowen[5]

[1] Department of Geography, The Pennsylvania State University, State College, USA
klippel@psu.edu
[2] School of Information Science and Learning Technologies,
University of Missouri, Columbia, USA
[3] Department of Geosciences, The Pennsylvania State University, State College, USA
[4] Teaching and Learning with Technology,
The Pennsylvania State University, State College, USA
[5] Fletcher L. Byrom Earth and Mineral Sciences Library,
The Pennsylvania State University, State College, USA

Abstract. Immersive technologies have entered the mainstream. To establish them firmly in educational curricula requires both practical and empirical assessments that ultimately lead to best practice and design recommendations. We report on a study that contributes to both. To enrich geoscience education, we developed an immersive virtual field trip (iVFT) that we evaluated in previous small-scale studies. In order to make it accessible to larger audiences we (a) developed a version of the iVFT for mobile devices (Oculus Go); and (b) used an evolving public VR infrastructure at The Pennsylvania State University. The results of an empirical evaluation are insightful in that they show that system characteristics are only partially predicting learning experiences and that required mainstream adoption, that is, making immersive experiences mandatory for all students in a class, still has its challenges. We discuss the results and future developments.

Keywords: Virtual field trips · SENSATIUM ·
Earth science education

1 Introduction

Immersive technologies have entered the mainstream. The historically wavelike development of excitement and rejection of immersive technologies [8] appears to have finally come to an end with the newest advancements (e.g., reducing cybersickness) and the computational infrastructure (e.g., affordable mobile solutions and high end solutions being installed in semi-public facilities). While some people still doubt that immersive technologies can be a medium of mass communication, there are many indicators telling a different story by illustrating strong

D. Beck et al. (Eds.): iLRN 2019, CCIS 1044, pp. 3–15, 2019.
https://doi.org/10.1007/978-3-030-23089-0_1

investments and the steadily rising number of users particularly in gaming and simulations [15].

The adoption of immersive technologies and associated experiences into classrooms and training is on its way, too [1,9]. As we are still on the verge of creating opportunities, infrastructure, and empirical evidence on the effectiveness of immersive learning experiences at scale (i.e., for the masses), we report here on an ongoing university-wide project catering to all three aspects: opportunities, infrastructure, and empirical evaluations. The focus of this project is immersive virtual field trips for earth sciences (geosciences and biology), but many of its elements are relevant for immersive learning in general. The project aims for a mainstream adoption of immersive learning environments and experiences into the day-to-day learning portfolio of instructors and students. We detail a number of critical ingredients of this ongoing project including the growing publicly accessible infrastructure, the design of immersive experiences at scale, and empirical validation and assessment of the learning experiences to evaluate design choices. We discuss a framework we developed for advancing the learning experience and ultimately the pedagogy of immersive virtual field trips. We then focus on a concrete immersive virtual field trip experience we developed in this context and report on a recent experiment we conducted with this experience yielding some rather unexpected results. The paper concludes with a discussion of critical future developments and challenges.

2   The Research Framework

Immersive virtual field trips (iVFTs) hold the promise to deliver access almost independent of space and time. Moving immersive learning into publicly accessible infrastructure is an important focus of our work as it allows for taking research teams out of the picture and testing immersive experiences accessible to all faculty and students in the future. In the studies reported in this paper, we used four locations: three locations (e.g., libraries) with dedicated VR spaces featuring HTC Vive systems[1] and one larger laboratory equipped with swivel chairs for mobile VR experiences (e.g., delivered though Oculus Gos[2] with the potential for delivery through other mobile devices).

Our research framework, guiding both our scaling efforts and empirical evaluations, has two main parts and is evolving (see [11]). First, we generally characterize the learning experience based on the kind of information and access the virtual field trip allows. This characterization is referred to as the virtual field trip taxonomy [10]. In a nutshell, we differentiate between *basic*, *plus*, and *advanced* iVFTs. Basic iVFTs replicate physical reality. Plus iVFTs allow for perspectives on physical reality not possible at the actual field site (e.g., drone images, 360° images collected on tall monopods, and comparison of spatially remote sites); however, the content still reflects actual physical field sites. Advanced iVFTs

---

[1] https://www.vive.com/us/product/vive-virtual-reality-system/.

[2] https://www.oculus.com/go/.

include simulations and models that go beyond capturing physical reality. Examples include looking under the hood of outcrops or simulating the genesis of a rock formation going back millions of years.

The second dimension in our framework focuses on immersive systems (referred to as xR systems in the following). We organize them along SENSATIUM, the SENsing-ScAlability Trade-off contInuUM (see Fig. 1, [11]). SENSATIUM reflects the sensing capabilities of different xR systems and associated costs. Greater sensing can be useful for creating more enriching experiences, producing a finer classification of different learning experiences, and understanding how and what types of interactions best facilitate learning. Yet, greater sensing comes at the cost of scalability (i.e., accessibility to fewer learners). Using SENSATIUM allows us to assess how much is gained by adding a more comprehensive portfolio of sensors to immersive learning environments and to describe what opportunities for adaptation are possible at which point in the continuum. In a nutshell, on the lower sensing side of the continuum we have xR systems such as the Oculus Go. These stand-alone headsets at the entry level (about $200) offer limited interactivity and capabilities for sensing human behavior, both actual and virtual. They allow for tracking rotational head movements but not translation. One step up, are systems like the HTC Vive which allows for room scale tracking of (physical) human movements. The standard Vive allows for both head and controller tracking to record advanced interactions and body movements. On the higher end of the continuum are systems like the Vive supplemented by both body and eye tracking. The basic version of body tracking requires Vive body trackers fixed to user feet, torso, and upper arms. This combination allows for a sophisticated recording of user interaction and behavior in an immersive learning environment.

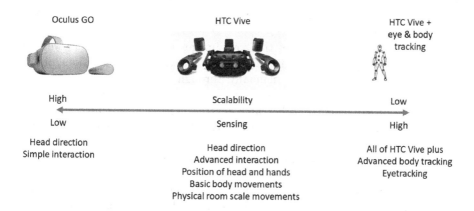

Fig. 1. SENSATIUM, the SENsing-ScAlability Trade-off contInuUM. (Source: [11]).

We combined these two dimensions into a research framework we recently presented at a workshop [11]. We advanced the framework over the course of three consecutive semesters running studies with nearly 150 participants. For this paper, in particular, we focus on a new study conducted in the fall of 2018, using the entire breadth of infrastructure available at the main campus of Penn State while specifically addressing practical questions of rolling out immersive experiences for entire courses. We also address questions along SENSATIUM, specifically the use of entry level, mobile VR systems (Oculus Go) in comparison to high-end consumer systems such as the Vive.

3   Evaluating Immersive Learning Experiences

3.1   Design

We briefly describe the main elements of the immersive virtual field trip (iVFT) we developed for the mentioned studies. A more in-depth description is available in [10]. This iVFT leads students to the Reedsville and Bald Eagle geologic formations accessible through an outcrop about 12 miles from Penn State. The iVFT is based on an actual field trip that is part of an introductory Geoscience course at Penn State. We used a combination of 360° images and structure-from-motion photogrammetry to capture the field site digitally. In our first studies, we used Unity3D[3] with an HTC Vive to realize an immersive, interactive experience; for the current paper, we additionally developed a mobile VR experience delivered through Oculus Gos. We give a brief overview of the materials we created and describe the differences between Vive and Go experiences.

The primary place-exploration is realized through high-resolution 360° images taken with a Panono camera with 108 K resolution. We collected 360° images not only at ground-level, but also at the height of 27' using a megamast (tripod). Such elevated views offer access to perspectives not available from ground level, increasing observations which often are critical to understanding an environment [19].

Despite the high-resolution of the 360° images used in this iVFT, we still enhanced students access to essential details of the outcrop and additional information usually found in the field manually, through interactive markers embedded in the 360° images, and higher resolution photographs. Students accessed this information using a controller and clicking a marker. Figure 2 shows an example of such additional information: a red box (marker) embedded into a 360° image. Upon selecting the marker, students saw a high-resolution image taken with a DSLR camera (Nikon D7200) and a diagram illustrating the formation mechanism of cross-bedding on the sandstone (Source: [13, slide 41]).

While 360° images are an efficient way to create immersive experiences allowing for some interactivity, many aspects of why field trips are used in earth science education require advanced interactivity offered only through 3D models. To allow students to perform the same activities virtually as in an actual field trip, we used structure-from-motion techniques [2] for parts of the outcrop and

---

[3] https://unity3d.com/.

Fig. 2. Example providing higher-resolution images embedded in the 360° images, and integrating additional content. A red marker in a 360° image (left) indicates the availability of additional information; here, a high-resolution DSLR image and a cross-bedding diagram (Source: [13, slide 41]).

created a 3D model of the Reedsville formation. Figure 3 (top left) provides some detail. At the actual outcrop students measure the thickness of layers along a section of the outcrop (location 6, see Fig. 4), while noting changes in lithology and grain size. The students used these observations to construct a stratigraphic column of a turbidite sequence, within the Reedsville formation. Students in the iVFT are able to change the ruler length and place it onto the outcrop surface to measure thickness of rock layers mimicking measuring activities at the actual site (Fig. 3, top right). The students first do a training exercise to learn to use the measurement tool. A data board, which displayed the set of measured widths, allowed students to review, organize and edit the data they collected (Fig. 3, bottom). The thickness data along with a screenshot of the outcrop model were sent to students after the experiment so that they could complete the official lab assignment, creating a stratigraphic column.

Figure 4 provides an overview of the Reedsville-Bald Eagle field site in the form of an aerial image. The numbers indicate locations where we took high-resolution 360° images. Locations indicated by yellow numbers allow users to experience the outcrop from an elevated perspective (27'). Locations with a white circle offered audio information. The blue arrow shows the location at which students measured the stratigraphy by accessing the 3D model (see also Fig. 3).

All this information was integrated into one scene in Unity3D. Furthermore the users were able to navigate between locations in the scene by following a predefined sequence of arrows using teleportation. The sequence of arrows were made available in a specific order resembling the storyline of the actual field trip. At the end of the experience, the users were provided with the opportunity to freely explore the virtual site, during which all the arrows representing different navigation points were made available at once. The opportunity to access the elevated perspective and return to the ground were indicated through red circles (something we may make more subtle in the future). When looking straight up or down, participants would see these circles at locations shown in Fig. 4. Clicking on a circle would switch a participant's perspective from ground to elevated and vice versa.

Fig. 3. Shown is an example of a 3D model created for parts of the Reedsville and Bald Eagle formations. Top left shows the outcrop model with an indication of where students were to measure. Bottom left shows a close-up of the outcrop model with the ruler tool used on top of an HTC Vive controller. Bottom right shows the virtual board where measurements are recorded and deleted. Top right shows a student performing the measurement. This material can be accessed on [10] for more information and interactivity.

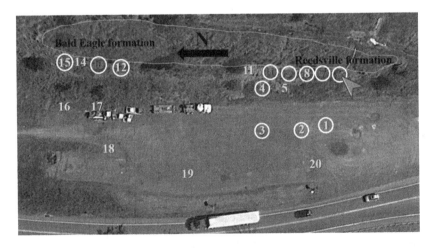

Fig. 4. Aerial image of the actual study area. We took 360° images from 20 locations. In contrast to our earlier study, we used high-resolution 360° imagery and included 15 elevated 360° images at 27' using a megamast (yellow numbers). 12 locations had audio guidance (white circles). Location 6 was the entry to a 3D model of the outcrop for measuring the stratigraphy (blue arrow). (Source: Google Maps) (Color figure online)

3.2 The Experimental Setup for the Oculus Go Condition (Compared to the Vive Version)

The VR-setup for the GO condition used a standalone Oculus Go head-mounted display with its synchronized handheld controller offering 3DOF orientation tracking and a field of view of 101° at a resolution of 2560 × 1440 pixels [14]. The virtual content rendered using the Unity3D game engine with an update rate of 60 Hz. The most substantial component was the measuring task. In contrast to our Vive version, users could walk around to operate a virtual ruler attached to his/her hand controller in 6DOF; the GO users were placed in front of the outcrop model. To generate length data, the user pointed a laser from the tip of the handheld controller to the outcrop model and pressed the touchpad to draw nodes on the rock surface. Each pair of nodes was connected by a straight line segment for length computation (Fig. 5, top).

Additionally, instead of allowing students to move around freely, they were seated in swivel chairs allowing them to turn their heads and bodies to perceive vestibular feedback (Fig. 5, bottom).

Fig. 5. Top: A student using the remote controller of the Oculus Go to perform the measurement. Bottom: 4+ students in the same lab session using Oculus Gos to experience the virtual field trip.

3.3 Participants

An important aspect in contrast to previous studies was that all students in the class (76) were required to participate in the iVFT because road construction turned the actual field site into a blast zone. Of these 76 students, 44 agreed to participate in this study and provided consent. 19 students used the Oculus Go (average age: 19.95, 6 female), 25 students used the HTC Vive (average age: 19.76, 10 female). Participation was encouraged and students were entered in a raffle for four creamery/food vouchers.

3.4 Procedure

The procedure to sign-up was different for the Vive and GO as three locations were equipped with HTC Vives (see Sect. 2) and one with GOs. Sign-ups for the Vive locations in the libraries ran through the libraries' space booking web platform. Students signed up for a time-slot 24 hours in advance. Upon arrival, they were greeted by a library employee who spent roughly five minutes orienting students to the VR equipment and how to access the field trip. Sign-up for the GO experience, however, was organized through a web-based calendar and up to six students could participate simultaneously. The iVFT experience lasted approximately 35 min for each individual session in both Vive and GO conditions (see Sects. 3.1 and 3.2 for review).

Before and after the iVFT, students were asked self-report and open-ended questions about spatial abilities, as well as their attitude and opinions toward the field trip experience. Lastly, students were asked to complete the lab assignment through the general class assignment system. More details can be found in Table 1 from the complementary documents[4].

4 Analysis and Results

Table 1 from the complementary documents describes the variables and instruments in detail. We first compared individual differences assessed through the Santa Barbara Sense of Direction (SBSOD) test and a technology enjoyment questionnaire. While there were no statistically significant differences in the latter, we found a significant difference in the sense of direction in favor of the GO users (GO: $M = 3.77$, $SD = .43$; Vive: $M = 3.19$, $SD = .67$), $t(41.0) = 3.49$, $p = .001$.

Next, we looked at student expectations with respect to their iVFT experience. While there was overall reasonable excitement about the experience, partially for practical reasons such as no travel, there was also a higher number of students not looking forward to using iVFT (28% in the Vive versus 10% in the GO). A chi-square test of independence to determine the relation between group and iVFT expectation showed no significant differences, $X^2(4, N = 44) = 5.01$, $p = .29$.

---

[4] https://sites.psu.edu/chorophronesis/files/2019/04/ILRN_Table1-szzgal.pdf.

We evaluated the learning experience based on subjective learning assessments as well as actual lab grades. In both cases, we found significant differences. Students using the GO assessed the quality of their learning experience significantly higher than Vive users (GO: $M = 3.47$, $SD = 1.02$; Vive: $M = 2.76$, $SD = 1.13$), $t(40.7) = 2.20$, $p = .03$. Students using the GO also received significantly higher lab grades than Vive users after removing outliers[5] (GO: $M = 23.63$, $SD = 0.99$; Vive: $M = 22.88$, $SD = 1.09$), $t(33.99) = 2.16$, $p = .04$.

Our enjoyment analysis centered on questions laid out in Table 1 from the complementary documents. In our comparison of GO and Vive users, there were no statistically significant differences (GO: $M = 3.54$, $SD = 1.07$; Vive: $M = 3.08$, $SD = .98$), $t(36.9) = 1.48$, $p = .15$.

From the media effects perspective, we were interested in users spatial situation model (SSM) as a critical component in place-based learning [17,18]. Comparing answers to the questions detailed in Table 1 from the complementary documents, we found no statistically significant differences between GO and Vive users (GO: $M = 3.65$, $SD = .71$; Vive: $M = 3.39$, $SD = .56$), $t(33.7) = 1.34$, $p = .19$.

As detailed in Sect. 2, GO and Vive have different systems characteristics. We therefore added questions on the usability of both systems, addressing aspects of simulator sickness (SS) and system evaluation (SE). None showed statistically significant differences between GO and Vive. Looking into ease of use, we found GO users provided a significantly more positive assessment (GO: $M = 4.34$, $SD = .87$; Vive: $M = 3.76$, $SD = .99$), $t(41.1) = 2.07$, $p = .04$.

We additionally evaluated the open-ended responses to identify the students' perspective towards the iVFT experience based on the device used. This analysis focused on developing codes to identify any differences between the Oculus Go and HTC Vive.

We used the hybrid inductive/deductive coding process described in [5] using the four questions from Table 1 from the complementary documents to structure the analysis. The researchers previously developed codes included in results from earlier studies [10] to provide the deductive list (Table 2 from the complementary documents[6]). Three individuals, two independent of the study, coded the data separately. Three consensus meetings enabled grouping and forming new codes. We validated the coding with Fleiss Kappa, for three independent coders, using a kappa of 0.8 or above as achieving consensus [16]. Using the Fleiss Kappa calculator [7], we calculated Kappa for five groups of codes by device.

Little differentiation between the two devices were observed in the responses. The key area students liked best were the ability to interact with the content and being able to access multiple forms of information at the same time. The students disliked the image quality, oftentimes also complaining of lack of features. One small difference, however, was the number of issues with discomfort

---

[5] The lab grades of two students in the GO condition and four students in the Vive condition were outside 1.5 times the interquartile range above the upper quartile and bellow the lower quartile. They were therefore excluded from the analysis.
[6] https://sites.psu.edu/chorophronesis/files/2019/04/ILRN_Table2-1axi8ar.pdf.

for the HTC Vive over the Oculus Go. The most identified benefit of using iVFTs was convenience. Lastly, two main ideas emerged as to what could be changed: added/improved interaction with the virtual content and improved image quality.

5   Discussion

The results, simply put, were rather different from our expectations and hypotheses. When we ported the iVFT experience to the GO, which sits much lower on SENSATIUM, we expected the values of our evaluation metric to be lower, that is, less positive in comparison to the Vive. There were simple objective characteristics of the GO that were nowhere near as sophisticated as the Vive. We discuss the results below, offering some additional insights into why the differences seem to be in direct contrast to our expectations.

While there were no differences in technology enjoyment, we did find statistically significant differences between the two test groups with regard to individual differences on the spatial ability (SBSOD scores). Whether or not these differences contribute to the results below is an important question that we cannot answer conclusively as there are a number of factors that contribute to the results. If anything, it is in contrast to recent findings that show users with low spatial abilities benefit from immersive learning experiences (e.g., [12]). In our evaluation, we find the group with lower spatial abilities also had reduced experiences. A current limitation, however, is we are not focusing on performance measures.

Going through the analysis, we found the Vive did not outperform the GO and that, if anything, the GO experience was favored by the students. As indicated above, even on metrics such as display fidelity and usability, where we—based on the system characteristics—expected advantages for the Vive but were proven wrong.

As described earlier in the paper and alluded to in the title, this study is conducted in the wild with an emerging but certainly not yet perfect infrastructure. It was also the first time that a class collectively participated in an immersive experience rather than participants being recruited on a volunteer basis. Taking all these aspects together, there are a number of possible explanations for our results: students for the first time had to use an infrastructure that does not provide a one-on-one experience with direct supervision by an experimenter knowledgeable about the experience. While this is true for the Vive students who signed up for public VR spaces; it is, in contrast, not the case for the GO users. As the GO experience is our most recent development, a team member supervised the experience to ensure everything went smoothly. While students did not comment on this aspect in the open-ended questions (see Table 1 from the complementary documents), it aligns with the many criticisms of virtual experiences that they are essentially individualized, not group experiences. While the experimenter is not technically part of the group, it might still factor into the overall experience. By contrast, while students using the Vive in the libraries were given an orientation at the beginning of their session and invited to ask for help if they encountered problems, students completed the bulk of the field trip alone in the VR room. The awe [3] that many first time users experience might have turned into the feeling of being lost without continuous guidance. This perspective is one aspect we are working on both practically and theoretically. Practically, we are working with the public VR spaces to insure students are guided and trained to deliver an optimal experience. Theoretically, we are working on experiences as part of an entire course which will allow for testing students' changing attitude towards immersive experiences when they participate in multiple ones. There were individual differences both in terms of students' spatial abilities but also in their attitude. There was a substantial number of students who were rather skeptical about the immersive experience in the Vive condition, which may have impacted our findings. This aspect deserves more attention and ideally a follow-up study with a larger participant pool allowing for better control of students' individual characteristics.

This last aspect might also explain the rather stark differences to our previous two studies. In studies where students participated on a voluntary basis, we found that all metrics comparing iVFT using an HTC Vive and actual field trip are in favor of the immersive experience. Compared to previous experiences and results, we find that quality of the learning experience overall is rated significantly different, $F(3, 82) = 11.61$, $p < .001$, $\eta_p^2 = .30$. A Tukey HSD test indicates that Vive participants in the current study (Fall 2018; $M = 2.76$, $SD = 1.13$) rated their learning experiences significantly lower than those in both Spring 2018 ($M = 4.3$, $SD = .97$; $p < .001$) and Fall 2017 ($M = 4.16$, $SD = .83$; $p < .001$).

Students' open-ended responses support the findings, showing little difference between the Oculus Go and Vive conditions. Overall, students placed focus on the qualities of the technology and less on the actual content of the trip. This technology-centric perspective overshadows any emergent ideas of information comprehension and positive perspective towards virtual field trips, where responses often noted concern for remembering content versus the usefulness of elevated views. Positive outlooks towards the potential of virtual field trips centered on the ideas of saving time, money, and enabling everyone access to the experience.

Lessons learned: (1) Immersive learning, like any other aspect of learning, is complex. In our particular case, we find the outcome of a learning experience is not exclusively determined by the system characteristics of a learning environment but by the learning environment holistically. (2) We are in dire need of large-scale studies on immersive learning. (3) Immersive learning experiences may not be for everyone.

6   Conclusions and Outlook

Immersive learning requires both basic research and studies in the wild. While the results of our first scaled experience were not what we expected, the lessons we learned and shared are valuable in understanding some substantial issues in scaling immersive learning experiences.

What our study shows is that it is not as simple as improving system characteristics, that is, just because the Vive has, on every measure, superior qualities compared to the GO, it does not automatically lead to improved learning outcomes. We need to think about several issues such as a pedagogy for immersive learning experiences (see [4,6]), evaluations that balance holistic, real world studies and basic research, and how immersive learning experiences can be scaled and made accessible by integrating them into existing portfolios of technologies offered at universities. Only time will tell whether students accept this new medium of learning, once it enters educational mainstream and the novelty effect wears off.

Acknowledgements. Dr. Klippel would like to acknowledge support for his contributions to this research by the National Science Foundation, grant #1526520.

References

1. Bursztyn, N., Shelton, B., Walker, A., Pederson, J.: Increasing undergraduate interest to learn geoscience with gps-based augmented reality field trips on students' own smartphones. GSA Today **27**(6), 4–10 (2017). https://doi.org/10.1130/GSATG304A.1
2. Carrivick, J.L., Smith, M.W., Quincey, D.J.: Structure from Motion in the Geosciences. Wiley, Chichester (2016). https://doi.org/10.1002/9781118895818
3. Chirico, A., Yaden, D.B., Riva, G., Gaggioli, A.: The potential of virtual reality for the investigation of awe. Front. Psychol. **09**, 1–6 (2016). https://doi.org/10.3389/fpsyg.2016.01766
4. Dede, C.: Immersive interfaces for engagement and learning. Science (New York, N.Y.) **323**(5910), 66–69 (2009). https://doi.org/10.1126/science.1167311
5. Fereday, J., Muir-Cochrane, E.: Demonstrating rigor using thematic analysis: a hybrid approach of inductive and deductive coding and theme development. Int. J. Qual. Methods **5**(1), 80–92 (2016). https://doi.org/10.1177/160940690600500107
6. Fowler, C.: Virtual reality and learning: where is the pedagogy? Br. J. Educ. Technol. **46**(2), 412–422 (2015). https://doi.org/10.1111/bjet.12135
7. Geertzen, J.: Inter-rater agreement with multiple raters and variables (2012). https://nlp-ml.io/jg/software/ira/
8. Jerald, J.: The VR Book: Human-Centered Design for Virtual Reality, ACM Books, vol. 8. Association for Computing Machinery and Morgan & Claypool Publishers, New York, NY and San Rafael, first edition edn. (2016). http://dl.acm.org/citation.cfm?id=2792790
9. Kamarainen, A.M., Thompson, M., Metcalf, S.J., Grotzer, T.A., Tutwiler, M.S., Dede, C.: Prompting connections between content and context: blending immersive virtual environments and augmented reality for environmental science learning. In: Beck, D., et al. (eds.) iLRN 2018. CCIS, vol. 840, pp. 36–54. Springer, Cham (2018). https://doi.org/10.1007/978-3-319-93596-6_3
10. Klippel, A., et al.: Transforming earth science education through immersive experiences - delivering on a long held promise. J. Educ. Comput. Res. (2019, in press)
11. Klippel, A., Zhao, J., Oprean, D., Wallgrün, J.O., Chang, J.S.K.: Research framework for immersive virtual field trips. In: 2019 IEEE Virtual Reality Workshop on K-12 Embodied Learning Through Virtual and Augmented Reality (KELVAR) (2019, in press)

12. Lee, E.A.L., Wong, K.W.: Learning with desktop virtual reality: low spatial ability learners are more positively affected. Comput. Educ. **79**, 49–58 (2014). https://doi.org/10.1016/j.compedu.2014.07.010
13. Little, W.W.: Introduction to sedimentary structures - part 1 [powerpoint presentation] (2014). https://www.slideshare.net/wwlittle/geol-370-3a-sd-structs-13-1228-96-ppi
14. Machkovech, S.: Oculus go review: The wireless-vr future begins today for only $199 (2018). https://arstechnica.com/gaming/2018/05/oculus-go-review-the-wireless-vr-future-begins-today-for-only-199/
15. PriceWaterhouseCoupers LLC: Global entertainment & media outlook 2018–2022: Trending now: convergence, connections and trust (2018). https://www.pwc.com/gx/en/entertainment-media/outlook/perspectives-from-the-global-entertainment-and-media-outlook-2018-2022.pdf
16. Schreier, M.: Qualitative content analysis in practice. SAGE Publishing (2012). https://uk.sagepub.com/en-gb/eur/qualitative-content-analysis-in-practice/book234633
17. Semken, S., Ward, E.G., Moosavi, S., Chinn, P.W.U.: Place-based education in geoscience: theory, research, practice, and assessment. J. Geosci. Educ. **65**(4), 542–562 (2018). https://doi.org/10.5408/17-276.1
18. Wirth, W., et al.: A process model of the formation of spatial presence experiences. Media Psychol. **9**(3), 493–525 (2007). https://doi.org/10.1080/15213260701283079
19. Zhao, J., Klippel, A.: Scale - unexplored opportunities for immersive technologies in place-based learning. In: 2019 IEEE Virtual Reality (VR). IEEE (2019, in press)

Special Relativity in Immersive Learning

Gregory Chu$^{(\boxtimes)}$, Irene Humer , and Christian Eckhardt

California Polytechnic State University, San Luis Obispo, CA, USA
{gdchu,ihumer,ceckhard}@calpoly.edu

Abstract. In this paper, we discuss our development, implementation and evaluation of an interactive, real-time, and real-scale virtual reality application used to understand the theory of special relativity. Since special relativity deals with non-trivial counter-intuitive subjects such as the twin paradox and the Lorentz contraction, we utilize an immersive VR experience to visualize these phenomena. In doing so, we attempt to teach the theory of special relativity in a manner different than conventional abstract methods. In this study, we tested a set of participants and examined their understanding of special relativity theory before and after engaging with the VR experience. Using the results, we inspected for any correlations between their perceived immersion during and after the simulation and their acquisition of special relativity theory.

Our study has shown that visualizing the phenomena of special relativity in VR led to high immersion among participants and increased knowledge about the theory of special relativity. With this work, we hope to build upon the collective knowledge about the effects of learning in a strong, visually pronounced, and highly immersive environment.

Keywords: Special relativity · Virtual reality ·
Immersive Learning · User study

1 Introduction

Special Relativity [1] is one of the most prominent developments in modern physics. Its effects capture people's interest, those of which are often described as counter-intuitive and contradictory to real life experiences of space and time. However, in teaching the subject, many students fail to develop an understanding of the fundamental concepts even after advanced instructions [2]. In part, misconceptions concerning Special Relativity Theory (SRT) stand as a barrier to mastering Einstein's mathematical formulations.

Our goal is to create an interactive and immersive simulation that improves users' skills with SRT [1] and resolve the challenges most people face with understanding the implications and intuition of Special Relativity [2].

Moreover, the use of our simulation extends beyond just the university level of education and into Secondary Education (S.E.) and anyone interested in SRT.

Early approaches like Gamow's *Mr. Thompkins in Wonderland* [3] attempts to educate readers about relativistic situations using a vivid description of a relativistic world where the speed of light is reduced to 30 mph.

© Springer Nature Switzerland AG 2019
D. Beck et al. (Eds.): iLRN 2019, CCIS 1044, pp. 16–29, 2019.
https://doi.org/10.1007/978-3-030-23089-0_2

Nowadays, computer simulations in two and three dimensions aim to add intuitive understanding of SRT. Virtual Reality (VR) makes it possible to immerse the learner into a Virtual Learning Environment (VLE) [4] that is enhancing, motivating and stimulating learners' understanding of certain events [5,6]. Our VLE scales velocities close to the speed of light revealing a relativistic world.

It has been shown that a carefully designed physics simulation can offer a level of comprehension that exceeds an understanding built during a traditional physics course [7]. Visual simulations can be highly engaging and educationally effective [7], especially if they have been carefully designed and tested. According to Adams et al. [7] simulations should encourage exploration and provide a high level of interactivity while limiting elements of distraction. They should be designed to offer enjoyment and avoid appearing intimidating or boring. Students must believe in the VLE in order to engage with it. In addition, students who believe they lack an understanding of the ideas presented by the VLE are more likely to explore and learn from the experience. Essentially, it is easier for students to build an understanding of scientific concepts unfamiliar to them when they engage with visual stimulation.

Hence, we believe providing a VLE to explore special relativity phenomena can improve students' conceptual understanding of Einstein's Theory of Special Relativity, a theory that is among the most misunderstood topics in modern physics, the specifics of which include: relativity of simultaneity, length contraction, and time dilation [2,9]. Our goal is for students to gain a complete conceptual understanding of the SRT, in particular time dilation (twin paradox) [10] and Lorentz contraction (aka length contraction) [11,12], as they outline the phenomena. In addition, we will pose questions regarding the twin paradox to help reveal students intuitive understanding of special relativity.

Already existing computer programs such as *PhysLet* [13], *Spacetime, Real-Lab* [14] and many others [15–17] offer 2D visualization and try to demonstrate to a student special relativity phenomena otherwise inaccessible to the human experience. In addition to two dimensional simulations, some authors have investigated 3D simulated environments such as *CAVE* [18,19] and *Real Time Relativity* [20,21] as well as VR for teaching special relativity [22]. One study by McGrath et al. [21] using *Real Time Relativity* was conducted on over 300 students. Students report a positive learning experience and see the subject area as being less abstract after use of the simulation. However, no analysis on the improvement of the student's understanding has been done.

Research on the effectiveness of those simulations is either incomplete [15,21] or just on a limited student population size [19] and assumes that the simulation will help to develop intuition on relativistic behaviors without any in-depth investigations [18], nor do any of them provide a large scale environment necessary to grasp the order of magnitude of SRT, such as including large stellar structures (galaxies) as well as smaller locations (solar system). This is of importance, since the Lorentz effect flattens the whole universe in flight direction, making it possible to traverse through the galaxy within seconds, depending on the speed. The dense stars of our galaxy, due to their numbers, are the major visual feedback to illustrate this effect.

The research presented in this paper focuses on investigating how VR experience can enhance students' knowledge and understanding of scientific topics. In particular, we look at how an individual's knowledge and application of SRT changes from before to after the use of a VR simulation and then gather data about each individual's level of immersion in order to conclude its effect on their learning [23]. Immersion with regards to VR is a cognitive state influenced by factors within and around a VLE. Immersion is composed of different psychological faculties such as attention, flow, engagement, planning and perception, and is qualified by a lack of awareness of time and the real world around an individual [24]. Additionally, it is the involvement and sense of existing in the simulated environment. Methods of measuring immersion have been investigated in subjective approaches [25], eye-tracking methodologies [26], non-interactive [8] and interactive media [23] using questionnaires [23], with latter one used in this work.

2   Methodology

We tested a group of n = 34 participants and conducted our research in four steps. Step 1 was to assess participants' demographics and existing skills in SRT using a pre-questionnaire. In Step 2, participants watched a lecture video about special relativity, developed by us. This video aimed to equip our participants with the most basic understanding of SRT to gain a fundamental level of abstraction. For step 3, participants engaged with the VLE experience. Finally, in step 4, participants answered post-questionnaire to assess their level of immersion and quantify any improvement in knowledge.

For this research, a real-time and real-scale simulation was developed to let the participants travel inside our solar system. The simulation included all 8 planets, and all moons bigger than 50 km in diameter, and allowed for user to navigate and explore the Milky Way with its diameter of 100,000 light-years (ly), in order to exhibit the large scale effects of SRT. In comparison to similar VLE's [13–17], the user will be immersed in a stereoscopic 3D environment by wearing a head mounted display (HMD), allowing free head movements.

The effect of Lorentz contraction happens only along the flight direction and is hardly visible from front view. To see the effect from the side, where it is most prominent, including Lorentz rotations [31], the flight direction and the view direction needs to be de-coupled, which is provided by the HMD. To achieve that in non-VR, 3D simulations must utilize two input methods, one for the flight direction and one for the view angle, which makes it over-complex to control, is in general not popular in games, and was consequently entirely left out in non VR approaches [18–21].

Prior and post to the VLE, a mandatory questionnaire that assessed the user experience was conducted. We collected demographics in the first questionnaire prior to the VR simulation, as well as education related question about the state of special relativity skills.

We identified two long existing myths in SRT: The first, that moving clocks appear slower in general, which is not true. In the twin paradox, which has profound evidences [27], there must be phases of observing faster passing time for one twin, in order for the other one to end up older when meeting again. In fact, when approaching, both clocks would observe the others running faster, but whoever is changing direction would delay this effect, resulting in different aging [10]. The second myth is the general statement, that spheres do not change its shape under Lorentz contraction, but this is only true if seen from the front, it indeed flattens by the flight-direction dimension.

Furthermore, a survey was conducted to make a connection in how far immersion is related to the learning outcome. We used two different sets of questions to assess the immersion in different categories about what participants felt during and after the VR experience [23,28].

We used two PC's equipped with an NVIDIA 1080Ti graphic cards each and Oculus Rift HMDs. Further on, OpenGL was chosen for the graphics programming and OpenVR to access the HMDs.

2.1   Pre-educational Video

The video [29] we developed aims to provide a basic framework and elemental level of understanding of SRT and consequently levels out bigger educational gaps of the participants. This pre-educational video does not answer the questions raised in the questionnaire of this work. One must rather derive the answers from a deeper understanding gained from the VR experience. It's purpose is solely to provide an abstract framework. It starts by deriving the Lorentz factor γ [12] and the term 'relativity' as well as the constant speed of light is postulated. Further on, the individual time frame, depending on γ is explained, followed by an introduction to Minkowski diagrams. These diagrams are platform for introducing the concept of simultaneously events from the perspective of an observer and a moving spaceship, stating, that the spaceship system has its own axis of simultaneously events, but keeping in mind the aspect of relativity. The observer and the spaceship must be able to derive the same observation about each other as long as they are not leaving their inertial frame of reference.

2.2   Galaxy Simulation

Development. Our VLE displays one million stars distributed across 100,000 ly (average disc diameter if the milky way) as well as all planets of our solar system, including the sun and all moons larger than 50 km in diameter. Due to the high density of stars close to the center of the milky way, we used it as landmark for one of our task, in order to have a better visual feedback illustrating the Lorentz contraction.

We developed the simulation in C++ and OpenGL, with a self written graphic engine specifically designed for displaying objects with massive size differences. As an example, our simulation's Earth rotated around the sun with $7,292115 * 10^{-5}$ rad/s which pushed the limits of 64 bit floating point precision. In another instance, when travelling on speeds close to the speed of light (c), the fraction $\frac{v^2}{c^2}$ of the Lorentz factor $\frac{1}{\sqrt{1-v^2/c^2}}$, in respect to the double-precision floating-point format, limits the speed at the eighth digit after the decimal and consequently does not allow to go closer to the speed of light. With a speed of $0.99999999c$, the spaceship would take several days to reach the center of the galaxy, which is not feasible for a user study. To overcome the double precision limitation, we used an arbitrary precision library [30] with 512 bit precision. Consequently, the maximum speed our simulation is $(1-10^{-24})c$. Arbitrary precision libraries however perform much worse than system-native floating point formats. Since our simulation runs in VR, every frame must be built in a time-frame $\frac{1}{90}$ of a second at maximum, in order to use the fix frame-rate requirement of the VR headset Oculus Rift of 90 frames per second (fps). To achieve the high frame-rate, we only utilize the arbitrary precision library to calculate the spaceship speed, position, as well as the positions of the planets and moons, based on their rotation.

As for the simulation itself, participants control a spaceship. The spaceship's cockpit consists of several panels, see Fig. 1. Starting in the upper-left corner is information to orient participants. The information includes the distance to a selected destination in light-years, the elapsed time relative to the spaceship, the elapsed time relative to Earth, and the current travel speed as a factor percentage of the speed of light. The spaceship's location is provided by a map displayed on the left. On the right side of the screen are autopilot controls which allow travel to any of the provided destinations. These destinations include all solar planets, the sun, and the galaxy's center and outer most bounds. Alternatively, participants can use the WASD keys on the keyboard to move around manually. The 'W' key accelerates the spaceship and 'S' stops it. The 'A' and 'D' keys rotate the screen left and right respectively. The flight direction is indicated by a red circle in the center of the screen, see Fig. 1. There is a pause button that can pause the simulation's time progression. At the bottom is the task window where participants can toggle through orientation instructions for the VLE and the three tasks we assigned them which we will elaborated on later.

The simulation always starts a participant's spaceship at Earth. Pressing the 'enter' key during the simulation will reset them back to this place. Pressing the space bar hides all screen and cockpit information as an attempt to decrease participants' distractions and increase immersion.

Simulation Tasks. We designed three tasks to highlight the educational goals.

In task 1, one should travel from earth to sun and back while focusing the time passing on earth, which will slow down while flying to the sun, but speeds up when traveling back to earth. The participants get informed, that the light takes approximately 8:20 min from sun to earth. Overall, when arriving back to

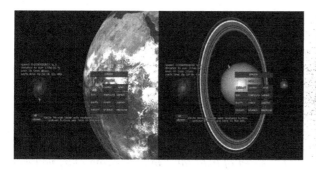

Fig. 1. Left picture: the cockpit view, including the autopilot, map, time and speed and the task bar. Middle picture: Uranus and its moon Ariel. The Lorentz contraction at a speed of 0.9999c flattening the spherical shape of the sun and the stars forming the galaxy in flight direction, while looking to the side. The background is color-reversed to raise the contrast. (Color figure online)

earth, approximately 16 min have passed on earth, while just some seconds with the close-to-light-speed, underlining the twin paradox. Task 2 repeats task 1 on a massively different scale: The participant should fly to the center of the galaxy and back. Given a distance to the center of 50,000 ly, 100,000 years will have past on earth. In task 3, the participants should perform a proximity flight towards the sun, getting close and passing by. During the flight, they should direct their view on the sun, experiencing the Lorentz contraction on a spherical object, see right image in Fig. 1.

2.3 Questionnaire

Prior and post to the VLE experience, participants were required to complete a mandatory questionnaire that assessed the knowledge and immersive experience. For the Likert-scale questions on both questionnaires, we used items numbered from 0–4, with the key being "Not at all" (0), "Slightly" (1), "Moderately" (2), "Fairly" (3) and "Very much so" (4). A control question was incorporated.

Pre-questionnaire. We collected the demographics, and Likert-scale questions *"How much do you think your education covered special relativity so far?"*, *"How well do you think you understand the basics of special relativity?"*, *"How well do you think you understand the principle of the twin paradox?"* and *"How well do you think you understand the principle of the Lorentz contraction aka length contraction?"*. In addition, we asked about the two common misconceptions of SRT: *"Moving clocks (regardless if coming closer or moving away) appear slower"* and *"Spheres under Lorentz contraction stay spheres."* Participants could answer with one of the following options: *"a true statement"*, *"a false statement"* or *"I don't know"*.

Post-questionnaire. We repeated asking the two questions about the common misconceptions from the pre-questionnaire, and further on *"You are in a spaceship and attempt to fly in minimum time (!) from one end of the galaxy to the other. How long does it take you (you, not earth) if the galaxy's diameter is 100,000 light years? You can fly and accelerate as fast as you wish, not exceeding the speed of light."* with the options *"100,000 years"*, *"a bit under 100,000 years"*, *"instantaneous"*, *"never"* and the correct answer *"nearly instantaneous"*.

Then, we asked six consecutive questions regarding the twin paradox: *"Two spaceships are leaving earth in opposite directions: Ship A (your ship) and ship B. Both are flying with 90% of the speed of light for a month. From afar, you can observe a watch on B. B's time is passing..."* (SRT1), *"To follow up to the last question: B is observing your watch as well and find out your watch is going..."* (SRT2), *"Continuing: B is still observing your watch and sees it:"* (SRT3), *"Now you brake hard, turn around and fly in B's direction, and with the same speed as B, keeping the distance. Once again, you are observing B's watch and find, it is:"* (SRT4), *"B decides now to meet up with you again and brakes until you catch up (while you maintain your speed). During that phase, you take a look at B's watch and see the time on B's watch is passing:"* (SRT5) and *"However, B checks your watch and finds the time on your watch is passing:"* (SRT6).

The answer options are (for all six questions the same): *"slower"*, *"faster"*, *"same speed as your time"*, *"at the beginning at the same speed, then faster"*, *"at the beginning at the same speed, then slower"*, *"at the beginning slower, then at the same speed"*, *"at the beginning faster, then at the same speed"*, *"at the beginning slower, then faster"* and *"at the beginning faster, then slower"*.

We consider the difficulty of this question-set as hard, but designed however, to rule out any trivial answers. To compare the results with a random answer sample: Given 9 possible answers per question, the average score results by picking randomly is $\frac{1}{9} = 0.111 = 11.1\%$ per question. Since the questions are consecutive, we anticipated a sequentially drop of correct answers.

Finally, we were asking immersive related questions [23,28] for during and after the VLE experience. The questions for 'during' assessed competence, sensory and imaginative immersion, flow, tension/annoyance, challenge, negative affects and positive affects. The questionnaire regarding 'after' investigates basic attention, temporal dissociation, transportation, challenge, emotional involvement and enjoyment.

3   Tested Group Demographics

Our testing group had a size of n = 34 and one can see their demographics in Fig. 2. In average, every participant was going through all 4 steps in approx 40 min.

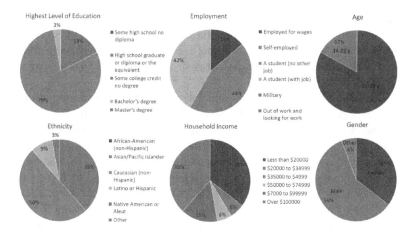

Fig. 2. Group demographics. The distribution of the participants age, level of education, employment status, ethnicity, gender and annual household income.

4   Results

Out of our testing group, 64.7% stated, that they had insufficient pre-education for understanding the SRT, 26.5% only a bit and 7.8% noted having been well educated for special relativity. This pre-education statement was not related to the actual existing knowledge, but rather about their secondary and partly tertiary education opportunities in SRT. 50% of the group did not understand the basics of SRT well prior. Within the other half, two participants stated to have profound knowledge about the topic, while the rest sees themselves on an immediate level. Only 17% claim to understand the twin paradox and the Lorentz contraction well and 20% to have some experience.

Evaluating the SRT myths, 29% believed incorrectly, that moving clocks, regardless of the flight direction, appear slower, and all of this subgroup stated to be equipped with pre-knowledge of the matter. The other 71% were uncertain of the answer. Among all participants, none believed the statement was false which was, in fact, the correct answer. This is a strong indication that many have either not been educated on the topic or hold an understanding of SRT that is incomplete. Lastly, 5.9% incorrectly believed that spheres remain spheres when undergoing the Lorentz Contraction while the rest said they did not know the answer.

The results of the SRT questions of the post-questionnaire can be seen in Fig. 3. The 'Moving Clocks' question could be clarified for 41% with a notable huge standard deviation (SD), while the second myth, the 'Spherical Shape' shows a definite improved results with 85% correct answers. Scores for the "Galaxy Travel" question scored lower in comparison. We believe this is because it requires participants to read the time displayed as text which was less visual and immersive for user. In future work, time displayed as text on the screen could be replaced by an analog clock to improve immersion and comprehension of the ideas presented in the simulation. Given the rudimentary knowledge of participants in this topic, our method could allow understanding of SRT to reach scores between 38−59%, see SRT questions 1–6 in Fig. 3. Since this questions are consecutive, the anticipated sequential score drop from SRT 1 to 6 is surprisingly not too pronounced.

Overall, the VLE experience significantly improved the understanding of SRT for our participants, given the facts, that (a) the group started in sum with minimal pre-knowledge, (b) the six consecutive SRT questions in the post-questionnaire are not answered in any material provided by us and must be derived from (the newly gained) understanding of the matter, (c) the six questions are directly challenging one of the SRT myths 'moving clocks are slower' which was shown in the pre-questionnaire to be a prevalent misconception among our participants, and finally (d) participants selecting randomly due to a lack of knowledge would result in scores in the rang of 11.1% when, it is evident, the scores are higher indicating at least an elementary knowledge of SRT.

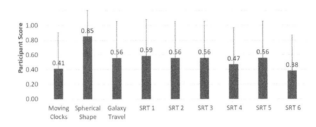

Fig. 3. Normalized, average score on SRT questions of the post-questionnaire.

In Fig. 4 the results of the assessment of the in-game experience felt during the VLE are shown in regards to seven components: Immersion, flow, competence, positive and negative affects, tension, and challenge. Each component is normalized to values between 0 and 1, where 0 indicates the lack of and 1 total agreement. The rating for positive affects was the highest with an average of over 0.8. The majority of participants enjoyed the simulation. This is underlined by the fact and in agreement with low scores in categories such as tension, annoyance and negative affects. We see the creation of a learning environment that ranks high in enjoyment as crucial for the learning process itself. Furthermore, the simulation did on average impose a low level of challenge (< 0.2) and this is despite the common difficulties known that students have with visualizations and the understanding of SRT. Overall, the users felt quite competent (> 0.7) and the scores for immersion and flow are very high (> 0.8 and > 0.65).

Our study has shown, that employing a real-time and real-scale VR-VLE as a teaching tool for SRT can offer learners enjoyment and a feeling of competence. We believe, that experiencing effects of special relativity in an immersive environment is an essential component for developing a deeper understanding.

Students were highly immersed in the gaming environment, they reported a loss of the connection with the outside world and a deep concentration on the VLE.

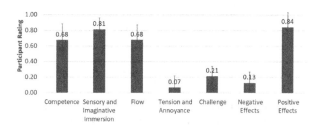

Fig. 4. Average rating of the immersion perceived during the VLE experience.

The evaluation of immersion after finishing the VLE can be seen in Fig. 5. It aims to assess the varying degrees of attention in the first three items 'Basic attention', 'Temporal dissociation' and 'Transportation' as well as anxiety through challenge, emotional involvement and enjoyment [28]. It is very clear, that the challenge felt after the VLE ranks noticeable higher, than during their VLE experience, which is, based on several interviews later, based on the difficulty levels of the 6 SRT questions. However, this had limited impact on the overall enjoyment.

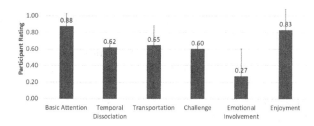

Fig. 5. Average rating of the immersion perceived after the VLE experience.

Upon further investigation, we split our group into two subgroups by their score on all nine SRT-related questions in the post-questionnaire and took a closer look at the upper third and lower third of scores. See Fig. 6 for the immersion assessed during and in Fig. 7 after the VLE. While several items got evaluated by both groups in similar ranges, and their difference becomes even less prominent in regards to the SD, the disparity for sensory and imaginative immersion with its lower SD in Fig. 6 is evident and is elevated for the lower third. The lower score on competence and the slightly higher one on challenge is, we believe intrinsic to participants who got exposed to SRT for the first time. Further on, there is a lower SD for basic attention, see Fig. 7, which we argue to be a result

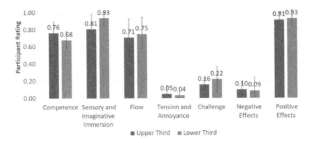

Fig. 6. Average rating of the immersion perceived during the VLE experience for participants who scored in the top (blue) and lower (orange) third. (Color figure online)

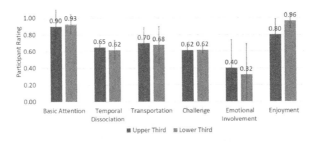

Fig. 7. Average rating of the immersion perceived after the VLE experience for participants who scored in the top (blue) and lower (orange) third. (Color figure online)

of less competence, but noticeable is also the higher overall enjoyment of the lower third of participants' scores.

Finally, we investigated the immersion for different improvement in the learning outcome. For that, we normalized the overall score of the nine SRT related questions of the post-questionnaire and subtracted a normalized factor derived from the four questions of their initial skills assessed by the pre-questionnaire. We split the participants into two groups again, focusing on the top and lower third in regards to improvement. See Fig. 8 for the participants immersion during and Fig. 9 post the VLE. Anxiety indicators 'tension and annoyance' and 'challenge' are elevated for participants, who were improving less, while most items in this figure are rather distinguishable by their SD, which is less widen for the 'most improved third'; a clear indicator for less frustration [23] and can also be seen in more basic attention and transportation in Fig. 9. At no point during the testing did we inform the participants whether or not their answers were correct. This leads to the expected conclusion, that participants who felt more anxiety improved less, but indicates a good validity of our measured data. However, overall the differences are not too distinct, which can be explained by the participants general enjoyment in Fig. 5 and positive affect score in Fig. 4.

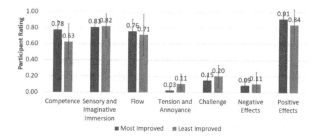

Fig. 8. Average rating of the immersion perceived during the VLE experience for participants who's score for improvement ranks in the top (blue) and lower (orange) third. (Color figure online)

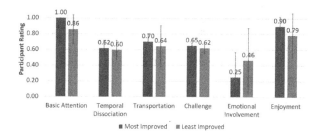

Fig. 9. Average rating of the immersion perceived after the VLE experience for participants who's score for improvement ranks in the top (blue) and lower (orange) third. (Color figure online)

5   Conclusion

In our work, we have shown that an immersive and interactive real-time and real-scale special relativity simulation in virtual reality provides a high level of immersion and enjoyment and has a significant positive learning outcome. We tested participants prior- and post to the VLE experience and developed additional learning material to convey an abstract mindset for understanding the special relativity theory. Our results indicate, that visual reinforcement of objects under Lorentz contraction as well as several task to experience the twin paradox improved the knowledge and skills in special relativity for our tested group. With the Lorentz contraction being profoundly visibly pronounced in our VLE, in a high positive answer rate, and consequently learning success was observed. Time dilation effects, which were connected to a text-readout in our VLE, were measured with definite gain of skills as well, but can be further improved with a more visible representation. Further on, we evaluated the immersion during and after the VLE experience. The results indicate, that students were highly immersed in the gaming environment, they reported a loss of the connection with the outside world and a deep concentration on the VLE.

6   Future Work

Our VLE incorporated three tasks to solve, which were related to Lorentz contraction and the twin paradox. We believe, a gamification of these tasks with a positive/negative reinforcement can increase the immersion and consequently the learning outcome. Investigating into a direct comparison of two different version of our VLE, one with gaming elements, the other without, can lead to a better understanding of immersive learning in general.

References

1. Einstein, A.: Relativity: The Special and General Theory, 1999th edn. Methuen & Co. Ltd., London (1924)
2. Scherr, R., Shaffer, P., Vokos, S.: Student understanding of time in special relativity: simultaneity and reference frames. Am. J. Phys. **69** (2002). https://doi.org/10.1119/1.1371254
3. Gamow, G.: Mr Tompkins in Wonderland. Macmillan (1940). https://dl.acm.org/citation.cfm?id=1124834
4. Pan, Z., Cheok, A.-D., Yang, H., Zhu, J., Shi, J.: Virtual reality and mixed reality for virtual learning environments. Universiti Teknologi Malaysia (UTM) (2006)
5. Kondo, K.: Augmented Learning Environment using Mixed Reality Technology. National Institute of Multimedia Education (2006)
6. Abdoli-Sejzi, A.: Augmented reality and virtual learning environment. Comput. Graph. **30** (2015)
7. Adams, W., et al.: A study of educational simulations Part I - engagement and learning. J. Interact. Learn. Res. **19**, 397–419 (2008)
8. Hong, R.: Immersion in reading and film as a function of personality. BSc thesis, Department of Psychology, University College London, U (2006)
9. Mermin, N.-D.: Lapses in relativistic pedagogy. Am. J. Phys. **62**, 11 (1994)
10. Einstein, A.: On the electrodynamics of moving bodies. Annalen der Physik **17**(10), 891 (1905). (End of ß4)
11. Dalarsson, M., Dalarsson, N.: Tensors, Relativity, and Cosmology, pp. 106–108. Academic Press, Boston (2015)
12. Lorentz, H.-A.: The relative motion of the earth and the aether. Zittingsverlag Akad. V. Wet. **1**, 74–79 (1892)
13. Belloni, M., Christian, W., Darcy, M.-H.: Teaching special relativity using physlets. Phys. Teach. **42**, 284–290 (2004)
14. Horwitz, P., Taylor, E.-F., Hickman, P.: Relativity readiness' using the RelLab program. Phys. Teach. **32**, 81–86 (1994)
15. Carr, D., Bossomaier, T., Lodge, K.: Designing a computer game to teach Einstein's theory of relativity. In: Computer Graphics, Imaging and Visualisation, pp. 109–114 (207)
16. Weiskopf, D., et al.: Explanatory and illustrative visualization of special and general relativity. IEEE Trans. Vis. Comput. Graph. **12**, 522–534 (2006)
17. Taylor, E.-F.: Space-time software: computer graphics utilities in special relativity. Am. J. Phys. **57**, 508–514 (1989)
18. De Hosson, C., Doat, T., Kermen, I., Vézien, J.-M.: Designing learning scenarios for a 3D virtual environment: the case of special relativity. Lat. Am. J. Phys. Educ. **1** (2012)

19. De Hosson, C, Kermen, I., Maisch, C., Parizot, E., Doat, T., Vézien, J.-M.: Learning scenario for a 3D virtual environment: the case of Special Relativity. HAL (2014). https://hal.archives-ouvertes.fr/hal-01663423
20. Savage, C., Searle, A., McCalman, L.: Real time reality: exploratory learning of special relativity. Am. J. Phys. **75** (2007). https://doi.org/10.1119/1.2744048
21. McGrath, D., Wegener, M., McIntyre, T.-J., Savage, C., Williamson, M.: Student experiences of virtual reality: a case study in learning special relativity. Am. J. Phys. **78** (2010). https://doi.org/10.1119/1.3431565
22. McGrath, D., Savage, C., Williamson, M., Wegener, M., McIntyre, T.: Teaching Special Relativity Using Virtual Reality. The University of Queensland (2008)
23. Jennett, C., et al.: Measuring and defining the experience of immersion in games. Int. J. Hum. Comput. Stud. **66**, 641–661 (2008)
24. Cairns, P., Cox, A.-L., Nordin, A.-I.: Immersion in digital games: review of gaming experience research. In: Angelides, M.C., Agius, H. (eds.) Handbook of Digital Games, pp. 337–361. Wiley, Hoboken (2014)
25. Chinta, R.: Measurements of Game Immersion through Subjective Approach. urn:nbn:se:bth-14825 (2012)
26. Cox, A., Cairns, P., Bianchi-Berthouze, N., Jennett, C.: The Use of Eyetracking for Measuring Immersion (2019)
27. Hafele, J.-C., Keating, R.-E.: Around-the-world atomic clocks: predicted relativistic time gains. Science **177**(4044), 166–168 (1972)
28. IJsselsteijn, W.-A., de Kort, Y.-A.-W., Poels, K.: The Game Experience Questionnaire. Technische Universiteit Eindhoven (2013)
29. Eckhardt, C: From Minkowski to Lorentz, a crash course in SRT. Youtube (2019). https://www.youtube.com/watch?v=tPM1k5UO6Fo
30. Sowa, T.: Bignum C++ library (2015). https://www.ttmath.org/
31. Mallinckrodt, A.-J.: Relativity theory versus the Lorentz transformations. Am. J. Phys. **61**, 760 (1993)

Immersive Learning for Scale and Order of Magnitude in Newtonian Mechanics

Trevor Brown$^{(\boxtimes)}$ ⓘ, Jason Lomsdalen$^{(\boxtimes)}$ ⓘ, Irene Humer ⓘ,
and Christian Eckhardt$^{(\boxtimes)}$ ⓘ

California Polytechnic State University, San Luis Obispo, CA, USA
{tbrown28,jlomsdal,ihumer,ceckhard}@calpoly.edu

Abstract. The purpose of this paper is to gain a better understanding on the role of immersive learning in regards to one's intuition on the order of magnitude and scale, by using projectile motion as an example of Newton mechanics. We developed a semi-tangible virtual reality (VR) application that serves as virtual learning environment (VLE). In this application, participants throw objects and explore the effects of different conditions, such as variations in gravity and air density. A questionnaire was conducted prior to and following the VR experience. Its purpose was to assess the participant's skill in estimating an object's behavior in varying conditions and their perception of the immersive experience. The VLE aimed to immersively train the participants to improve their perception of the scale and order of magnitude of key variables in Newtonian Physics. Our studies have shown that a semi-tangible virtual reality application improves the intuition of the scale and order of magnitude for the given Newtonian sample system and provide a highly immersive experience.

Keywords: Immersive learning · Newton · Newtonian mechanics ·
Order of magnitude · Scale · Perspective · Virtual · Reality ·
Learning · Environment · VR · VLE

1 Introduction

To gain an understanding for scale and order of magnitude in Newtonian mechanics, deep-seated preconceptions that conflict with classical instructions have been reported [1]. Learners tend to hold scientifically incorrect ideas about physics concepts in general, and about force and motion concepts in particular. The conceptual difficulties in mechanics have been well documented [12,14,15,22] and a considerable body of literature in science education has been formed [16,20,21]. To overcome the limitation of current immersive experience in a typical classroom setup, there have been various attempts to create a virtual learning environment (VLE) regarding Newton mechanics. 2D approaches, such as *Newton's Playground* [18] or 3D applications, such as *Physics's Playground* [19] that exploit the strengths of our immersive virtual environment, or *NewtonWorld*,

© Springer Nature Switzerland AG 2019
D. Beck et al. (Eds.): iLRN 2019, CCIS 1044, pp. 30–42, 2019.
https://doi.org/10.1007/978-3-030-23089-0_3

a collection of virtual worlds designed to explore the potential utility of physical immersion and multi-sensory perception to enhance science education [13] found significant pretest–posttest physics gains and have been studied thoroughly [17]. Nowadays VLE's aim to add intuitive understanding of Newton mechanics by immersing the learner in order to enhance, motivate, and stimulate learners' understanding of certain mechanics [3,4]. Carefully designed physics simulations can even offer a level of comprehension that exceeds an understanding built during a traditional physics course [5].

This work aims to measure learning outcomes and the entanglement with immersion by investigating competence improvements in intuition and abstraction regarding scale and order of magnitude. For that, a VLE was created which lets participants throw an object of a certain mass under different settings of gravity and air-density. A pre- and post application test examining their skills was conducted. The VLE aims to train the learner to deduct a better result on the post-questionnaire, rather than directly leading to correct answers.

To enhance the immersion, VR was being used in combination with a haptic controller for throwing the object, a ball, making it necessary to perform a real object-throwing body movement. Such pedagogical design elements were described and analyzed well to create a process of structuring learning situations that create constructivist experiences [24]. According to Desai et al. tangible systems are less complex to use and they require less time to encode and retrieve associated knowledge to use them intuitively. They are associated with low domain transfer distance and easy discoverable features [23].

To assess the immersion during the VLE experience, different metrics have been explored such as eye-tracking methodologies [10], subjective approaches [9] and non-interactive [6]. Questionnaires are used in this work to measure immersion in interactive media [8] and provide a good framework of testing participants of a VLE [7,11].

2   Methodology

We tested our VLE on 33 participants. By conducting our research in three different steps we were able to accurately track the immersive learning effect on the participants. We began by having the user take a survey to collect demographic information and a quiz to get a baseline reading for their understanding of Newtonian mechanics (step 1). The quiz was followed by the VR application (step 2), and finally a post application survey (step 3).

For this research, we developed a model for users to learn about gravity and surface pressure. This model consisted of five environments with different conditions. By altering the gravity and surface pressure in each environment, the application lets the participants explore different conditions and learn about the scale and order of magnitude in Newtonian mechanics. In comparison to other applications on two-dimensional screens, ours used realistic environments and a first person point of view. Further on, by utilizing a head mounted display (HMD) and touch sensors, participants were able to move their head freely and use virtual hands to interact with the application.

Prior to and immediately following the VR experience, participants were required to complete a survey that analyzed their user experience and tested their knowledge regarding the scale and order of magnitude of Newtonian mechanics for various kinematic variables. Furthermore, the survey gathered data about the immersion felt by users during and after the VLE.

2.1 Baseline Data Collection

First, we needed to get an initial reading of the user's perceived expertise and their actual expertise on the topic of Newtonian mechanics. We achieved this goal in the form of a quiz consisting of ten questions, where users would estimate the distance a ball would travel under different conditions. Participants were provided with an initial environment to compare to the question environments, but were not given any information about how gravity and surface pressure affect projectiles.

2.2 Application

Development. Our application transports participants to five different planetary bodies. Four of these environments are based on realistic locations in our solar system. See Table 1. One environment was reserved as a sandbox environment where users could adjust the gravity and surface pressure themselves, allowing the user to explore different combinations.

Table 1. The four environments participants could explore in the application and their corresponding gravity and surface pressure.

Planetary body	Gravity	Surface pressure
Earth	$9.8\,\mathrm{m/s^2}$	1 bar
Earth's Moon	$1.6\,\mathrm{m/s^2}$	0 bar
Mars	$3.7\,\mathrm{m/s^2}$	0.01 bar
Pluto	$0.7\,\mathrm{m/s^2}$	0.00001 bar

The application was developed using Unity, C#, and the Oculus Rift, including their touch sensors. The Unity Asset Store allowed us to easily immerse our users with realistic landscapes. See Fig. 1. C# scripts allowed participants to record and display the information about each throw, switch scenes without breaking immersion, have unlimited ball throws, and change the environmental settings. The users were able to modify the gravity to any value between $.001\,\mathrm{m/s^2}$ and $20\,\mathrm{m/s^2}$ and the surface pressure to any value between 0 bar and 10 bar. To calculate the exact distance a ball was thrown, we took the difference between the position of the ball as it leaves the user's hand and the position when the ball collides with the ground.

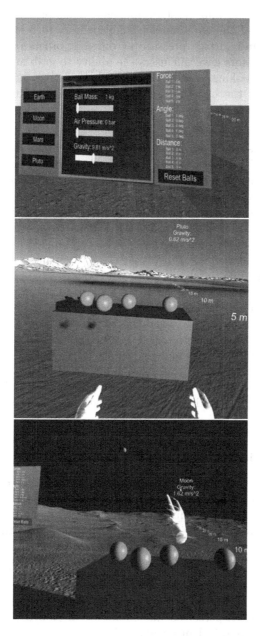

Fig. 1. Application photos. (Top) U.I. board for displaying throw information, sliders to adjust sandbox environment variables, and buttons for switching environments. (Middle) A user preparing to throw a ball on Pluto. (Bottom) A user observing their ball toss on the Moon.

Notably, the immersion wouldn't be possible without the HMD attached touch sensors. VR is an important component to this project because the first person perspective of the environment enabled users to better experience the effects of gravity and surface pressure at different orders of magnitude. The HMD and touch sensors gave our users the ability to grab and release balls by making a fist and looking around the scene by rotating their head. To exert a throwing force on the ball the users had to physically replicate a throwing motion with the touch sensors.

Application Tasks. We designed three tasks for our participants to accomplish in the application. The goal of these tasks was to help the users learn how the scale and order of magnitude of gravity and surface pressure affect the distance a projectile will travel.

To do this we had the user begin Task 1 in a familiar environment (Earth) and pick up balls with the Oculus touch sensors. The participants would then throw balls until they were approximately throwing at a 45° angle, with a flight distance of 4.6m. At this point we determined that the participants were comfortable in the application and able to reliably throw the balls.

Task 2 directed the users to proceed to the next environment, the Moon. The participants would then throw all five balls and observe the distance they traveled. The participants then repeat this process on Mars and Pluto.

Task 3 instructed the user to travel to the sandbox environment and throw balls to notice if the distance and trajectory of the ball resembles any environment they had already been in. After a few throws they would change the environmental variables and repeat the process until they had thrown balls in environments with high, medium, and low gravity and with high, medium, and low surface pressure.

2.3   Questionnaire

Before and directly after step 2, participants were required to complete a mandatory questionnaire approved by the Cal Poly Institutional Review Board. We used unique identifiers to link user's surveys without compromising their anonymity. To survey the user's immersive experience, we utilized the Likert-scale. The scale numbered responses from 0–4, with the key being "Not at all" (0), "Slightly" (1), "Moderately" (2), "Fairly" (3) and "Extremely" (4).

Initial Survey. In the initial survey, we asked a single Likert-scale question to gauge participant's self-perceived understanding of Newtonian mechanics. We also collected participant's demographic info.

We then asked ten questions regarding the distance a ball will travel under different orders of magnitude of both gravity and surface pressure. The velocity of the ball, the launch angle, and the mass of the ball were constant throughout each question, but the environmental variables, gravity and surface pressure, would vary. Notably, we gave the participants the horizontal distance a ball would travel for an example situation with the following conditions: $F_{grav} = 9.8\,\mathrm{m/s^2}$ $P_{sp} = 1\,\mathrm{bar}$ Users were then instructed to answer the following questions: How far would the mass travel if launched at a 45° angle at $7.0\,\mathrm{m/s^2}$ on...

1. Venus? (gravity: $8.87\,\mathrm{m/s^2}$, surface pressure: 92 bar)
2. Mercury? (gravity: $3.7\,\mathrm{m/s^2}$, surface pressure: 0 bar)
3. Titan? (gravity: $1.352\,\mathrm{m/s^2}$, surface pressure: 0 bar)
4. Carme? (gravity: $0.17\,\mathrm{m/s^2}$, surface pressure: 0 bar)
5. 55 Cancri e? (gravity: $78.3\,\mathrm{m/s^2}$, surface pressure: 0 bar)
6. Neptune at high altitude? (gravity: $11\,\mathrm{m/s^2}$, surface pressure: 30 bar)
7. an Earth-sized planet with high atmospheric pressure? (gravity: $9.8\,\mathrm{m/s^2}$, surface pressure: 20 bar)
8. on a Mercury-sized planet with high atmospheric pressure? (gravity: $3.7\,\mathrm{m/s^2}$, surface pressure: 20 bar)
9. a Carme-sized planet with high atmospheric pressure? (gravity: $0.1\,\mathrm{m/s^2}$, surface pressure: 20 bar)
10. a Earth-sized planet with twice the gravitational pull? (gravity: $18.2\,\mathrm{m/s^2}$, surface pressure: 1 bar)

2.4   Calculating Survey Question Answers

Our goal with this study was to create a VLE rather than a true simulation of Newtonian mechanics on different planetary bodies, so we let some aspects remain constant throughout the experiment. For our question results, we set the temperature and viscosity for each environment as a constant. We assumed a temperature of 25 Celsius, and an absolute viscosity to be $\sim 1.810^{-5}\,\mathrm{Ns/m^2}$. Selecting these to be constants gave us a dynamic friction coefficient C_d of 0.5 on the ball for each environments. For each question we also kept the following constants in order to measure strictly the user's understanding of how gravity and surface pressure affect the distance a ball travels. $m_{ball} = 1.0\,\mathrm{kg}$ $v_i = 7.0\,\mathrm{m/s^2}$ $\Theta = 45.0°$

Post-survey. Immediately following the VLE, participants were required to complete a survey that analyzed their experience, and then given the same quiz as at the pre-questionnaire.

3   Participant Demographics

The initial survey collected participant's demographic information such as age group, location, gender, ethnicity, highest education, annual household income, employment, and marital status. We found that 64% of our participants were male and 36% were female. 88% of our participants were pursuing a college degree and 70% of our participants make less than $20,000 annually. For age, level of education, employment status and ethnicity, see Fig. 2.

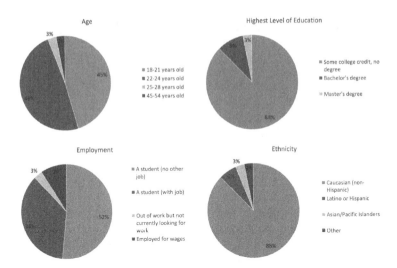

Fig. 2. Participant demographics. The distribution of the participants age, level of education, employment status, and ethnicity.

4   Results

On average, participants rated themselves a 1.96 on a scale of 0 to 4 when describing their understanding of Newtonian mechanics (0 indicating a lack of understanding and 4 complete understanding). Comparing the results of the initial quiz to the final quiz we found that 76% of participants made more accurate estimations after using the VR application.

Table 2. Distribution frequencies and test hypothesis probabilities

Level	Count	Probability	Hypothesis probability
Didn't show learning	116	0.35152	0.50000
Showed learning	214	0.64848	0.50000
Total	330	1.00000	1.00000

Table 2 shows the binomial distribution of survey results. Of the total 330 questions asked, 215 questions improvement from the initial survey to the final survey (Table 3).

Table 3. Binomial test

Binomial test	Level tested	Hypothesis probability (p1)	p-value
Ha: Prob (p > p1)	Showed learning	0.50000	**<.0001***

When examining question results, we compared the difference between the initial estimate and final estimate to the calculated expected value. We defined a guess that "showed learning" as one where the difference between their guess and the expected value decreased after using the application. A guess that "did not show learning" was one that grew farther away from the expected value after using the application. By classifying the quiz estimations in this way, each question was reduced to one of two possible outcomes; "showed learning" or "did not show learning." We saw a participant's estimation for each question as independent from each other because each question was unique. Thus, we were able to create a Binomial Distribution of the data. Our null hypothesis was that our VLE does not help one understand the scale and order of magnitude in Newtonian mechanics. We set our hypothesis probability to 0.5, and calculated an exact one-sided binomial test that looked for a probability greater than the hypothesized value. This resulted in a p-value of $<.0001$. Since our p-value is less than 0.05 we were able to reject our null hypothesis and state that there is enough evidence to suggest that the alternative hypothesis, that our VLE does help one understand the scale and order of magnitude in Newtonian mechanics, in particular projectile trajectory, can be accepted.

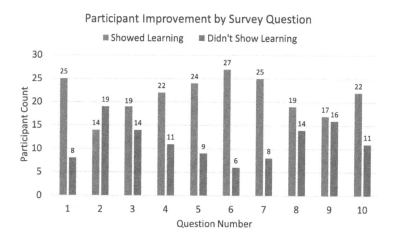

Fig. 3. Survey improvement results

We also calculated a binomial distribution for each question individually, see Fig. 3. We assumed the same null hypothesis as before, that Virtual Reality does not help one understand scale and order of magnitude in Newtonian mechanics and set our hypothesis probability to 0.5. Then calculated an exact one-sided binomial test, that looked for a probability greater than the hypothesized value. We calculated the test probabilities and got the following p-values respectively for questions 1 through 10: (0.0023, 0.8519, 0.2434, 0.0401, 0.0068, 0.002, 0.0023, 0.2434, 0.5, 0.0401). Since our p-value is less than 0.05 for questions 1, 4, 5, 6, 7, and 10 we were able to reject our null hypothesis for those questions.

This suggests that the alternative hypothesis, the VLE does help one understand the scale and order of magnitude in Newtonian mechanics, can be accepted. Questions 2, 3, 8, and 9 resulted in p-values > 0.05 and we were unable to reject the null hypothesis. We expect this behavior is because our participants initially guessed close to the calculated value for questions 2 and 3. We attribute the p-values of questions 8 and 9 to the underestimated effects of surface pressure in high-pressure environments.

An additional way we examined the quiz result data was through the average bounded difference between the estimates and the expected value. Because of the high variability in the order of magnitude from participant to participant in this application, extreme outliers were not uncommon and would greatly modify the average estimate for each question. In order to account for these outliers, we used the following approach: $diff = |actualvalue - median|$, $UpperBound = median + (2*diff)$, and $LowerBound = median - (2*diff)$ We took the absolute value of the difference between the median of the estimates for that question and the actual value. Next, for any outlier that was outside of the calculated UpperBound or LowerBound we snapped it to the bound it was closest to.

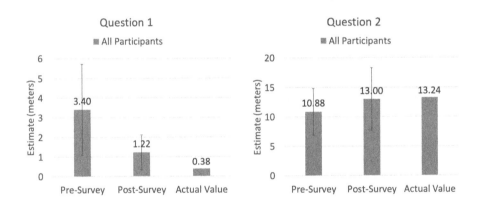

Fig. 4. The average bounded response of Questions 1 and 2.

In Figs. 4, 5, 6, and 7 you can see that the average guess grew closer to the the accurate result after the participant used the VR application.

As you can see in Fig. 8, Questions 9 and 10 both show that the average guess grew less accurate after using the application compared to the calculated result. Question 9 asked "How far would the mass travel if launched at a $45°$ angle on an Carme-sized planet with high atmospheric pressure? (gravity: $0.1 \, \text{m/s}^2$, surface pressure: $20 \, \text{bar}$)" and had an initial average estimation of $17.74 \, \text{m}$. After using the application the average estimation increased to $22.01 \, \text{m}$, when the actual value was $1.74 \, \text{m}$. It is important to note that estimates after using the application had a standard deviation of 18.78 which indicates a high degree of uncertainty.

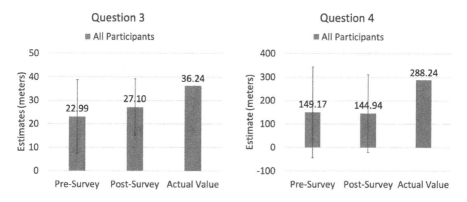

Fig. 5. The average bounded response of Questions 3 and 4.

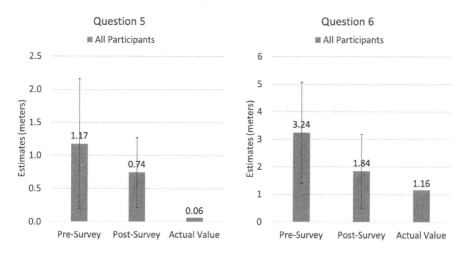

Fig. 6. The average bounded response of Questions 5 and 6.

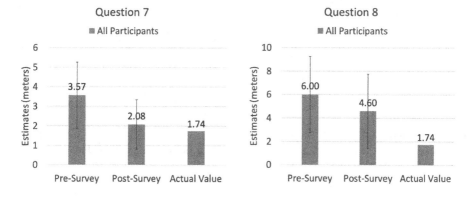

Fig. 7. The average bounded response of Questions 7 and 8.

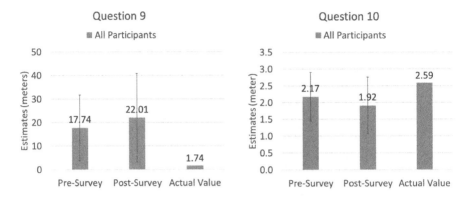

Fig. 8. The average bounded response of Questions 9 and 10. These were the only questions to show (on average) a less accurate estimate after the application.

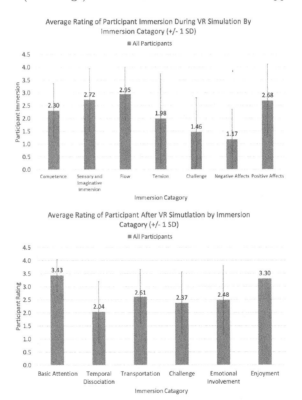

Fig. 9. Immersion feedback from participants. (Left) This data is the polling that happened during the application usage. (Right) This data is the polling that happened after using the application.

Question 10 displays a similarly high standard deviation, but a much lower degree of error. In question 9, average estimation error ranged from 16 m to 20.27 m whereas the average estimation error in question 10 ranged from .42 m to .67 m. When contrasted with Fig. 3 we can see that the major of users actually improved their estimate, but those who did not improve made estimations that were a high order of magnitude away from the actual answer, resulting in an less accurate post application average estimation.

On average, the top third of our participants "showed learning" on 8 questions, while the bottom third (on average) "showed learning" on only 5 questions.

Surveys were used to evaluate the VLE experience during and after the using the application. Figure 9 shows the results of both surveys. The surveys collected the users reactions to categories listed in both graphs of Fig. 9 and showed a definite high rate of enjoyment, the general high rate of attention indicators (basic attention, temporal dissociation and transportation) and the surprisingly high emotional involvement. Notably, participants rated the challenge of the VLE greater after experiencing the VLE. This is because their overall perception encompassed the entire experience, including the questionnaires.

5   Conclusion

Through our research we have found that a semi-tangible application in virtual reality provides a high level of immersion and enjoyment. In addition, the results from the pre- and post- survey indicate a positive learning outcome for the majority of our participants. This was concluded by data supporting their gained knowledge on the importance of scale and order of magnitude in Newtonian mechanics.

Furthermore, the surveys reveal a high level of user attention due to the VLE's immersive nature. Hence, the first person perspective and kinetic actions required by the VLE create a powerful learning tool for teaching abstract scientific concepts.

References

1. Brown, D., Clement, J.: Classroom teaching experiments in mechanics. In: Duit, R., Goldberg, F., Niedderer, H. (eds.) Research in Physics Learning: Theoretical Issues and Empirical Studies, pp. 380–397. IPN, Kiel (1992)
2. Pan, Z., Cheok, A.-D., Yang, H., Zhu, J., Shi, J.: Virtual reality and mixed reality for virtual learning environments. Universiti Teknologi Malaysia (UTM) (2006)
3. Kondo, K.: Augmented Learning Environment using Mixed Reality Technology. National Institute of Multimedia Education (2006)
4. Abdoli-Sejzi, A.: Augmented reality and virtual learning environment. Comput. Graph. **30** (2015)
5. Adams, W., et al.: A study of educational simulations Part I - engagement and learning. J. Interact. Learn. Res. **19** (2008)
6. Hong, R.: Immersion in reading and film as a function of personality. BSc thesis, Department of Psychology, University College London, U (2006)

7. Jennett, C., et al.: Measuring and defining the experience of immersion in games. Int. J. Hum. Comput. Stud. **66**, 641–661 (2008)
8. Cairns, P., Cox, A.-L., Nordin, A.-I.: Immersion in digital games: review of gaming experience research. In: Angelides, M.C., Agius, H. (eds.) Handbook of Digital Games, pp. 337–361. Wiley, Hoboken (2014)
9. Chinta, R.: Measurements of Game Immersion through Subjective Approach. urn:nbn:se:bth-14825 (2012)
10. Cox, A., Cairns, P., Bianchi-Berthouze, N., Jennett, C.: The Use of Eyetracking for Measuring Immersion (2019)
11. IJsselsteijn, W.-A., de Kort, Y.-A.-W., Poels, K.: The Game Experience Questionnaire. Technische Universiteit Eindhoven (2013)
12. Dede, C.J., Salzman, M.C., Loftin, R.B.: virtual realities for learning complex and abstract scientific concepts, VRAIS (1996)
13. Dede, C.J., Salzman, M., Loftin, R.B.: The development of a virtual world for learning Newtonian mechanics. In: Brusilovsky, P., Kommers, P., Streitz, N. (eds.) MHVR 1996. LNCS, vol. 1077, pp. 87–106. Springer, Heidelberg (1996). https://doi.org/10.1007/3-540-61282-3_10
14. van der Linden, A., van Joolingen, W.: A serious game for interactive teaching of Newton's laws. In: VRCAI 2016 Proceedings of the 3rd Asia-Europe Symposium on Simulation and Serious Gaming, pp. 165–167 (2016)
15. Kaufmann, H., Meyer, B.: Physics education in virtual reality: an example. Themes Sci. Technol. Educ. Spec. Issue **2**, 117–130 (2009)
16. Tomara, M., Tselfes, V., Gouscos, D.: Instructional strategies to promote conceptual change about force and motion: a review of the literature. Themes Sci. Technol. Educ. **10**(1), 1–16 (2017)
17. Winn, W.: The impact of three-dimensional immersive virtual environments on modern pedagogy. HITL Technical report R-97-15. Discussion paper for NSF Workshop. Human Interface Technology Laboratory, University of Washington, Seattle, WA, 30 May 1997
18. Shute, V., Ventura, M., Kim, Y.J.: Assessment and learning of qualitative physics in Newton's playground. J. Educ. Res. **106**, 423–430 (2013)
19. Kaufmann, H., Meyer, B.: Simulating educational physical experiments in augmented reality. In: SIGGRAPH Asia '08 ACM SIGGRAPH ASIA 2008 Educators Programme (2008). Article No. 3
20. Clark, D.B., Nelson, B.C., Chang, H.-Y., Martinez-Garza, M., Slack, K., D'Angelo, C.M.: Exploring Newtonian mechanics in a conceptually-integrated digital game: comparison of learning and affective outcomes for students in Taiwan and the United States. Comput. Educ. **57**(3), 2178–2195 (2011). https://doi.org/10.1016/j.compedu.2011.05.007
21. San Chee, Y.: Virtual reality in education: rooting learning in experience. Invited talk. In: Proceedings of the International Symposium on Virtual Education 2001, Dongseo University, Busan, South Korea, pp. 43–54. Symposium Organizing Committee (2001)
22. Desai, S., Blackler, A., Popovic, V.: Intuitive interaction in a mixed reality system. In: Design Research Society, Brighton, UK, 27–30 June 2016 (2016)
23. Desai, S., Blackler, A., Popovic, V.: Intuitive use of tangibles Toys. In: IASDR (2015)
24. Gardner, M., Elliott, J.B.: The Immersive Education Laboratory: understanding affordances, structuring experiences, and creating constructivist, collaborative processes, in mixed-realitysmart environments. Trans. Futur. Intell. Educ. Environ. **1**, 1–13 (2014)

Contribution Title Conceptual Framework for Virtual Field Trip Games

Amani Alsaqqaf[✉] and Frederick Li

University of Durham, Durham, UK
Amani.z.alsaqqaf@dur.ac.uk

Abstract. Field-based learning is essential in a number of different study disciplines in secondary education as well as in higher education. However, the reduction of field trips for many reasons, such as the limitation in time and expenses increases the demand for alternatives solutions. There is a need for an alternative way to provide learners with rich field trip and fieldwork experience. Advanced technology, such as educational games are a promising medium to design and develop virtual field trips. This study aims to provide a conceptual framework to facilitate the designing of virtual field trip games.

Keywords: Conceptual framework · Game based learning · Virtual field trip

1 Introduction

Field-based Learning (FBL) is learning by first-hand experience, outside the restrictions of the classroom walls [1]. FBL is essentially in a different field of study; however, there is a reduction of field trips in all levels of learning in the UK and around the world for a number of reasons, such as expense limitations and safety issues. In fact, there is a need for an alternative solution, and Virtual Field Trips (VFTs) in a game environment [2] are a promising area of research. Game-based Learning (GBL) is defined as the use of games in teaching and learning. Studies have proven the effectiveness of GBL [3]. GBL has been used in real field trips as a supporting technology for FBL [4].

FBL and GBL are two different methods of learning, which share some similarities such as learning theories. Experiential Learning Theory (ELT) is a well-established theory that utilised in both FBL and GBL, as well collaborative learning [5]. On the other hand, one of the differences is the setting of the learning environment which is important to FBL because the learning environment represents a fundamental source of learning content. Learners have to observe and analyse the field (forest, museum, theatre, or zoo) which is the learning environment. While in GBL, learning content is embedded in a game environment with the main purpose of motivation and engagement. Then environment settings are used in GBL to engage and immerse learners to get that embedded learning material, whilst FBL considers the learning environment as learning content itself. The contribution of this study is facilitating the design of Virtual Field Trip Games (VFTGs) for game designers and educators by providing a conceptual framework to support the alternative solution of field trip reduction.

© Springer Nature Switzerland AG 2019
D. Beck et al. (Eds.): iLRN 2019, CCIS 1044, pp. 43–55, 2019.
https://doi.org/10.1007/978-3-030-23089-0_4

2 Related Works

Technology can be applied to FBL to enrich field experience and enhance learning. The utilisation of technology in relation to FBL is divided into three categories: technology supported by using mobile devices in real field trips [6], remote access field trip [7], and virtual field trips. Virtuality can be achieved with multimodal presentations by using Google Maps, photographs of field site, or video clips along with verbal information [8], or with advanced technology, such digital games to provide richer meaning of virtuality as a 3D model representation of space with different level of authenticity and complexity of real-word field, lab, or museum [9]. Literature shows that there is real use and need to apply technology, such as serious games [10] to support field trips.

Frameworks and models to support designing GBL in general are found in literature and analysed to two groups. The first group is focused on one specific issue related to game design such as scenarios [11], one genre of digital game (massively multi-player online role-playing games) [12], motivation [13], or designing assessment [14]. The main limitation of this group is that it does not cover all game designing aspects, nor learning requirements. The second group is more comprehensive and covers most aspects of game design. For example, Experiential Gaming Model [15] aims to integrate learning theory within game design to design GBL. Flow theory and its main characteristics are emphasised to enhance the positive experience of players which means more engagement with learning. The model applies a specific learning theory, experiential learning theory, and is focused on the importance of clear goals with immediate feedback. Two main elements are not included in this model: social interaction, and assessment. Focusing on one learning theory could be considered a disadvantage which limits game designers and educators to build the game based only on this theory. Some frameworks are considered inclusive; however, they miss important elements of the learning process, such as feedback and assessment [16, 17]. Other frameworks overwhelm designers with many aspects of learning and game designs with complicated structures [17] and without providing clear guidelines [18]. The literature displays the need for an alternative solution for field trip reduction. Previous studies show interests on VFTG, and there are a few attempts [10, 19] which try to provide more than high-fidelity presentation. A number of conceptual frameworks for GBL/serious game design are available in literature, but to my knowledge no framework for designing VFTGs have been found. The contribution of this paper is to provide a conceptual framework that facilitates and enhances the quality of designing VFTGs, and formulates experiential learning theory (ELT) with game machinations.

3 The Framework

The VFTG framework consists of three phases: learning modeling, game modeling, and course authoring. The aim is to create a connection between learning theories relating to FBL and game design (see Fig. 1). It starts from learning modeling that combines two components: ELT and task model. Learning modeling forms the basis of designing VFTG with an important theory (ELT), and is followed by the task model that will shape the design of tasks in relation to ELT's stages.

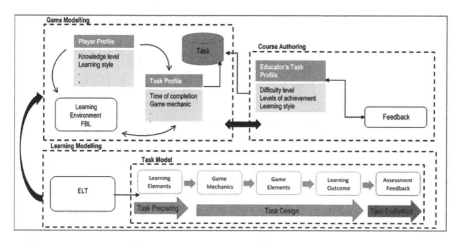

Fig. 1. The VFTG framework.

Then result of learning modeling is developed further in game modeling by utilising profiling technique (player and task) in addition to characterising the learning environment within the game environment and connecting it to the actual field relating to the FBL structure. It is a two-directional process between game modeling and course authoring to finalise task design. In fact, course authoring contributes to game modeling by manipulating some learning variables to fit different learning objectives by educators.

3.1   Learning Modeling

Learning modeling forms the basis of designing VFTGs by providing an understanding of Kolb's Experiential Learning Theory (ELT) which is essential for FBL. The theory is explained in the following section to game designers by applying the concepts of game machinations; symbols' meanings can be found in [20]. In addition, task model is provided as a second step in learning modeling based on Task-Based Learning (TBL). The task model delivers a guide to game designers with a theoretical approach of designing game tasks for field trips and connecting task designing to both learning theories and game mechanics.

Experiential Learning Theory. This is considered to be one of the most used learning theories in FBL [21], and consists of four stages. Concrete experience is the recall of previous knowledge or perceived new knowledge by experiencing the concrete with sensing and immersing in real situations. Reflective observation encourages reflection on experience. Abstract conceptualisation includes analysing, thinking, or planning through symbolic presentation. Active experimentation is about doing things. These four stages are performed in cycle and can be started in any stage and repeated as needed. Learners can start the cycle from any point but must touch all four bases. The theory originally defines four learning styles: diverging, assimilating, converging and accommodating, which depend on the preference of the learner. This preference results from personality type, life experience, and cultural influences.

Fig. 2. Concrete experience CE.

Game machinations framework [20] is a tool to visualise game mechanics and test the internal economy. This study uses game machinations to explain ELT as the game's internal economy, which connects learning elements to game mechanics such as feedback loops and results in facilitating educational game design and implementation. The first stage of ELT is concrete experience which is identifying knowledge by experience or recalling previous experience. This is a simple machination where player's knowledge is abstracted as interactive *source Task* to complete a task. The difficulty of the task is represented as a *gate* with 50% chance of completing the task based on the player's skill level and producing resource as knowledge to store in *level1 pool* (see Fig. 2).

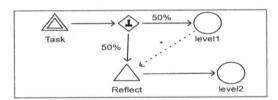

Fig. 3. Reflective observation RO.

Reflective observation is thinking and reflecting on player's experience from first stage and is a mental activity, but it could be encouraged with activities such as discussion. In (Fig. 3), reflection forms a *source Reflect*, which will be activated in two different situations. A trigger state connection from the *level1 pool* to *source Reflect* will activate the reflection in the first situation where the player expected to complete the task. The second situation is indicated by *gate* with probability of reflecting if the player couldn't complete the task. The player needs to reflect whether he/she completed the task successfully or not showing that player will still learn something. In the second stage, the player should reflect, which results in producing resources in level2 pool. The third stage, abstract conceptualisation, is about analysing, hypothesising, and planning to experiment in the next stage. This process can be done with a loop of reflecting and analysing until forming a final plan (see Fig. 4). The loop starts from the *converter Analyze* which convert resources in *level2* to hypothesis and plan to store in *level3 pool*. Collecting resources in *level3 pool* will activate the *interactive gate* then the player can reflect again by activating *source Reflect*.

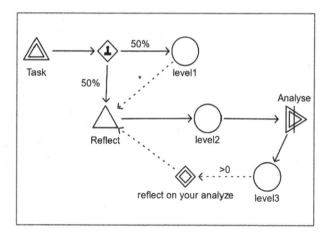

Fig. 4. Abstract conceptualization AC.

At the final stage, active experiment, the player needs to practise what he/she learned from the previous stages. In (Fig. 5), this final step is abstracted with *do experiment converter*. At the end of each stage, the player's knowledge is developed to the next level of achievement (*level1*: concepts, *level2*: comprehensive understanding, and *level3*: analysing, *level4*: synthesis) until constructing a full new knowledge in the last level4. At the end of the cycle, the player is expecting feedback (FB) to start a new cycle. Assuming that the player's knowledge and skill is improved, that will increase the difficulty the task in next cycle by one.

Task Model. Tasks in field trip games should be shaped based on the understanding of the four stages of ELT and task or tasks designed to represent each stage and allow players to go through them all. Task model comes as a second step to design tasks for specific stage based on the following model. TBL is a learning theory that proved to be

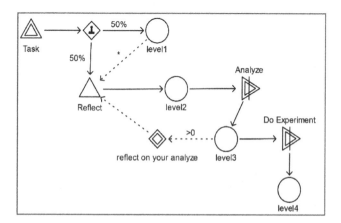

Fig. 5. Active experiment AE.

effective in teaching languages and using a task as a unit of analysis. As a part of this VFTG conceptual framework, where designing learning is constructed around tasks, a task model provides general instructions to help game designers to plan tasks. The task model consists of three steps: task preparing, task design, task evaluation (see Fig. 1).

Task preparing consists of defining some elements that are required for planning learning tasks for VFTs within the game environment. These elements are objectives, complexity: time & location, difficulty, and authenticity. Learning objectives have to be specified as a first step where clear objectives develop a motivation to complete the task. The complexity depends on manipulating time and location, short time and one location is the less complex task and will be maximised with longer time and more locations. The difficulty of the task should be increased relative to the player's progress and level of skills, and balanced based on flow theory [22]. The last element for creating a task is authenticity, and it can be achieved by 10 characteristics: real-world relevance, ill-structured, complex, required variety of recourse to solve, create opportunity to collaborate/reflect, beyond domain-specific subject, integrated with assessment, leads to create whole product, and allows a diversity of outcomes [23].

The Task Design step involves three components: game mechanics, game elements, and learning outcomes. The game designer is required to choose appropriate game mechanics (running, searching, managing resources, role-playing, constructing, or tactic strategy) for learning elements that are defined in the first step such as applying searching game mechanic for observing learning task, or using constructing mechanics to gain new knowledge. Then, they have to select game elements (presentation, narrative, identity, interaction and choices) that facilitate the chosen game mechanics. For example, multimodal presentation and interaction can enable searching mechanics, while identity can enhance role-playing and social interaction mechanics. The expected learning outcomes should be specified in addition to the way of capturing the player's learning outcomes to be evaluated in the next step.

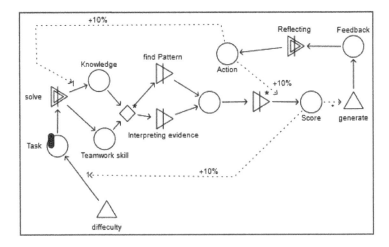

Fig. 6. Evaluation model.

Task evaluation and Feedback (FB) should be linked to game mechanics and elements to reduce learning interruption. The evaluation model in (see Fig. 6) explains the process of assessment and providing feedback using game machinations. The evaluation starts after solving a task by the player, a *converter Solve* represents the solving process by the player and converts a task to two resources *knowledge* and *teamwork skill* which form learning outcomes. A *gate* will collect both knowledge and teamwork skills and distribute them automatically to two converters: *find pattern* & *interpret evidence*. The aim of this step is to interpret evidence of performance and find behaviour pattern. That leads to automatic *converter* to assign *Score*. Any change in resource *Score* will activate an automatic source *generate* to provide *Feedback*. Each time a player is assigned *Score*, a label modifier will increase the rate of source *difficulty* to maintain the balance between an improved player's skills and the difficulty of the next task. Also, the player has to reflect and act on the giving FB via interactive converter *Reflecting* which will increase the rate of solving task and constructing knowledge and skills in the next step.

This is the main goal of formative assessment where FB will help the learner to reduce the gap between the actual and desired learning outcome. In addition, multi-modal presentation could be used to shows the variety of presenting FB. Also, FB will enhance the flow. Based on experiential gaming model [15], immediate and appropriate FB facilitates the flow experience.

3.2 Game Modeling

The game modeling phase enhances the connection that has already been established between learning elements and game design in learning modeling. The game modeling focuses on two elements that are essential to VFTs: learning environment, and profiling (task and player). Task profiling is an extension of the task model to finalise designing games with task characteristics that can be determined by game designers, while other characteristics can be defined by educators after game design. Learning to FBL. In addition, this framework considers player profiling to enhance learning environment is a fundamental part of designing VFTGs for this framework links itand playing experience at the same time. In fact, player profiling works as the middle point between task profiling and learning environment because the player interacts with each of them and the player's characteristics affect the design of tasks and learning environment. Finally, task profiling and learning environment are connected where the best learning happens within the learning context and the learning environment has to be designed to provide that context of tasks (see Fig. 1).

Learning Environment. The next step in VFTG design is connecting actual field to game environment by defining field settings. Realism, multimodal interactions, Multi-role, and complexity are characteristics that support transforming and linking between the two environments (game and field).

Realism is interpreted as authenticity of objects, events, and activities to mimic the field trip experience. Authentic presentation is essential for VFTs, because it provides a virtual field to learners that should replace the actual field to some level of fidelity.

However, authentic presentation should be used as it is needed to support the content in aim to achieve the learning/training goals.

Multimodal interaction, where all senses are allowed to be used to learn and solve tasks, must be considered in designing games of FBL as it is in actual field trips. The reason behind that is the effectiveness of FBL grounded on interactions with the environment of the field. That can be achieved by providing tasks that engage the player to interact with the learning environment, learning materials, and peers (social interaction) which all add to the learning context.

Multi-role allows the learner to play many roles (observer, data collector, and analyser) to complete tasks. The role of students in traditional classrooms is most likely a passive role, waiting for knowledge from teachers and following guidelines. However, in the FBL it is holistic and multi-role learning. That is what game designers of virtual filed trip games must consider when designing leaning experience, permitting the learner/player to experience different roles which would increase the motivation for playing and performing tasks.

Complexity comes from combining realism, multimodal interaction, and multi-role characteristics, which would result in the complex environment player has to face. Complexity has to be balanced in designing not to overwhelm the learner/player and at the same time provide a virtual field trip game environment that will enhance engagement and immersion.

Profiling. This proposed framework applies profiling technique to record and analyse task and player. The aim of profiling is to change and adapt gameplay as needed. Task profiling (Table 1) stores characteristics distinguishing each task, such as game mechanic or time of completion, to help game designers planning task and gameplay around it. Table 1 displays the main task characteristics. However, these characteristics can be extended as needed by the designer.

Table 1. Profiling.

Player profile	Task profile
Knowledge level	Time of completion
Constructed knowledge	Modal
Developed skills	Expected subtasks
Learning style	Position
Task completion	

Also, player profiling (Table 1) based on knowledge/skill level at the start of the game in addition to learning style or player preferences are all characteristics that can be used to adapt tasks for individual players. Some of these characteristics are fixed during gameplaying, such as learning style while others will be updated after completion of each task or ELT cycle, such as knowledge level.

3.3   Course Authoring

Course authoring deals with a few elements that can be fixed designed or adapted by educators' visions of teaching as part implementation. The proposed framework considers authoring to allow educators to contribute to game designing which is a demand by educators to save the cost of designing new games with different learning objectives. Educators need to participate in defining task profiling based on their domain experts and to personalise tasks for their students. Difficulty level, different levels of achievement, learning style are task characteristics that should be determined by educators.

In real field trips, students usually receive limited FB while performing tasks. However, teachers provide FB to the final product of the whole field trip activities after the real field trip. The framework of VFTGs analysed FB mechanism in learning to enhance the provision of FB in VFTGs. As a result, the proposed framework applies the profiling concept to FB mechanism in course authoring with the aim of designing the provision of FB in real-time inside VFTGs. As mentioned before, FB is an important component of task model, course authoring is a better way to formulate FB characteristics by permitting educators to specify their requirements regarding to FB. That would improve FBL in a games environment over real field trips by delivering FB to each learner after completing a task. FB can be categorised as: immediate, or delayed FB based on time of provision. Level of information that is carried out in the FB message can be knowledge of result – KR (answer is correct or not), knowledge of correct answers – KCR, and elaborated feedback – EF (guiding or hint to find correct answers). With the dramatically developed and improved technologies, FB can be displayed to students on different modality: visual, auditory, haptic and even multimodal form. Based on the importance of FB, the proposed framework is included in course authoring to give educators the chance of determining the characteristics of FB that provided for each task. These characteristics are: timing (immediate, delayed, or per request from student), frequency (depends on student's efficiency of completion, more frequent with low level), content (KR, KCR, or EF), functionality (explicit, or implicit), or modality.

4   Evaluation

In order to evaluate the framework, qualitative analysis is conducted. It is a preliminary evaluation study of the conceptual framework in which we explored the experts' perception of the usability and usefulness. The goal was to obtain experts' feedback in order to identify issues before starting implementation of the case study. Seven game designers and 13 educators participated in answering the questionnaire, giving a total of 20 participants. They are mainly from UK, but it also involved participants from USA, and S.A.K. The questionnaire and summary of the proposed framework are provided via Bristol Online Survey. Invitations were sent via emails and followed by reminders after few days. The questionnaire aimed to answering the following research questions:

Can the framework provide a connection between learning theories and game design?

Is the framework easy to apply for both game designers and educators?

There were 13 questions designed to answer the first research question. Ten questions required answers based on a five-point Likert scale (Strongly Agree = 5, Agree = 4, Neutral = 3, Disagree = 2, strongly Disagree = 1), and three open-ended questions for opinion and suggestions. The System Usability Scale (SUS) [24], which is a well-established questionnaire for measuring usability is used. It contains 10 items of attitude Likert scale to subjectively evaluate the usability in global view. In addition, there were personal questions that focus on knowledge of game designing and filed-based learning.

It should notice that SUS scores are calculated in composite way and produce a single usability score from 0–100.the average usability score of the conceptual framework is 69.3, which is above the average. T-tests shows there is a significant difference between game designers and educators regarding to usefulness of the conceptual framework. Regarding to intention to use the framework, the majority in favour of using the framework (probably yes 45%, definitely yes 15%). The association between intention to use the framework and occupational status (game designers 71% and educators 53%) are visible. As compared to educators, game designers are more tending to declare plans to use the framework in the future. Three responses suggested developing high-level skills and considered while designing VFTGs as additional concept to be included in the conceptual framework. In conclusion, there is a moderate support for the framework, and can be improved.

5   Prototyping

A prototype of a virtual field trip game is in the process of implementation based on the VFTG conceptual framework. The game is being developed to provide a player-driven experience of natural hazards. It is designed around the mission of surviving by understanding and analysing those phenomena. The learning content is based on natural hazard topic (volcanos) from national curriculum in England: Geography – Key Stage 3. Target audience is secondary school students, and the world Design is presenting Bali which is an island that contains three volcanoes: Mount Batur, Mount Agung, and Mount Bratan. Player has to survive in island of volcanos by observing and collecting data. Player has to complete quests (see Fig. 7) such as preparing survival kit to be able to access a link for volcanos' status alert. Another quest encourages player to explore the island by shooting fires with water gun. It is an element of fun to motivate player to learn while shooting and collecting gems (common mineral found in volcano's lava). The quests in addition to narrative all guided by the conceptual framework and blinded with ELT. The game design started by understanding the ELT cycle based on the conceptual framework and formulating each stage along with resources and their flow as an internal economy. In the first stage (concrete experience), players will recall some previous experience about volcanos by naming a volcano's parts. For each correct answer (volcanos' part), one object of survival kit (food, water, flash light, mask, aid kit) in case of eruption will appear somewhere on the island. That should be followed by the second stage (reflective observation), where player encouraged to reflect by collecting information about volcanos in the island such as type, name, and status (see Fig. 8) and record them in a table.

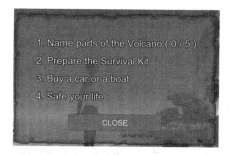

Fig. 7. List of quests.

Fig. 8. Volcano emits gas

In the stage of abstract conceptualisation, which is the third, players need to plan based on analysing, and hypothesise from observation and collecting data. Players are asked to write their hypothesis and plan in a text box to answer what is the situation on the island and what player should do to survive. That leads to the last stage, which is active experiment: the player experienced natural hazard (volcano) and has to do something to survive based on concrete experience (recall some knowledge about volcanos), reflecting on knowledge and experience from first stage, and analysing/ planning. The resource that results in completing each stage should be: *level1*: concepts about volcanos, *level2*: understanding the situation on the island, *level3:* analysing the status of volcanos and planning, *level4*: escape to far area from volcano or leave the island. The process of designing continued by modeling tasks, through three steps as shown in Table 2. More than one game mechanic and element are used in the task of each stage. The learning outcomes are represented as resources of each stage.

The game modeling phase consists of learning environment characteristics and pro-filing. The learning environment is created to be realism as Bali Island, the nature (trees, ocean, day and night), terrain is built with height map of real data, and volcano eruption signs. In fact, Bali is a rich environment with natural landmarks, variety of

Table 2. Task model implementation.

Task preparing	Task design		Task evaluation
	Game mechanic	Game element	
Learning objective: understand volcano and how to cope with a natural disaster	Exploring constructing	Narrative and multimodal presentation	Evaluating the resources of each stage: level1, level2, level3, and level4
	Managing resources		
Complexity: one location and many tasks	Physics	Interaction with learning materials and environment	
		Control of choices shooting and running	

plants and ancient temples. In addition, the learning environment is created to permit multimodal interaction with the island, to explore volcanos, to collect a survival kit, and to access learning materials. A player has access to a daily report of volcano status as a source of information.

The environment is designed to allow players to play in multi-role tasks such as volcanologist and survivor. The complexity of environment is balanced by providing a medium level of realism, limiting roles to two, but allowing unlimited interactions. The task profiling is determined based on the Table 1 by estimating time completion for tasks of each stage. All the tasks are designed to be multimodal (visual, auditory, text, motion). The first stage consists of a task with two subtasks, and the rest without subtasks. The position of all tasks was not limited to one specific spot on the game environment. However, player profile is part of the future work. Course Authoring is used to permit an educator to decide to provide the correct answer (knowledge of result) and how many chances to give a player.

6 Conclusion and Future Work

FBL requires alternative methods than a regular real field trip, and GBL can provide promising solution. The VFTGs framework provides a connecting between learning elements to game elements relating to FBL. The framework addresses some of the limitations found in previous frameworks, such as considering one learning theory or focusing on a few elements. The framework applies three important theories for FBL (Experiential Learning Theory, FBL, and task-based learning). In addition to emphasising assessment and FB which are essential components of learning, the framework is simplified to provide guidance which is a feature missed in many previous frameworks.

Future work of this research includes quantitative evaluation of the conceptual framework by testing the prototype game in a learning experiment with secondary school students. The focus can be on measuring learning performance and motivation by pre- and post-tests in addition to analysing gameplay data. A player test of the usability and stability of the game has to be conducted first. One of the most important future pieces of work which is in process of developing involves teamwork skills model as part of this conceptual framework to encourage collaboration and competition. VFTGs design should consider high-level skills that are required in the 21st century workplace.

References

1. Lonergan, N., Andresen, L.W.: Field-based education: some theoretical considerations. High. Educ. Res. Dev. **7**(1), 63–77 (1988)
2. Van Eck, R.: Digital game-based learning: it's not just the digital natives who are restless. Educause Rev. **41**(2), 16 (2006)
3. Hamari, J., et al.: Challenging games help students learn: an empirical study on engagement, flow and immersion in game-based learning. Comput. Hum. Behav. **54**, 170–179 (2016)

4. Kamarainen, A.M., et al.: EcoMOBILE: integrating augmented reality and probeware with environmental education field trips. Comput. Educ. **68**, 545–556 (2013)
5. Sung, H.-Y., Hwang, G.-J.: A collaborative game-based learning approach to improving students' learning performance in science courses. Comput. Educ. **63**, 43–51 (2013)
6. Welsh, K.E., et al.: Student perceptions of iPads as mobile learning devices for fieldwork. J. Geogr. High. Educ. **39**(3), 450–469 (2015)
7. Palaigeorgiou, G., Malandrakis, G., Tsolopani, C.: Learning with drones: flying windows for classroom virtual field trips. In: 2017 IEEE 17th International Conference on Advanced Learning Technologies (ICALT), IEEE (2017)
8. Lenkeit Meezan, K.A., Cuffey, K.: Virtual field trips for introductory geoscience classes (2012)
9. Burden, D., et al.: Fieldscapes–Creating and Evaluating a 3D Virtual Field Trip System (2017)
10. Argles, T., Minocha, S., Burden, D.: Virtual field teaching has evolved: benefits of a 3D gaming environment. Geol. Today **31**(6), 222–226 (2015)
11. Luo, L., et al.: Design and evaluation of a data-driven scenario generation framework for game-based training. IEEE Trans. Comput. Intell. AI Games **9**(3), 213–226 (2017)
12. Eseryel, D., Guo, Y., Law, V.: Interactivity 3 design and assessment framework for educational games to promote motivation and complex problem-solving skills. In: Assessment in Game-Based Learning, pp. 257–285. Springer, Berlin (2012)
13. Alexiou, A., Schippers, M.C.: Digital game elements, user experience and learning: a conceptual framework. Educ. Inf. Technol. **23**, 1–23 (2008)
14. Graafland, M., et al.: How to systematically assess serious games applied to health care. JMIR Ser. Game. **2**(2), 11 (2014)
15. Kiili, K.: Digital game-based learning: towards an experiential gaming model. Inter. High. Educ. **8**(1), 13–24 (2005)
16. De Freitas, S., Jarvis, S.: A framework for developing serious games to meet learner needs (2006)
17. Arnab, S., et al.: Mapping learning and game mechanics for serious games analysis. Bri. J. Educ. Technol. **46**(2), 391–411 (2015)
18. Amory, A.: Game object model version II: a theoretical framework for educational game development. Educ. Technol. Res. Dev. **55**(1), 51–77 (2007)
19. Boulos, M.N.K., Hetherington, L., Wheeler, S.: Second life: an overview of the potential of 3D virtual worlds in medical and health education. Health Inf. Libr. J. **24**(4), 233–245 (2007)
20. Adams, E., Dormans, J.: Game Mechanics: Advanced Game Design. New Riders, Indianapolis (2012)
21. Kolb, D.: Experimental Learning: Experience as the source of learning and development. Prentice Hall, Englewood Cliffs (1984)
22. Csikszentmihalyi, M., Csikszentmihalyi, I.: Beyond Boredom and Anxiety, vol. 721. Jossey-Bass, San Francisco (1975)
23. Herrington, J., Oliver, R.: An instructional design framework for authentic learning environments. Educ. Technol. Res. Dev. **48**(3), 23–48 (2000)
24. Brooke, J.: SUS-A quick and dirty usability scale. Usability Eval. Ind. **189**(194), 4–7 (1996)

Design Considerations for Haptic-Enabled Virtual Reality Simulation for Interactive Learning of Nanoscale Science in Schools

Mary Webb[1]([⊠]), Megan Tracey[1], William Harwin[2], Ozan Tokatli[2],
Faustina Hwang[2], Ros Johnson[3], Natasha Barrett[2], and Chris Jones[2]

[1] School of Education, Communication and Society,
King's College London, London, UK
mary.webb@kcl.ac.uk
[2] School of Biological Sciences, University of Reading, Reading, UK
[3] The Abbey, Reading, UK

Abstract. This paper reports on a study which investigated whether the addition of haptics (virtual touch) to a 3D virtual reality (VR) simulation promotes understanding of key nanoscale concepts in membrane systems for students aged 12 to 13. We developed a virtual model of a section of the cell membrane and a haptic enabled interface that enables students to interact with the model and to manipulate objects in the model. Students, in two schools in England, worked collaboratively in pairs on activities designed to develop their understanding of key concepts of cell membrane function. Results of pre-and post-tests of conceptual knowledge and understanding showed significant knowledge gains but there were no significant differences between the haptic and non-haptic condition. However, findings from observation of the activities and student interviews revealed that students were very positive about using the system and believed that being able to feel structures and manipulate objects within the model assisted their learning. We examine some of the design challenges and issues affecting the perception of haptic feedback.

Keywords: Haptics · Virtual reality · Cell biology · Science learning

1 Introduction

This paper is based on a study that aimed to examine the value of haptic-enablement to support the development of conceptual understanding of membrane structure and function in students aged 12–13. Our research objectives were to: (1) design and develop a haptic-enabled 3D VR model of the plasma membrane that would enable students to explore difficult concepts of membrane structure and function through multisensory collaborative activities; (2) investigate whether or not the ability to feel the interactions through haptics affected students' development of understanding of concepts and (3) examine students' perspectives on the interactive learning experience and the advantages and limitations of the system. In order to achieve (2), we aimed to design an interface in which haptics could be enabled, or disabled, such that the user could still interact with the model but had only visual cues.

© Springer Nature Switzerland AG 2019
D. Beck et al. (Eds.): iLRN 2019, CCIS 1044, pp. 56–67, 2019.
https://doi.org/10.1007/978-3-030-23089-0_5

While previous haptic interfaces supported only a single point of contact, recent developments in haptic technology have enabled the deployment of two-fingered haptic devices with which users can pick up and move objects and feel the forces exerted on those objects [1]. Thus, a haptic-enabled interface for a simulation can enable people to manipulate objects directly in a 3D VR environment much more realistically than is possible through more standard interfaces such as mouse and tracker ball.

In this paper, we first discuss the theoretical framework. Then we explain the principles and design of the VR environment that we developed for this study and the haptic-enabled interface designed to explore the VR environment. We then discuss the nature of the interactive learning environment and activities that we developed based on findings from previous studies [2]. The methods for collecting data, results and discussion of findings then follow. Finally, we consider the implications for future design and use of haptic-enabled VR environments in school science.

2   Theoretical Framework

It has long been recognised that the ability to visualise and to manipulate objects in the imagination is a crucial skill for learning science [see for example 3] but this has not been easy to achieve through the 2-D representations and static 3-D models frequently in use in science classrooms [4, 5]. Previously, Webb et al. [2] argued that the potential benefits, for learning science concepts, of the addition of haptics to a 3D VR simulation derive from: (1) the known general benefits of multisensory learning compared with uni-sensory [6]; (2) engagement and motivational effects of a more realistic experience; and (3) the more specific possibility that haptic interaction will support the visualisation that is necessary for understanding many key processes in science [3].

A possible theoretical foundation for the suggested improved learning associated with haptic support for visualisation comes from two main cognitive theories. First, Dual Coding Theory [7, 8] which proposes that distinct interconnected systems for different sensory modalities act synergistically. Secondly, Cognitive Load Theory as it applies to individual interaction with computer systems [9] and also in relation to collaborative learning [10]. Cognitive Load Theory [11] suggests that whilst learning, an individual's working memory is put under cognitive load as new information is attempted to be processed. In VR systems, information is commonly processed visually or to a lesser extent auditorily; haptic devices provide sensory feedback in the form of touch, so based on Dual Coding Theory it is proposed that having another channel of information in a different modality may help alleviate the cognitive load and aid learning.

3   Understanding Cell Membranes at Lower Secondary Level

Based on considerations of the existing curriculum, the following key concepts were to be developed with students aged 12–13:

1. The cell membrane is a barrier to the movement of some substances whereas others pass through freely.

2. Substances move in the cellular fluid by diffusion and some substances are able to continue moving by diffusion through the membrane.
3. The movement of substances that are able to freely diffuse depends on their individual diffusion gradients.
4. The cell membrane is a dynamic structure in which membrane proteins "float".
5. Carrier proteins enable the movement of some substances through the membrane by attracting a specific molecule and changing shape as the molecule passes through the channel of the transporter.

For the students, aged 12–13, who were the subjects in our investigation, their usual study of cell membranes includes examination of cell preparations under the light microscope, where cell membranes appear as a thin line stained with a dye. These practicals are accompanied by teaching and discussion with 2D and 3D diagrammatic representations of how membranes function to control movement into and out of cells. It is likely that some of the significant student comprehension problems and misconceptions of the functioning of cell membranes result from poor models and representations currently used for teaching [12, 13]. Therefore, using a 3D VR simulation may help to overcome these issues.

4   Design of the VR Environment

Designing the VR environment presented several challenges. First, cell membranes and the ways in which they control the movement of substances into out of cells are very complex so achieving a realistic model, for example by using real images was impossible. Therefore, it was necessary to identify suitable iconic ways of representing structure and function. In summary, key considerations for the design of the model included:

4.1   Level of Complexity

Identifying a level of complexity that would be sufficiently accurate not to lead to misconceptions while being feasible to be modelled in a VR environment and not too complex for students to understand.

4.2   Scale Considerations

Representing the relative size and scale of the nanoscale structures so that they would be manipulable within a confined space given that the workspace dimensions of the haptic device with multi-finger manipulation were 30 cm along the x-axis, 23 cm along the y-axis and 40 cm along the z-axis.

4.3   Haptics

Modeling the haptic forces in such a way that students would be able to feel forces and manipulate the structures.

Representing the elements of the model to scale presented significant challenges. Methods for measuring the size of nanoscale particles accurately are still under development and typically there are various different techniques such as x-ray crystallography and fluorescence resonance energy transfer [14]. For the purposes of this investigation, approximate sizes are adequate and Table 1 enables comparison of the typical approximate measurements of the structures of interest. It is apparent, from Table 1, that representing molecules for manipulation in the VR environment with the cell membrane requires compromise on scale. For example, if an oxygen molecule is represented at the size of a blueberry (~ 1 cm), representing the cell membrane to scale would make it 30 cm thick.

Table 1. Some typical approximate measurements relevant to the model

	Typical approximate measurements	Approximate average dimension in metres
Cheek epithelial cell (diameter)	50–80 μm	$6 * 10^{-5}$
Plasma membrane (thickness)	6–9 nm	$7 * 10^{-9}$
Membrane protein	3–6 nm 20–110 nm	$4 * 10^{-9}$ $60 * 10^{-9}$
Glucose molecule (diameter)	1 nm	1×10^{-9}
Oxygen molecule/Sodium ion	0.1–0.5 nm (Sodium slightly smaller)	1×10^{-10}

Fig. 1. View of part of the cell membrane model

The details of the molecular bilayer of the cell membrane were not considered to be important for students aged 12 to 13 to understand. Therefore, in order to represent the articles to be manipulated approximately to scale in relationship to each other, we compromised on representing the membrane as a relatively thin straw-coloured barrier with some hexagonal shapes indicating that the membrane consists of many separate molecules. The screenshot in Fig. 1 shows the cell membrane model near the start of the activity. Pale cream structures penetrating through the membrane represent the membrane proteins. Some of the membrane proteins are modelled as glucose transporters based on the GLUT1 transporter, as far as its structure and function is known [15]. Small particles were represented, as far as possible, by their coloured atoms, following the CPK (Corey, Pauling, Koltun) colouring convention. For example, carbon dioxide and oxygen molecules can be seen in Fig. 1. The particles modelled are shown in Table 2.

Table 2. Particles incorporated into the model

Particle	Colour	Type of model
Oxygen atom	Red sphere	Space filling
Carbon atom	Black sphere	Space filling
Potassium ion	Dark purple sphere	Space filling
Sodium ion	Light purple sphere	Space filling
Glucose molecule	Light blue blob	Approximate shape without atomic detail

5   The Interactive Learning Environment and Activities

The user can interact with the system via two points of contact of the thumb and index finger on the same hand (either left or right), represented as blocks in the model (see Fig. 1). The interface uses a thimble device shown in Fig. 2. In the model, the finger and thumb are able to move freely through the cell membrane but when the user grabs hold of an object in the model, such as a glucose molecule, if the haptics is enabled, the user feels the object and any forces acting on that object, such as those resulting from concentration gradients.

Fig. 2. Haptic interface   **Fig. 3.** Students using the system

In the non-haptic condition, the user interacts using the same interface but the haptics is turned off in the software, so the user must rely on visual cues to grab objects. When the user makes contact with one of the substances the "Label" changes to show the name of the substance (carbon dioxide, oxygen, glucose, sodium and potassium). When haptics is enabled, the user can feel forces on the substances, as kinaesthetic force feedback at the fingertip, depending on their concentration as (s)he moves a molecule or ion. During the simulation, users can add more molecules and ions, thus changing the concentration gradient. When a user pushes a glucose molecule towards a glucose transporter, in the haptic enabled condition, the user feels the force as the molecule is drawn into the transporter protein and the model simulates the glucose transporter changing shape as it transports the glucose molecule through the membrane.

As shown in Fig. 3 students worked in pairs, where one student (the pilot) was immersed in the VR environment using the interface and the head-mounted display, while the other student (co-pilot) had the same view of the 3D environment on a standard computer screen. The students swapped roles halfway through the activities. The pilot controlled the interaction with the VR environment while the co-pilot directed the activity by: reading the instructions and questions on the worksheet; controlling some aspects of the model through the keyboard and writing the answers onto the worksheet. The worksheet activities directed the pilot to perform a series of actions on objects in the model while observing visually and feeling how they moved: (1) moving membrane channel proteins within the membrane; (2) observing the movement of coloured particles; (3) touching and grabbing oxygen and glucose molecules; (4) moving an oxygen molecule into the cell and (5) moving a glucose molecule into the cell. The worksheet also instructed the students to predict and discuss their ideas.

The design of this learning environment was informed by a series of investigations with previous prototypes and discussions with teachers and students [2] which found that designating their distinct and essential roles as pilot and co-pilot encouraged the students to collaborate on an equal basis. Furthermore, working with a co-pilot who was not immersed enabled the pilot to feel immersed and to explore the VR environment confidently while also feeling grounded in the classroom. The following were the main design principles:

1. to focus students' attention on the haptic interaction and feel of the structures through the activities and questions on the paper-based worksheet
2. to encourage students to learn collaboratively by discussing their ideas
3. to encourage students to formulate their ideas precisely.

6 Research Methodology

The study was carried out in a boys' school and a girls' school with students who were in their first term of Year 8 (aged 12–13). Both schools were independent and selective, so the students were of relatively high academic ability. Opportunist sampling was used, based on which students could be freed from lessons to take part in the study which was carried out in one of the school science rooms. Pairs of students were assigned randomly to the haptic or non-haptic condition in equal numbers and the students were not informed of this difference. In all, data was obtained from 32 pairs of students: 16 pairs in haptic enabled condition, 16 pairs in non-haptic condition. In order to be able to compare results between the two conditions, students worked through the activity using the worksheet without teacher support; technicians were on hand to deal with technical issues with the hardware and software.

In line with ethical considerations, the purpose of the study was explained carefully to the students and their's as well as their parents' consent for the data collection was obtained. As some students were only exposed to the non-haptic condition in this study, in a follow-up study later in the academic year, we ensured that all students had the opportunity to experience the haptic condition.

A test of biology knowledge, based on the key concepts listed above, was administered before and straight after the activities. While students were undertaking the activity (approx. 40 min) they were video recorded and observed by members of the research team who made notes on how students engaged with the activities and with each other. The research team later reviewed the notes and videos in order to identify advantages and limitations of the system and interaction. Following the activity, students were interviewed in pairs using a 20-min semi-structured interview. Transcripts of the interviews were subjected to thematic analysis utilising inductive coding by two independent researchers based on a process of negotiated agreement [16] which reached 96% agreement.

7   Results

Observations of students during activities showed that both those in the haptic and non-haptic condition were engaged with the tasks and most pairs worked well together to support each other in interacting with the system and answering the questions. Only two of the students had previously used VR systems and therefore the experience was novel and exciting for nearly all of them. Generally, students quickly became familiar with the system and were able to use it effectively in both haptic and non-haptic conditions. Here, we examine findings from analysis of the knowledge tests, interviews and observations in relation to knowledge gains, students' interactions with the system and each other and students' perceptions of using the system and any difficulties they encountered.

7.1   Knowledge Gains from the Activities

Analysis of the test scores, shown in Table 3, using a 2 × 2 mixed analysis of variance showed significant knowledge gain between the pre- and post-knowledge-test results; $F(1,62) = 66.18$, $p < 0.001$. The mean score of the pre-tests ($M = 23.87$, $SD = 5.73$) was significantly lower than the mean score of the post-tests ($M = 30.97$, $SD = 6.32$.) However whether the participants were in the haptic or non-haptic condition did not affect significantly the change in scores; $F(1,62) = 1.40$, p = .24.

A one-way analysis of variance showed that there were no significant differences in the pre-test scores for haptic ($M = 25.19$, $SD = 5.40$) and non-haptic ($M = 22.56$, $SD = 5.82$) conditions; $F(1,62) = 3.45$, $p = .066$. There was also no significant

Table 3. Comparison of pre-and post- test results for knowledge

Descriptive Statistics

	Condition	Mean	Std. Deviation	N
Pre-test Score	haptic	25.19	5.40	32
	nonhaptic	22.56	5.82	32
	Total	23.87	5.72	64
Post-test Score	haptic	31.25	6.03	32
	nonhaptic	30.69	6.68	32
	Total	30.97	6.32	64

difference between the post test scores for haptic ($M = 31.25$, $SD = 6.03$) and non-haptic ($M = 30.69$, $SD = 6.68$) condition; $F(1, 62) = .13$, $p = .73$.

7.2   Student Perspectives on Using the System

The results from the thematic analysis of student interviews pertaining to students' perspectives on using the system and difficulties that they encountered are summarised in Table 4. All the pairs of students reported in the interviews that they found the system generally easy to use but they were encouraged to be specific about where they had difficulties.

Table 4. Summary of thematic analysis of student interviews

Theme	Number of items coded		
	Total	Haptic condition	Non-haptic condition
Difficulties	307	162	145
- Thimble device issues	21	14	7
- Grasping particles	43	17	26
- Space restriction	17	11	6
- Task difficulty	30	21	9
- Technical problems - software	60	31	29
Liked features	161	72	89
Feel forces	16	14	2
Feeling in general	18	9	9
Moving things	37	16	21
Seeing	75	24	51

7.3   Difficulties in Using the System and Technical Problems

Of the more than 300 data items, from the interviews, coded as difficulties, only 30 were about difficulties with the activities. Observations also confirmed that students were able to perform the activities although they found answering questions challenging which may have contributed to encouraging them to discuss and learn. There were some system problems, particularly with the thimble devices so it was necessary to stop and restart the system in order to adjust the thimble devices. Students' comments showed that such problems were twice as prevalent in the haptic compared with the non-haptic-enabled condition (See Table 4) and this was confirmed by observations. Thus, there were more interruptions in the haptic-enabled condition because of the juddering of the haptic interface which tended to dislodge the thimble devices. These problems were quickly resolved by technicians or the students themselves and generally did not interfere with the progress of activities although it is possible that they affected the students' thinking processes and interaction between the students. Technical problems with the software were equally prevalent in the haptic and non-haptic condition but were resolved quickly by restarting the system. A notable minority of pairs, both in haptic and non-haptic conditions, said that they found difficulty in grasping the objects in the system. Such comments were more frequent in the non-haptic condition.

7.4   Students' Perspectives on Using the System

All the students believed they gained a better understanding through using the VR system especially compared with more traditional methods of teaching and learning such as listening to the teacher or viewing static diagrams. The thematic analysis showed that, of the "liked features", seeing the model was most commented upon but it is notable that comments about "seeing" were twice as prevalent in the non-haptic condition. Being able to grasp and move the objects was also frequently commented on both in the haptic and non-haptic condition. For example, when asked what they liked about the system, one student commented:

> "Yeah, if you look at a diagram and you're told, well, oxygen can move freely, you don't necessarily take that in as much as if you actually could pick it up and move it, and you can see that it can move pretty freely."

Most students in the haptic condition commented that they liked to be able to feel the objects, for example:

> "It is really cool…you can actually feel the objects that you touch and it's, it's not like in a computer."

Overall, the thematic analysis suggested that the students appreciated being able to physically manipulate the model and thought that the system would support their learning.

As there were no differences in the number of data items coded to the "moving things" theme between the haptic non-haptic conditions, this supports the hypothesis that the haptic feedback is not necessary to aid manipulation. Furthermore, some students in the non-haptic system described their manipulation of the cell model with 'feeling' words, despite the lack of haptic feedback. Comments from the non-haptic students referred to being able to 'touch' things in the system. Some were well aware of the lack of feel and found being able to grasp objects with their fingers, but not feel them, quite strange, for example:

> "we couldn't actually feel them in a way.... It's really weird, it's like you can see you're moving something, but you can't feel like actually sense that you're moving it."

Others thought that they were somehow compensating by imagining the "feeling" of what they were seeing, for example:

> "I didn't feel too much, actually, with the haptic feedback… But ..I think it really will improve kind of being able to feel the resistance, cos you can kind of feel it in what you're seeing.".

Observations also suggested that students in the haptic condition were not all feeling the forces to the same extent.

8 Discussion and Conclusion

Findings from the pre-and post-tests revealed that students had better understanding of the subject matter after undertaking the activities with the system. Furthermore, findings from the interviews together with observations of the activities and videos showed that the students: were engaged with the system; they worked well together in their pairs to complete the tasks; found the experience fun and interesting and believed that they were learning. As there was no significant difference in knowledge gains between the haptic and non-haptic condition, in this study, turning off the haptics so that students could not actually feel the objects appears not to have affected their learning of the concepts involved. Observations of the students while they were undertaking the activities as well as students' own perspectives confirmed that turning off the haptic feedback generally did not inhibit the students from interacting with the system and carrying out the activities. Therefore, students were able to compensate for the lack of feel through visual cues. Indeed, as explained earlier, some of the students in the non-haptic condition discussed that they experienced a kind of feel, which is consistent with findings from recent research in pseudo-haptics in which pseudo-haptic feedback is created or promoted by visual cues [17].

As observations suggested that students did not all feel all the forces to the same extent, it is possible that the haptics in the system did not provide sufficient force for all students to perceive and this is also consistent with findings that haptic perception varies between different people [17]. Furthermore, it is possible that the various interruptions caused by technical problems, the novelty of the system and the engaging visual displays which would tend to be prominent owing to the visual dominant effect [18] interfered with their haptic perception.

Whether or not the haptic feedback is critical for students' learning, the addition of haptics to a VR system does provide a more complete and authentic experience. Furthermore, some students found the experience of being able to grasp objects without feeling them strange. Currently, the addition of haptics to VR systems presents significant technical challenges. Currently, haptic interfaces are relatively expensive whereas the cost of VR systems with 3D visual interfaces are reducing. If, as expected, it becomes possible to provide relatively inexpensive haptic interfaces to VR systems, then it will be important to identify the relative learning benefits and issues associated with haptic feedback in various situations.

While this investigation was of necessity conducted outside of their normal lessons and no elements of the usual interaction with a teacher were included in the activities, it is expected that normally a teacher would be able to support and scaffold the activities thus focusing students' attention to relevant phenomena including the haptics.

Limitations of the study include the relatively small number of participants which was limited by the availability of haptic devices. Furthermore, the study was conducted in selective schools so the students were not representative of the whole population of 12 to 13-year-olds.

Acknowledgments. The authors are pleased to acknowledge support for this work from the Leverhulme Foundation project '3D Learning in a Rich, Cooperative Haptic Environment'. We are also pleased to thank our colleagues on this project Jon Rashid, Carleen Houbart, Phil James, Richard Fisher, and Simon Bliss as well as all the students who participated.

References

1. Tokatli, O., et al.: Haptic interactions to support biology education: navigating the cell. Euro haptics, Imperial College, London (2016)
2. Webb, M., et al.: The potential for haptic-enabled interaction to support collaborative learning in school biology. In: Resta, P., Smith, S. (eds.) Society for Information Technology & Teacher Education International Conference 2017, pp. 927–935. Association for the Advancement of Computing in Education (AACE), Austin (2017)
3. Tuckey, H., Selvaratnam, M.: Studies involving three-dimensional visualisation skills in chemistry: a review. Stud. Sci. Educ. **21**, 99–121 (1993)
4. Gilbert, J.K.: Visualization: a metacognitive skill in science and science education. In: Gilbert, J.K. (ed.) Visualization in Science Education. MMSE, vol. 1, pp. 9–27. Springer, Dordrecht (2005). https://doi.org/10.1007/1-4020-3613-2_2
5. Webb, M.: Impact of IT on science education. In: Voogt, J., Knezek, G. (eds.) International Handbook of Information Technology in Primary and Secondary Education. SIHE, vol. 20, pp. 133–148. Springer, Boston (2008). https://doi.org/10.1007/978-0-387-73315-9_8
6. Shams, L., Seitz, A.R.: Benefits of multisensory learning. Trends Cogn. Sci. **12**, 411–417 (2008)
7. Paivio, A.: Mental imagery in associative learning and memory. Psychol. Rev. **76**, 241 (1969)
8. Paivio, A.: Intelligence, dual coding theory, and the brain. Intelligence **47**, 141–158 (2014)
9. Wong, A., Leahy, W., Marcus, N., Sweller, J.: Cognitive load theory, the transient information effect and e-learning. Learn. Instr. **22**, 449–457 (2012)
10. Kirschner, P.A., Sweller, J., Kirschner, F., Zambrano, R.J.: From cognitive load theory to collaborative cognitive load theory. Int. J. Comput.-Support. Collaborative Learn. **13**, 213–233 (2018)
11. Sweller, J.: Cognitive load theory, learning difficulty, and instructional design. Learn. Instr. **4**, 295–312 (1994)
12. Flores, F., Tovar, M.E., Gallegos, L.: Representation of the cell and its processes in high school students: an integrated view. Int. J. Sci. Educ. **25**, 269–286 (2003)

13. Malińska, L., Rybska, E., Sobieszczuk-Nowicka, E., Adamiec, M.: Teaching about water relations in plant cells: an uneasy struggle. CBE-Life Sci. Educ., **15**, ar78 (2016)
14. Hellenkamp, B., et al.: Precision and accuracy of single-molecule FRET measurements—a multi-laboratory benchmark study. Nat. Methods **15**, 669–676 (2018)
15. Deng, D., et al.: Crystal structure of the human glucose transporter GLUT1. Nature **510**, 121 (2014)
16. Campbell, J.L., Quincy, C., Osserman, J., Pedersen, O.K.: Coding in-depth semistructured interviews: problems of unitization and intercoder reliability and agreement. Sociol. Methods Res. **42**, 294–320 (2013)
17. Culbertson, H., Schorr, S.B., Okamura, A.M.: Haptics: the present and future of artificial touch sensation. Ann. Rev. Control Robot. Auton. Syst. **1**, 385–409 (2018)
18. Lukas, S., Philipp, A.M., Koch, I.: Switching attention between modalities: further evidence for visual dominance. Psychol. Res. PRPF **74**, 255–267 (2010)

Disciplinary Applications: Special Education

Formative Design and Evaluation of an Immersive Learning Intervention for Adults with Autism: Design and Research Implications

Matthew Schmidt[1], Dennis Beck[2(✉)], Noah Glaser[1], Carla Schmidt[3], and Fahad Abdeen[2]

[1] Department of Instructional Design and Technology,
University of Cincinnati, Cincinnati, OH, USA
{matthew.schmidt,glasernh}@ucmail.uc.edu
[2] Department of Curriculum and Instruction,
University of Arkansas, Fayetteville, AR, USA
{debeck,fabdeen}@uark.edu
[3] Department of Special Education, University of Cincinnati,
Cincinnati, OH, USA
schmicd@ucmail.uc.edu

Abstract. We present here the formative design and evaluation of Virtuoso, an immersive learning intervention for adults significantly impacted by autism. The intervention consisted of two components: a spherical, video-based VR intervention, and a headset-based VR intervention. VR-based interventions such as Virtuoso have garnered a modest basis of empirical support, but more is needed. The focus of the intervention was on using public transportation. Usage testing utilized multi-methods, including observational and survey methods. Results suggest a very positive user experience for participants using both video-based and headset-based VR, indicating the video-based condition was more relevant and easy to use. Implications for design and future directions for research related to VR-based interventions for individuals with autism are discussed.

1 Introduction

Findings from the evaluation of a virtual reality (VR) learning intervention named "Virtuoso" that was designed for adults with autism spectrum disorder (ASD) are presented in this paper. Components of Virtuoso that were evaluated consisted of two parts: (1) a spherical video-based virtual reality (SVVR) application, and (2) a headset-based, immersive virtual reality learning environment. Although many case studies exist on VR learning interventions, a reliable empirical basis that supports generalization of learning effects of VR for individuals with ASD does not exist. Many VR learning interventions focus on children and adolescents with high-functioning autism. Very little research has been performed on individuals who are more severely impacted by ASD. Likewise, little research focuses on using VR for adults with autism. Virtuoso focuses on adults enrolled in a day program that is geared towards more severe

© Springer Nature Switzerland AG 2019
D. Beck et al. (Eds.): iLRN 2019, CCIS 1044, pp. 71–85, 2019.
https://doi.org/10.1007/978-3-030-23089-0_6

manifestations of autism. The evaluation findings presented here serve as a potential entry point in addressing this gap in the literature, specifically targeting a population that has been traditionally underrepresented in VR learning intervention research.

2 Background

The impact of autism spectrum disorder is substantial, with one out of every 68 people being affected in the United States [1]. The American Psychiatric Association [2] characterizes autism as a spectrum of impairments that fall into the categories of (1) social, (2) communicative, and (3) behavioral. Challenges across these domains lead to difficulties related to adaptive skills, that is, practical, everyday skills needed to live in and meet the requirements of your environment, including the skills needed to care for yourself and interact with others. The research base is replete with quality exemplars of interventions designed to stimulate and develop adaptive skills, but obstacles to these best practices can be significant costs, geographically distant locations, and limited providers [3].

Many of the most recent learning interventions have used information and communications technologies (ICTs) [4, 5] as therapeutic interventions for individuals with ASD [6–8]. One area of ICTs, immersive technologies, can include many varieties and types, including virtual worlds, virtual reality, and video games. Many VR learning interventions only permit one person at a time to use the application due to experimental controls [8–10]. However, some educational technology research has explored the effectiveness of other multi-user, collaborative activities [11–13]. Some use the trace data generated by multi-user interactions in VR environments for data mining, providing new insights into collaborative learning [15]. The photographic realism of these environments is helpful in representing real world activities as well as embodiment as avatars that promote socio-communicative activity [14–16]. When working with individuals with ASD, VR environments enable researchers and practitioners to finely tune input stimuli, visual fidelity, and interactivity to create interventions that are uniquely attuned to the specific needs of specific learners with ASD [17].

Until recently, a significant barrier to the diffusion of VR technologies has been cost. However, the use of VR has recently increased with the corresponding decreasing costs of VR hardware and software. This is especially true for spherical video-based virtual reality (SVVR), in which users interact through head motions with the content within a first-person video environment [18]. SVVR features the use of 360-degree video to render the representation of the virtual environment, which the user can experience using a head-mounted display (HMD). These videos are created using 360-degree video cameras, which have become increasingly affordable.

Digitally modeled fantasy environments or recreations of real-world settings have been the staple of VR environments for years, but with the commercial availability of spherical video-based virtual reality, this could be changing. Developing video-based VR is less complex and less expensive, and thus more accessible in educational contexts [19]. Indeed, SVVR could help to bridge the gap between research and practice in the field of educational VR. However, despite the potential affordances of the technology, there remains a near absence of empirical and pedagogical support [20]. This paucity of support extends to individuals with ASD.

3 Methodology

A day program for adults with ASD at a large midwestern university was the setting for Virtuoso usage testing and evaluation. The day program focuses on individuals with significant communication and behavioral challenges associated with ASD. Participants are paired with a peer mentor that helps guide them through a personalized daily schedule. An interdisciplinary team of academic and clinical professionals designed and developed Virtuoso, coming from fields as diverse as special education, applied behavior analysis, ASD, instructional design, educational technology, and immersive learning. The encompassing purpose of Virtuoso was to assist day program participants to overcome one of the most cited barriers for individuals with disabilities – the use of public transportation [21, 22]. The Virtuoso team used applied behavior analysis principles in combination with immersive technologies and special education curriculum to develop a pilot public transportation training prototype.

As previously stated, the VR environments explored in this study include both SVVR (Virtuoso-SVVR) and traditional VR (Virtuoso-VR). For our Virtuoso-VR setting we used a digitally modeled recreation of a real-world setting – the large midwestern university where the day program is located (Fig. 1). The Virtuoso-SVVR environment is a spherical video environment of the same university. Virtuoso-SVVR was developed as an Android app that uses a video modeling format to present tasks (Fig. 2). The Google VR SDK for Unity with Android in 4K resolution was used for app development. A Samsung Gear 360 camera was used for all video recording. Day program participants used the gyroscopic controls of Android smartphones, a Google Cardboard HMD, or a Google Daydream HMD to control the application. The 360-degree videos follow a day program staff member prompting the viewer to engage in sequenced activities: (1) determining where to catch the shuttle, (2) walking to shuttle stop, (3) checking a university app to determine when shuttle will arrive, and finally (4) getting on shuttle.

Fig. 1. Participants walk together to the shuttle stop on the university campus.

Fig. 2. Screenshot of Virtuoso-SVVR illustrating the 360-degree view as represented in the Google Cardboard HMD.

The Virtuoso-VR intervention was developed using the High Fidelity (https://highfidelity.com/) virtual worlds toolkit, an open-source, multi-user application for constructing and implementing immersive environments. The VR environment was both social and interactive, meaning it allows for real-time creation, reorganization, and alteration of 3D assets. Day program participants interacted verbally with others in the environment using microphone-equipped headsets and were visually represented using avatars. The Virtuoso-VR environment allowed day program participants to interact with the 3D environment while also interacting socially with others. The social interaction was guided by a day program staff member (the "online guide"). The virtual space was structured to allow practice the same transportation skills as were used in the Virtuoso-SVVR application within a virtual replica of the university.

We describe here our formative evaluation of our interventions that train participants in transportation skills. A multi-methods, design based research approach was used to guide the Summer, 2018 formative evaluation. This included a usability evaluation and survey completion among five day program participant. Purposive sampling was used to identify day program participants based on level of independence, acuity score, and scores on standardized assessments. Firstly, training was conducted with participants in how to use both types of VR environments. Secondly, participants were asked to perform tasks using Virtuoso VR environments. Completion of these tasks in Virtuoso-SVVR took 8.2 min on average, while the same tasks took 9.3 min on average using Virtuoso-VR. All sessions were video and audio recorded for analysis and researchers took detailed field notes. After completing the tasks, each day program participant completed a version of the SUS [23] that the research team had modified to simplify its language.

3.1 Research Questions

Our research questions were:

1. How do usage test participants rate the ease-of-use of the Virtuoso SVVR and Virtuoso-VR interventions?
2. What is the nature of usage test participants' user experience with the Virtuoso SVVR and Virtuoso-VR interventions?
3. To what extent do the Virtuoso SVVR and Virtuoso-VR interventions meet the design goals of being feasible, relevant, and easy to use?

3.2 Intervention

Both the VR and SVVR Virtuoso interventions were evaluated across a variety of hardware and software.

The Virtuoso-SVVR intervention is described as follows:

1. One participant used the SVVR app on the Motorola zForce smartphone with no HMD
2. Two participants used the Motorola zForce smartphone with a Google Cardboard HMD
3. Three participants used the Motorola zForce smartphone with a Google Daydream HMD

The Virtuoso-VR intervention is described as follows:

1. One participant used a desktop VR configuration with monitor, keyboard, and mouse
2. Four participants used HTC Vive HMD with controllers on the Windows 10 platform
3. One participant used HTC Vive HMD with Xbox 360 controller on Windows 10 platform

For analysis, we investigated independent observations of the Virtuoso-VR and Virtuoso-SVVR videos from two raters along the coding scheme categories of (1) usability errors, (2) technology induced errors, and (3) amount of time elapsed for each video segment. Interobserver agreement scores and inter-rater reliability Kappa values met and exceeded established agreement metrics. To approach the question of the nature of user experience, inductive qualitative coding methods were employed with the goal of achieving categorical saturation.

4 Results

4.1 Agreement and Reliability Analyses

In this study, we compared independent observations from the two raters along the coding scheme categories of (1) usability errors, (2) technology induced errors, and (3) amount of time elapsed for each segment [24, 25]. A simple interobserver agreement (IOA) calculation was performed by taking the number of agreements between the independent observers in each categories and dividing by the total number of agreements plus disagreements in each category and multiplying by 100. Results indicated very high interobserver agreement for time frame (.875), usability errors (1) in the Virtuoso-SVVR condition. Results also indicated very high interobserver agreement for time frame (.906), usability errors (.909) and technology induced errors in the Virtuoso-VR condition.

Inter-rater reliability was calculated using the Kappa statistic. Kappa was calculated by taking the difference of the relative observed agreement among raters and the hypothetical probability of chance agreement divided by one minus the hypothetical probability of chance agreement (or K = (Po − Pe)/(1−Pe)), the results of which are provided in Table 1.

Table 1. Kappa calculations for usability errors, technology induced errors, and amount of time elapsed for each segment in the Virtuoso-SVVR and Virtuoso-VR usage study.

	Virtuoso-SVVR Kappa	Virtuoso-VR Kappa
Usability errors	1	0.8739255014
Technology induced errors	1	1

4.2 Results: Nature of Participants' User Experience

4.2.1 Analysis

To answer our second research question, "What is the nature of participants' user experience with the Virtuoso-SVVR and Virtuoso-VR interventions?" we used an iterative qualitative data analysis approach. To begin, a trained graduate student applied open coding processes [26], first reading through transcripts multiple times and creating preliminary labels to describe and begin to apply semantics to the data. These labels were used to create a provisional set of codes and coding definitions. These codes were refined using an axial coding process [27] that employed the five "intellectual habits of mind" outlined in Hubbard and Power [28]. The trained graduate student recursively reviewed the coded transcripts and coding categories to ensure identified concepts and themes accurately reflected participants' voices.

Following this, we explored relationships between the emergent themes, leading to identification of new codes and themes and further underscoring the relevance of identified themes. Through this process, we identified two overarching themes specifically related to the nature of user experience (accessibility and user affect). We also identified a number of passages that have implications concerning generalization. A listing of the categories and codes that emerged from this qualitative process can be found in Table 2.

To further explore the semantic and conceptual properties of the coded data, the graduate student worked with a professional researcher to cluster coding categories using affinity mapping techniques and associated them with the overarching themes in a concept map. By constructing this concept map, themes and clustered coding categories were organized in a downward branching hierarchical structure. This process

Table 2. Qualitative codes and operationalizations

Code		Operationalization
Affect	Joy, fun, or excitement	A participant expresses a positive state of affect including statements of joy (e.g., having fun), or excitement with their experience in the intervention
	Willingness to return	A participant expresses desire to return to use the intervention again during their session
Accessibility	Physical accessibility	The intervention's content and/or possibilities for action have implications for physical accessibility
	Cognitive accessibility	The intervention's content and/or possibilities for action have implications for the cognitive accessibility
	Cybersickness	A participant states or physically exhibits symptoms of cybersickness
Generalization	Usefulness/Relevance	A participant comments on the usefulness or applicability of content and/or activities in the intervention
	Recognizability of Assets/Realism	A participant matches assets in the intervention with real-world counterparts or when they comment on the realism of assets or actions in intervention
	Real-world connections	A participant describes connections between tasks/activities in the intervention with analogous tasks/activities in the real-world

helped to reveal structural affinities among the coding categories and ultimately to make connections between our thematic categories and our research question focusing on the nature of user experience.

4.2.2 Findings

Generally speaking, the nature of usage test participants' user experience can be characterized as particularly enjoyable, despite a variety of usability errors and technological bugs. The Virtuoso-SVVR intervention was more stable than the VR intervention, with only one serious bug being observed. Overall, the Virtuoso-SVVR intervention was perceived as being highly usable, having strong physical and cognitive accessibility, having simple controls, and being well received by study participants. For instance, Participant 2 indicated strong curiosity and interest with the Virtuoso-SVVR application: "Oh…Wait…I'm a little—how did you formulate this? This is awesome." In contrast, the VR intervention proved to have somewhat unpredictable stability. This was in large part due to the immaturity of the underlying High Fidelity virtual worlds toolkit software, which was still in development. This led to routine and sometimes predictable system instability and crashes. However, despite the instability, participants were surprisingly tolerant of errors and eager to engage with the software.

By "error tolerance", we refer to participants' willingness to continue to experience, finish, and find satisfaction with the system over the course of a usage testing session, in spite of usability errors and technical instability. For example, participant 2 said his favorite part was just moving around, "Just trying to mess around with the controls. Yes. It was very simple the moment you get used to like... The controls were simple. The controls are very simple." This quote came from his second session with the VR environment that took 3 min longer than his first usage of this environment, largely in part to the fact that there were six coded instances of system crashes. Despite the prominent problems observed during the session, this participant still found it to be enjoyable and seemingly had a high error tolerance. We found evidence of error tolerance across Virtuoso-VR and Virtuoso-SVVR, with average rates of 0.32 errors per minute for participants using Virtuoso-SVVR, and average rates of 1.24 errors per minute for participants using Virtuoso-VR. Despite these errors, no participant asked to leave the usage test, no participants expressed dissatisfaction with either of the intervention platforms, and participants, on the whole, expressed a sense of joy and excitement with using the intervention. Analysis of usage session videos and transcripts suggest that this error tolerance potentially could be related to the reinforcing nature of the intervention.

4.2.3 Affect

By "affect," we refer to how participants expressed themselves in relation to mood, feelings, and attitudes during usage testing. Statements were found in nearly all sessions indicating positive affect related to Virtuoso. For example: RESEARCHER: "So, you also said you had fun. What did you find fun?" P2: "Just trying to mess around with the controls." Some participants also indicated that they were excited to leave and tell their friends about Virtuoso. Participant 4 stated many times, "I would love to tell my friends about that." This sentiment was shared by Participant 5 when asked if he would tell his friends about Virtuoso: "I would."

It appears that participants overwhelmingly found their usage test experience to be enjoyable. After completion of their session, some asked if they could come back and use the system again. In fact, Participants 1 and 2 returned for multiple sessions. Many participants described our systems as "cool." Participant 5 asked when we would be releasing our project to the public: "How do the others use the app or get it?...Is this a mobile app that you can get for the iPad?" We do however note that the affect and error tolerance experienced by our participants is based on the caveat that they spent a limited amount of time in Virtuoso. More exposure and usage with the same rate of errors could change the affective state of our participants.

4.2.4 Accessibility

While user experience was positive, analysis uncovered accessibility challenges which could be exacerbated with prolonged exposure to the system. While most participants quickly learned to use the system, notable concerns arose around three dimensions of accessibility: (1) physical accessibility, (2) cognitive accessibility, and (3) cyber sickness.

Physical accessibility. Physical accessibility issues were observed as participants sought to gain fluency using the VR controllers - the Google Daydream remote and the HTC Vive controller (see Table 2). While most users gained fluency quickly with controls, others faced challenges. For instance, Participant 1 struggled to operate the Vive's default controllers due to psychomotor impairments. The Virtuoso system was designed to support alternative input devices for situations such as this; thus, we were able to replace the Vive controller with a Microsoft Xbox 360 controller. This replacement alleviated the accessibility issues for this participant.

Cognitive accessibility. In designing Virtuoso, we set out to instantiate design standards that could address challenges related to using technologies for people with cognitive disabilities [29]. We paid particular interest to supporting executive functioning, language, literacy, perception, and reasoning. For example, instead of using text-only, we applied multiple means of representation via images and numbers paired with written text for activity schedules, maps, icons, signage, navigation supports, etc. Participants were able to utilize these features with the exception of Participant 3, who had challenges navigating and working his way through the Virtuoso-SVVR application. He inadvertently skipped one of the tasks when completing the usage test because he was unable to identify the button he was asked to select. For the following Virtuoso-VR test, the online guide read all text to the participant to address these accessibility issues.

Cybersickness. Research suggests that a majority of users can experience symptoms of cybersickness after just ten minutes in a VR platform (Table 2) [30]. Noting that the majority of research related to cybersickness has focused on people who are neurotypical, we characterized cybersickness as an accessibility issue given that our target population was prone to sensory processing issues. Following each usage session, we asked participants if they felt discomfort and if they were experiencing symptoms of cybersickness.

Of the participants that used the Google Daydream, none of them reported feelings of physical discomfort. Three of the five participants stated that they did not experience any symptoms of cybersickness such as headaches, eyestrain, dizziness, or nausea, however Participant 2 related the following:

RESEARCHER: Why are you leaning back? *P2:* I'm disorientated.

RESEARCHER: What do you mean by 'disorientated?' *P2:* Like that... [inaudible]. Okay. [exasperated tone] Oh boy!

RESEARCHER: Can you tell me how you physically feel? *P2:* Like [tone rising] whooooo boy!

RESEARCHER: Like dizzy or a headache? *P2:* Oh no, it's somewhat dizzy and somewhat out on the roof.

RESEARCHER: Okay. Do you need a drink or water or something? *P2:* I'm fine.

RESEARCHER: Okay... *P2:* So, I don't think virtual reality is for me.

Interestingly enough, despite the claim that "I don't think virtual reality is for me," Participant 2 insisted on returning to complete the second part of that day's session and later asked to return the following day for a second usage test. In subsequent testing sessions, Participant 2 did not demonstrate or communicate any further cybersickness. This may be an indication of an overall positive, enjoyable, and enthusiastic affective state towards Virtuoso.

4.2.5   Generalization

Virtuoso includes elements of the natural environment with the goal of exploiting functional contingencies that exist in the real world, which are thought to promote training and reinforcement of desired skills [9, 31]. Therefore, one of our design principles was centered around creating an environment that participants could relate to, would find realistic, and would convey a sense of presence or a feeling of really "being there."

We found that users found our environment to be useful and realistic, commented on the recognizability of the assets, and were able to match where they were within the virtual environment with corresponding real-world locations. In Virtuoso-VR, participants recognized the adult day program office space and, when prompted, were able to walk to their personal workspaces and those of their friends. Using Virtuoso-SVVR, Participant 2 was immediately able to recognize his location in the Impact Innovation offices and reacted positively: "Oh. Wait. I'm a little—that's the plant thing... ... before you come in. And that's the work [space]" Participant 4 was also able to recognize many of the assets: "I know where those seats are... It's outside by Dyer Hall. That's right. Where the new café is. That's right. And it's University Square straight ahead. I recognize that hat you got on too, Greg."

After usage testing concluded, some participants were also able to identify their current location relative to the environments and tasks portrayed in the Virtuoso environment, suggesting some degree of generalization. Participant 4 was asked, "Do you think you can find that shuttle stop outside?" He responded positively and was able to look out the window and point to the shuttle stop that he had visited in the virtual environment. In another session, Participant 5 indicated he might be able to identify the location of the bus stop:

RESEARCHER: Do you feel like it was realistic? *P5:* I do.

RESEARCHER: Do you feel like if I asked you to point out where that bus stop was, do you think you could point where it was? *P5:* Probably.

5   Discussion

5.1   Applications for Virtuoso Intervention

5.1.1   Accessibility and Error Tolerance

Accessibility was the first overarching theme that was derived from the nature of the participants' experience. This is important, as accessibility and thus error tolerance was a design principle of Virtuoso, which was based on the Universal Design principle of tolerance for error, which focuses on minimizing hazards and the adverse consequences of accidental or unintended actions [32]. In this study we defined error tolerance from a participants perspective, as their willingness to continue to experience, finish, and find satisfaction from the system despite usability errors and prominent technical mishaps throughout the course of the usage study. Error tolerance is inextricably linked to accessibility as it measures participants' ability to persist in a task despite the presence of these errors.

Errors can originate in any of the processes that a user goes through to perform an action [33]. Furthermore, it is usually assumed that errors are not the fault of the user if determined by factors outside of their control [34]. This parallels our categorization of errors as technology-induced and usability related. Our results showed some evidence of error tolerance among users. Despite an error rate of 1.24 times per minute for participants using the collaborative 3D virtual learning environment, no participant asked to leave the usage test and no participant expressed dissatisfaction with the platforms. Interestingly, participant usability errors were much more frequent in the Virtuoso-VR environment compared to the Virtuoso-SVVR environment. We can also see the type of usability error in both environments involved the user not understanding instructions or the language or labels used in the interface (physical and cognitive accessibility), while technology induced errors were more frequent in the Virtuoso-VR environment. Research in the field of error management explores the effects of factors like cognitive abilities, resources (e.g. time, memory and attention) and control strategies on performance and learning [35]. It is possible that these specific types of errors were present due to the unique challenges experienced in the areas of physical and cognitive accessibility present in individuals with ASD. If so, future research should consider how accurate measurement of specific participant abilities in these areas can result in better design of *Virtuoso* that may in turn result in a lower presence of these kind of errors.

5.1.2 Affect

Affect was the second overarching theme that was derived from the nature of the participants' experience. In this study we defined affective state of being as how the participants expressed themselves in relation to their moods, feelings, and attitudes. In our study, participants on the whole expressed an intense sense of joy and excitement with using both of the learning environments. Participants specifically mentioned their ability to navigate, and the realism of the environment as sources of their positive affect. The intensity of the positive affect was also shown through their spoken desire to share *Virtuoso* with their friends and family.

Affective cues are insights into the emotions and behaviors of individuals with ASD, and as such the ability to utilize the power of these cues is critical given the importance of human affective information in human-computer interaction [36], the significant impacts of the affective factors of individuals with ASD on intervention [37], and the core social and communicative vulnerabilities that limit individuals with ASD to accurately self-identify affective experiences [38]. Some VR systems have been formulated to monitor the affective response of individuals with ASD using physiological signals and subsequently manipulating aspects of social communication in response [39]. If *Virtuoso* stimulates intense positive affect from participants, then future design iterations should consider how to capitalize on that positive affect to reinforce learning and performance.

5.1.3 Generalization

Generalization was the third overarching theme that was derived from the nature of the participants' experience. We defined generalization as observable changes in behavior in settings different from the training environment and "across stimuli, responses, and time" [31] (p. 721). Stokes and Baer [40] identified nine techniques designed to promote generalization, which were later categorized into three broad principles [31], including taking advantage of natural communities of reinforcement, training diversely, and incorporating functional mediators.

Our results showed some evidence of generalization of the adaptive skills learned in *Virtuoso*. This supports one of the design principles of Virtuoso, nature communities of reinforcement [41, 42] as well as other research that suggests that a high visual fidelity and realistic representation of assets helps to promote generalization for people with autism [9]. Participants in Virtuoso easily recognized their location in both the Virtuoso-VR and Virtuoso-SVVR environments, although more so in the latter environment. Also, after the usage test, some of them could remember the tasks and places in the immersive environments and connect them to where they were at on the campus and in a specific building. suggesting some degree of generalization. This has clear implications for future iterations of *Virtuoso*, in which a redesign of the Virtuoso-VR environment using Unity 3D is planned. Unity is an integrated design environment where the "visible pieces" of a game can be put together with a graphical preview and using a controlled "play it" function. Its advantages include higher visual fidelity and realistic representation of assets than the currently used High Fidelity platform. As a result, we hope that this will in turn increase generalization of adaptive skills among future *Virtuoso* users.

5.1.4 Limitations

This research is limited in that it is based on a qualitative analysis of a small sample of participants. Therefore the generalizability and applicability of our findings may not apply in other contexts and with other populations. This notwithstanding, autism is a low incidence disability, and therefore research involving smaller sample sizes and single-subject designs is prevalent [43].

6 Conclusion

The work of *Virtuoso* is very relevant to those designing immersive learning experiences for adults with disabilities. Both kinds of VR environments used in this study haven't been studied enough in the literature and are becoming much less expensive and easier to use and implement. Additionally, the formative evaluation of Virtuoso described above could be could be helpful to others interested in designing training content for generalization.

Other disability areas which experience deficits in executive functioning among individuals could benefit from similar interventions, (e.g., Down syndrome, traumatic brain injury, cognitive impairment, etc.). The social validity of any intervention approach is, of course, an important consideration, and especially among those that would be considered a vulnerable population. How can we make Virtuoso more and more accessible, relevant, and easy to use? How can we make the methods, processes, technologies, and training content developed by Virtuoso widely available? These questions should be always at the forefront of our minds, and perhaps we may bridge the gap between what virtual reality environments have often promised, but not fulfilled [9].

In this paper, we presented the full range of results, including lessons learned and implications for research and practice and how these findings shape the design principles of our educational design research. These findings provide unique insights into developing training interventions in adaptive skills for adults with ASD, and may lead to greater degrees of independence, thus increasing the potential to impact overall quality of life.

References

1. Centers for Disease Control Autism and Developmental Disabilities Monitoring Network. Prevalence of autism spectrum disorder among children aged 8 years. Atlanta, GA (2014). http://www.cdc.gov/mmwr/preview/mmwrhtml/ss6302a1.htm?s_cid=ss6302a1_w
2. American Psychiatric Association: Diagnostic and Statistical Manual of Mental Disorders (5th edn.). Washington, DC (2013)
3. Zhang, L., Warren, Z., Swanson, A., Weitlauf, A., Sarkar, N.: Understanding performance and verbal-communication of children with ASD in a collaborative virtual environment. J. Autism Dev. Disord. **48**, 1–11 (2018)
4. Barton, E.E., Pustejovsky, J.E., Maggin, D.M., Reichow, B.: Technology-aided instruction and intervention for students with ASD: a meta-analysis using novel methods of estimating effect sizes for single-case research. Remedial Spec. Educ. **38**(6), 371–386 (2017)
5. Boucenna, S., et al.: Interactive technologies for autistic children: a review. Cogn. Comput. **6**(4), 722–740 (2014)
6. Goodwin, M.S.: Enhancing and accelerating the pace of autism research and treatment: the promise of developing innovative technology. Focus Autism Other Dev. Disabil. **23**(2), 125–128 (2008)
7. Grynszpan, O., Weiss, P.L., Perez-Diaz, F., Gal, E.: Innovative technology-based interventions for autism spectrum disorders: a meta-analysis. Autism **18**(4), 346–361 (2014)
8. Odom, S.L., et al.: Technology-aided interventions and instruction for adolescents with autism spectrum disorder. J. Autism Dev. Disord. **45**(12), 3805–3819 (2015)
9. Rutten, A., et al.: The AS interactive project: single-user and collaborative virtual environments for people with high-functioning autistic spectrum disorders. Comput. Anim. Virtual Worlds **14**(5), 233–241 (2003)
10. Parsons, S.: Authenticity in virtual reality for assessment and intervention in autism: a conceptual review. Educ. Res. Rev. **19**, 138–157 (2016). https://doi.org/10.1016/j.edurev.2016.08.001
11. Trepagnier, C.Y., Olsen, D.E., Boteler, L., Bell, C.A.: Virtual conversation partner for adults with autism. Cyberpsychol. Behav. Soc. Netw. **14**(1–2), 21–27 (2011)
12. Jarrold, W., et al.: Social attention in a virtual public speaking task in higher functioning children with autism. Autism Res. **6**(5), 393–410 (2013)
13. Lorenzo, G., Pomares, J., Lledó, A.: Inclusion of immersive virtual learning environments and visual control systems to support the learning of students with asperger syndrome. Comput. Educ. **62**, 88–101 (2013)
14. Moore, D., Cheng, Y., McGrath, P., Powell, N.J.: Collaborative virtual environment technology for people with autism. Focus Autism Other Dev. Disabil. **20**(4), 231–243 (2005)

15. Schmidt, M., Laffey, J.:. Visualizing behavioral data from a 3D virtual learning environment: a preliminary study. In: IEEE Proceedings of the 45th Hawaii International Conference on System Science (HICSS), pp. 3387–3394 (2012). https://doi.org/10.1109/HICSS.2012.639

16. Wang, X., Laffey, J., Xing, W., Ma, Y., Stichter, J.: Exploring embodied social presence of youth with autism in 3D collaborative virtual learning environment: a case study. Comput. Hum. Behav. **55**, 310–321 (2016)

17. Wallace, S., Parsons, S., Bailey, A.: Self-reported sense of presence and responses to social stimuli by adolescents with autism spectrum disorder in a collaborative virtual reality environment. J. Intellect. Dev. Disabil. **42**(2), 131–141 (2017)

18. Glaser, N.J., Schmidt, M.: Usage considerations of 3D collaborative virtual learning environments to promote development and transfer of knowledge and skills for individuals with autism. Technol. Knowl. Learn. (2018). https://doi.org/10.1007/s10758-018-9369-9

19. Hwang, G.-J., Jong, M.S.Y., Shang, J.: Call for papers. Interact. Learn. Environ. **26**(4), 566 (2018)

20. Brown, A., Green, T.: Virtual reality: low-cost tools and resources for the classroom. TechTrends **60**(5), 517–519 (2016)

21. Fowler, C.: Virtual reality and learning: where is the pedagogy? Br. J. Educ. Technol. **46**(2), 412–422 (2015)

22. Allen, S.M., Moore, V.: The prevalence and consequences of unmet need: contrasts between older and younger adults with disability. Med. Care **35**(11), 1132–1148 (1997)

23. Carmien, S., Dawe, M., Fischer, G., Gorman, A., Kintsch, A., Sullivan Jr., J.F.: Socio-technical environments supporting people with cognitive disabilities using public transportation. ACM Trans. Comput.-Hum. Interact. (TOCHI) **12**(2), 233–262 (2005)

24. Brooke, J.: SUS-A quick and dirty usability scale. Usabil. Eval. Ind. **189**(194), 4–7 (1996)

25. Khowaja, K., Salim, S.S.: Heuristics to evaluate interactive systems for children with autism spectrum disorder (ASD). PLoS One **10**(7), e0132187 (2015)

26. Nielsen, J.: 10 usability heuristics for user interface design. Nielsen Norman Group, 1(1) (1995)

27. Benaquisto, L.: Open coding. In: Given, L.M. (ed.) The SAGE Encyclopedia of Qualitative Research Methods, p. 582. SAGE Publications Inc., Thousand Oaks (2008). https://doi.org/10.4135/9781412963909.n299

28. Simmons, N.: Axial coding. In: Allen, M. (ed.) The Sage Encyclopedia of Communication Research Methods, pp. 80–82. SAGE Publications Inc., Thousand Oaks (2017). https://doi.org/10.4135/9781483381411.n33

29. Hubbard, R.S., Power, B.M.: The Art of Classroom Inquiry: A Handbook for Teacher Researchers, Revised edn. Heinemann, Portsmouth (2003)

30. Steel, E.J., Janeslätt, G.: Drafting standards on cognitive accessibility: a global collaboration. Disabil. Rehabil. Assistive Technol. **12**(4), 385–389 (2017)

31. Cobb, S.V., Nichols, S., Ramsey, A., Wilson, J.R.: Virtual reality-induced symptoms and effects (VRISE). Presence Teleoperators Virtual Environ. **8**(2), 169–186 (1999)

32. Stokes, T.F., Osnes, P.G.: An operant pursuit of generalization – republished article. Behav. Ther. **47**, 720–732 (2016)

33. Connell, B.R., et al.: The principles of universal design. NCSU (1997). http://www.ncsu.edu/ncsu/design/cud/about_ud/udprinciplestext.htm. Accessed 22 Feb 2019

34. Wickens, C.: Engineering Psychology and Human Performance. Charles E. Merrill, Columbus (1984)

35. Noroozi, A., Khan, F., MacKinnon, S., Amyotte, P., Deacon, T.: Determination of human error probabilities in maintenance procedures of a pump. Process Saf. Environ. Prot. **92**, 131–141 (2012)

36. Zhang, Y., Goonetilleke, R.S., Plocher, T., Liang, S.-F.M.: Time-related behaviour in multitasking situations. Int. J. Hum.-Comput. Stud. **62**, 425–455 (2005)
37. Picard, R.W.: Affective Computing. MIT Press, Cambridge (1997)
38. Seip, J.A.: Teaching the Autistic and Developmentally Delayed: A Guide for Staff Training and Development. British Columbia, Delta (1996)
39. Hill, E., Berthoz, S., Frith, U.: Brief report: cognitive processing of own emotions in individuals with autistic spectrum disorder and in their relatives. J. Autism Dev. Disord. **34**(2), 229–234 (2004)
40. Welch, K.C., Lahiri, U., Liu, C., Weller, R., Sarkar, N., Warren, Z.: An affect-sensitive social interaction paradigm utilizing virtual reality environments for autism intervention. In: Jacko, J.A. (ed.) HCI 2009. LNCS, vol. 5612, pp. 703–712. Springer, Heidelberg (2009). https://doi.org/10.1007/978-3-642-02580-8_77
41. Stokes, T.F., Baer, D.M.: An implicit technology of generalization. J. Appl. Behav. Anal. **10**(2), 349–367 (1977)
42. Stokes, T.F., Fowler, S.A., Baer, D.M.: Training preschool children to recruit natural communities of reinforcement. J. Appl. Behav. Anal. **11**(2), 285–303 (1978)
43. Case-Smith, J., Weaver, L.L., Fristad, M.A.: A systematic review of sensory processing interventions for children with autism spectrum disorders. Autism **19**(2), 133–148 (2015)

Learning Through Experiences: Accessible Fabricated Dioramas for the Visually Impaired

Myrsini Samaroudi[(✉)] and Karina Rodriguez Echavarria

Centre for Secure, Intelligent and Usable Systems,
University of Brighton, Brighton, UK
{M.Samaroudi,K.Rodriguez}@brighton.ac.uk

Abstract. This paper investigates digitally fabricated replicas and how these contribute as novel interpretative means to support visitor experiences in cultural heritage contexts. The paper's main contribution is the evaluation of the experience that visually impaired users had with a 3d printed relief of a Victorian environmental display, or diorama, from the Booth Museum of Natural History in Brighton (UK) along with a pervasive audio mobile application. Our intention is to illuminate the subtleties, interests and learning through experiences with objects and supporting interpretative applications in the cultural heritage sector.

Keywords: Digital fabrication · 3D printing ·
Environmental displays · Dioramas · Visually impaired · Museums ·
Audience research

1 Introduction

Digitally fabricated artefacts, or replicas, can be defined as objects that have been produced by using digital technologies and refer to or depict cultural heritage (CH) artefacts. The production pipeline of replicas includes: a. digitally capturing the shape and appearance of an object with 3D imaging technologies; b. processing the data; and c. using fabrication technology to recreate it (e.g. with a 3D printer) and applying all necessary post-processing steps.

Over the last decades, 3D imaging technologies and consequently digital fabrication products have become popular due to reasons which are mostly related to the technology becoming more accurate, cheaper and easier to use. Following this trend, the CH sector has been an important field to test technologies for a variety of purposes when managing cultural heritage assets (e.g. conservation, exhibition planning, packaging and other). Amongst the most important applications of digital fabrication are these that belong to the realm of communication, information dissemination, interpretation and learning [18, 19, 26, 27].

At the same time, context-aware ubiquitous applications are gradually gaining more space in CH settings aiming to support users when exploring collections,

© Springer Nature Switzerland AG 2019
D. Beck et al. (Eds.): iLRN 2019, CCIS 1044, pp. 86–100, 2019.
https://doi.org/10.1007/978-3-030-23089-0_7

based on personal information and needs [6,7]. Combining ubiquitous applications and the physical aspect of digitally fabricated replicas has the potential to enhance CH experiences in ways that were not possible before. Hence, new opportunities for accessing a more democratised cultural heritage arise [17,18] through experiences which: allow people to become involved with the physicality of CH objects; embrace the "Design for All" principles [8]; aim to enhance learning and appreciation of CH resources, perceived in terms of a constant constructive dialogue between the individual, contextual factors and actual life connotations [12,13,15]. The possibilities are immeasurable if we also consider that the physical aspect of a replica can be edited and customised to satisfy specific audience groups -such as the visually impaired community- according to their requirements and circumstances [26], while being transparent and conscious about design and fabrication choices. Nonetheless, a number of questions arises regarding the effectiveness of these experiences for learning and enjoyment of cultural heritage, as it happens with the introduction of all new technologies in the CH sector [10].

Fig. 1. (a) Dioramas at the Booth Museum; (b) the selected diorama; (c) 3D printed relief; and (d) interface of the mobile application.

This paper presents the evaluation of an experience focusing on visually impaired users interested in natural history. The research pertains to the exhibits of the Booth Museum of Natural History in Brighton (UK) and its collection of Victorian dioramas [28] which have been designated as being of national importance [24]. These dioramas are not accessible for visually impaired users as they are enclosed in glass displays (Fig. 1a). Therefore, an application was developed in order to assist visually impaired users to explore a diorama from the Booth Museum. The chosen diorama showcases a kittiwake standing on a rock and gazing across the horizon (Fig. 1b). The proposed solution enables the tactile exploration a 3D printed relief (Fig. 1c) in conjunction with a context-aware audio mobile application using proximity beacons (Fig. 1d). The audio description provides information about the diorama, the relief, the bird's species and the sound of the kittiwake's call. More information about the design of the relief and the application can be found in [25].

The paper is structured as follows: Sect. 2 presents related work. Section 3 describes the case study where the relief and mobile application were deployed and the evaluation findings. Finally, Sect. 4 presents the discussion and conclusions along with future work.

2   Related Work

3D replicas have already served a variety of purposes in managing CH resources [3,26]. Recently, they were also introduced to communicate CH information within interpretative and creative scenarios. To date, there are not many evaluation reports in literature regarding replicas in experiential frameworks. More rare are reports concerning the experience of visually impaired users.

[19] refer to an evaluation of tactile paintings given to visually impaired people. [22] talk about the qualities of tactile paintings, stating that a more comprehensive study should be planned in the future. In later evaluations of replicas with blind and partially sighted visitors, [23] assess users' feedback using both quantitative and qualitative methods focusing on materiality and interaction with replicas. In one of their latest publications, [21] evaluate a gesture-based system to experience tactile paintings. They deploy techniques of quantitative nature for the evaluation, reflecting the traditional aspects of user experience (UX). [5] similarly evaluate paintings with visually impaired users quantitatively focusing on the readability, recognition and comprehension of objects after explorations with a decreasing difficulty level. Finally, [1] evaluate a system to assist blind and partially sighted people when experiencing full 3D replicas in museums deploying observations and interviews. However, they mostly focus on usability which is measured in terms of task success, time and number of errors.

By looking at these examples it becomes understood that the evaluation of similar experiences deploying replicas is an active and interesting field of research. Our effort focuses on addressing holistically the questions around replicas and their effectiveness to support visually impaired users in novel ways.

3   Case Study

3.1   Evaluation Design and Participants

A case study to investigate how a specific target audience responds to multiple aspects of a context-dependent CH experience with the use of a 3d printed relief was designed. The study's target audience involved adult visually impaired participants. The evaluation took place at the Booth Museum and at the premises of the Blind Veterans charity in Brighton (Fig. 2). The initial intention was to test only within the museum's context. However, soon it became obvious that this would not be feasible, as very few visually impaired people visit the museum outside of an "organised activity".

To address the questions about the contribution of the replica and application in the experience, both quantitative and qualitative data were collected.

Fig. 2. Testing the relief and application with a visually impaired user.

Data collection methods included video recordings, observations, questionnaires, interviews and focus groups. The topics of investigation draw on relativist constructivist theories, exploring contextual learning [12–14] and visitor agendas in terms of personal, social and physical context. The evaluation also examines the outcome of the experience through a set of themes reflecting learning and CH appreciation in the broader sense as proposed -amongst others- by [2,9]. These refer to: awareness/knowledge; engagement/interest; attitudes; behaviours; skills.

3.2 Findings

The data that are analysed reflect the opinions, ideas and overall evaluation of the experience with the 3D printed relief and audio context-aware application from eleven (11) participants. For the analysis of data, we use a thematic structure focusing on the personal, social and physical context [11].

Personal Context. Six (6) participants were women, (two blind and four partially sighted). Men participants were five (5) (three partially sighted and two blind). All blind participants had previous sight memory. Only one participant was a Braille reader. Older ages are over-represented in the study, because most participants were members of the Blind Veterans Charity, where younger people constitute a "valuable minority" as one participant stated.

All participants came from a white ethnic background and live in the south part of England. Participants had different levels of knowledge/experience and expectations/motivations with regards to museum visits, interaction with objects and background information. Only two (2) had visited the Booth museum in the past, even though eight (8) of them live less than fifteen (15) miles away from it. Most of the participants' past or current occupation was not related to CH either (only two had relevant work experience).

People had limited experience in touching objects in museums (Fig. 3a). Such finding is not surprising as only in the last decades CH organisations started

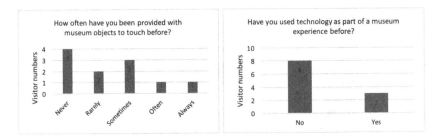

Fig. 3. (a) Previous experience in touching objects; (b) previous experience in using IT.

integrating touch as a rather fundamental way to experience heritage for the visually impaired and other audience groups [4,16]. The only participants who had regular opportunities to touch objects were the two with relevant professional experience, hence enjoyed "privileged institutional" access to artefacts. Information technology (IT) had not been part of most people's experiences in museums either (Fig. 3 b). Such finding might be related to the age of participants, as two out of the three with previous IT experience in CH settings were of a younger age and belonged to the group of 50–59 year olds.

Table 1. Tendencies in participants' expectations.

Expectations (tendencies)	Representative people's comments
Tactile experience	"I expected that the presentation would be different and that we wouldn't find glass displays. We have got to be able to touch"
Feedback session	"I had a vague idea of what we have done here" "Touching a relief while hearing the audio description of a box in front of me."
No expectation/Not sure about it	"I didn't really know what to expect" "I had no idea"
Find out and participate	"I am always interested in what is going on"
Learn about 3D printing	"I am interested in 3D printing"

In terms of people's expectations, the intention was to find out what people were looking forward to doing during the visit or exploration. Five main tendencies have been recognised (*see* Table 1). Most comments can be explained as the result of an organised activity. It is very rare to find in CH research and beyond examples of feedback collection from visually impaired users outside of an "institutional" framework. Such remark highlights the still existing societal incapacity to provide access to infrastructures for visually impaired people on a regular basis. Therefore, "outings" to museums might still impose physical and cognitive barriers for people with some kind of disability.

Quite similar are the results when examining people's interests concerning the collections of the museum. Five tendencies were noted: interest in the general collection; interest in the birds' collection; no specific interest; interest in fossils; interest in "whatever is accessible". For many participants visiting a museum is an opportunity to socialise and enjoy an activity that brings a change to their daily routines, without having a specific interest in the museum's collections.

Social Context. The first thing to examine as for the social context of the experience is the composition of each exploration. Both sessions were part of "scheduled" events. The place of the data collection dictated whether people came accompanied or not. At the Booth Museum, three out of the four participants had a volunteer who came with them, whereas at the Blind Veterans' institute all participants were on their own. In two cases, where the participants had their "helper" along, it was observed that the helper occasionally was in charge. Blind or partially sighted people were relying on them in many instances during the exploration. Helpers would often guide the participant to sit and help find the relief; motivate them to interact with it; and provide confirmation or assistance. The environment in all cases was not crowded as trials took place in pre-booked rooms. When the participants had hearing aids, external noise made listening to the audio description and focusing on it more difficult.

Physical Context. The physical context refers to the CH object itself, hence the diorama which was present in all sessions. Then, the location and its atmosphere are examined. At the Booth museum, a small room serving as storage space with shelves full of dioramas was provided. The particular smell of the museum (due to specimens) was noticeable. At the premises of the Blind Veterans, the room was in a busy area of the building. People generally seemed more comfortable in the premises of the Blind Veterans, as this was a place they knew, whereas they were relying on other people to move around at the Booth museum. Thus, even though the museum might imply a more "original" experience in spatiotemporal terms, there is a trade-off, as people are not fully confident in exploring independently exhibits and collections yet. Therefore, the portability of 3d printed replicas might be of great importance in order to facilitate access to museum content out of its physical boundaries.

Eight (8) out of the eleven (11) participants found both the exhibit and replica easily and they were attracted by it. As for the interpretative means, most people noticed the Braille label, but they did not pay much attention to it. The only participant who was a Braille reader, identified it immediately by touch and read "kittiwake" aloud. The interpretative means that participants paid most attention to are presented in Fig. 4a. Most participants paid attention both to the relief and the audio description. Those who had partial sight occasionally turned to look at the display (maybe to corroborate information). Two participants explored all means at the same time. One participant only focused on the audio and the diorama. This person, though, had enough sight to rely on it. The only participant who focused mostly on the audio, found it difficult to explore the relief while listening to the description. This person had visual memory and had not acquired tactile skills at an early stage of life.

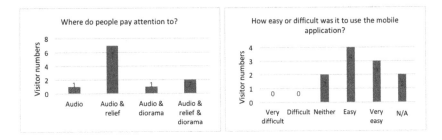

Fig. 4. (a) Attraction to interpretative media; (b) usability evaluation.

Regarding the usability aspect of the application, most people found it "easy" or "very easy" to use (Fig. 4b). However, phones with the application running were given to the users. Providing the devices was deemed necessary as it was not possible to know whether people had smartphones. In addition, lending devices to visitors consists a common practice for museums. Few participants found it difficult to rate the ease of use of the application, as they could not perceive how it worked since they had not done anything. Such a remark might highlight the difficulty in evaluating ubiquitous IT applications especially when involving participants of a certain age who might not be familiar with technology.

The audio description was also rated by users. Almost all of them were "satisfied" (5 out of 11) or "very satisfied" (5 out of 10) with it. Some participants commented positively about the inclusion of the actual kittiwake's call, as listening to it made the experience more complete. The soundwave representation on top of the relief was commented in various ways. Some participants could not understand its purpose, whereas others found it "novel" and "interesting". Another participant said that he would like it to have a more flexible/soft feeling.

When evaluating the features of the relief, the users were asked about its tactile properties. For sensitivity reasons, a general question about the visual appearance of the relief was included too. People were also questioned whether they would want any of the features of the relief to be changed. The majority of partially sighted people were "satisfied" or "very satisfied" with the shapes on the relief, but blind people's opinions were mixed. Few people mentioned that they found it difficult to distinguish the elements on the rock. When asked about possible changes on the relief, only one partially sighted user suggested that the representation "could be more defined with deeper detail".

As far as it concerns other comments about the relief's features, some users liked the fact that it is portable. People's opinions about the texture of the relief varied. Some were satisfied with it, whereas others wanted it to have different textures; another user expressed a desire for realistic organic textures; and one suggested using lines/dots on the seaweed and whelk eggs to differentiate them, without exaggerating as this would confuse users. As for the visual properties of the relief, two participants expressed their desire for more colour and another one stated that she would want more visual information only if the diorama was not present. One participant pointed out that a large print label would be useful and another one wanted some parts of the relief to be coloured in black.

The Outcome-Perception of the Experience. All qualitative data were analysed to illuminate the experience under specific themes. Inevitably there was a level of overlapping as many responses were coded under more than one themes.

Table 2. Awareness/knowledge related to the experience.

Subthemes	Quotes
Awareness	"I thought it was interesting to actually feel and understand how totally blind people can determine what they are like"
Making sense of something	"Well the description itself gave me an understanding of what was in front of me"
Broader understanding	"I like the bit where it played the sound... Before the audio played, I guessed it was some form of seagull from the shape. So, it has broadened that"
Difficulty in understanding	"Because I find this very difficult you know"
Using previous knowledge/experience	"... well I had a vague idea, because I've always lived by the sea. So, I'm quite aware of what seabirds are like. But not the specific species. I didn't know about the actual bird itself" "I understand about soundwaves due to my background"
Learning facts	"I am surprised that during the winter they go to sea"
Expanding information	"The only bit that wasn't mentioned in there was that there is kittiwakes on, if there is any left, on Seaford Edwards"

People's feedback reflecting **awareness, knowledge** and understanding as effects of the experience ranges from making sense, to learning facts and deepening understanding about the diorama. One partially sighted user developed a better understanding (thus awareness) about blind people's interaction with objects. Other participants used previous knowledge during the identification process, while one person expanded information based on facts that he already knew. However, some people expressed a level of difficulty to perceive the relief or stated that the experience did not help them to understand better the exhibit. The main subthemes as for awareness and knowledge are presented in Table 2.

The level of **engagement** and **interest** that participants demonstrated is witnessed by acts or comments related to emotions, surprise and generally the creative aspect of the experience. Observational data with regards to engagement are closely connected to people's skills. Those who were able to locate the elements on the relief often demonstrated joy or expressed themselves with affirmation sounds. Some users looked surprised when listening to the kittiwake's call and touching the soundwave. The users who kept tuning in and out of the relief seemed to lose and find their interest, depending on the success of the identification process. Nonetheless, they all kept coming back to the relief to engage with the exploration. Only one participant demonstrated disappointment and seemed disconnected. Further qualitative data provide more information about engagement and interest. All subthemes along with representative quotes can be found in Table 3. Combining senses was something that users appreciated, while

Table 3. Types of engagement with the experience.

Subthemes	Quotes
Using senses	"... you were using three senses in a sense, because you are using your listening skills, your feeling skills and your vision. I was using all three. That was interesting"
Desire for creative activity	"Well I thought I was gonna come in and paint you see... But I would tell them to get somebody to paint them"
Reminiscence/memory recall	"I used to love birds, but unfortunately I can't see them now. And in my garden, I get all sorts of birds. But I can't see them, unless they are very close to me. They don't do that very often"
Feelings	"Almost felt that you are actually looking at the real thing"
Enjoyment	"I enjoyed the sound of what the bird made" "... it didn't tell you go and explore, it took you through stage by stage, which I think was better, so the guidance"
Moderate/no interest	"As I enjoy most things. I have just enjoyed it yes"
Surprise	"The model of the bird and the bird itself. I think it is very pretty. And that is a kittiwake?" "I like the idea of actually doing the sound of the kittiwake that was on top. That is a really nice idea"
Imagination	"And then to be able to do the description with the relief gave me an understanding of putting back into a shape, back into my mind. So basically, what I was able to do in the recesses of my mind, it was to imagine..."
Connection to past interest	"And I love the idea of the tactile sound. But that comes because of my... basically because of my background in engineering"

many emphasised the importance of the audio guidance. Few people did not particularly engage. Another user perceived the experience in a more emotional way, associating it with memories. The imaginative effect of the experience was also noted. Connecting enjoyment with past interests was one of the types of engagement demonstrating the power of associations with people's lives [15].

Table 4. Attitudes related to the experience.

Subthemes	Quotes
Opinions	"When you can't see, you have got to handle something"
Self-confidence	"It gives me much more freedom of the feeling of being part of the real world"
Ethical considerations	"On the other hand, it would turn people off if they had dead birds on their hands"
Attitudes of/towards/regarding organisations	"...I do think as a visually impaired person we are not catered for, not just in museum, but generally." "Totally encourages people to visit a museum..."
Attitudes towards/about other people	"We need young people to be understanding the world around us" "I would also like to see people who have lost their sight as adults not to sit around at home, but to be able actually to do the things they used to do when they had sight and still be able to enjoy them and be able to access and therefore find that love back again"

The **attitudinal** aspect of the experience reflects on people's principles, values, self-esteem and possible behavioural changes. To explore attitudes, participants were asked about the value of having 3D printed objects in museums. The resulting subthemes are presented in Table 4. Most participants recognise the value of handling replicas in museums. Many users, implied that CH organisations do not yet provide what is needed for the visually impaired. Such provision would motivate people who have lost their sight to do the things they used to enjoy, but could also help young congenitally blind people to better understand the world. In this sense, similar experiences could support basic human rights with regards to accessibility, equality and education. Interestingly, a participant mentioned the idea of "freedom" as a consequence of engaging with the relief. Lastly, one participant highlighted ethical considerations about stuffed birds' handling. An issue that replicas might be able to address.

The exploration of the relief with the support of the audio application constituted an activity through which people were challenged to use their listening, thinking and tactile **skills**. Some participants were skilled in combining their senses to identify the elements of the relief, following meticulously the audio description. Other users occasionally identified elements and occasionally seemed lost. However, all kept coming back to the relief to "exercise" their senses. One participant with remaining vision kept closing his eyes while navigating on the relief in an effort to isolate his listening and tactile skills from the interference of sight. Later, he referred to blindness awareness.

Table 5. Skills related to the experience.

Subthemes	Quotes
Tactile skills	"This is a new venture. Feeling is a different finding"
Combination of skills	"It is difficult to have to keep moving while the description lasts"
	"... you are using three senses in a sense, because you are using your listening skills, your feeling skills and your vision"
Communication skills	"No, I don't think I could explain it properly, I'm sorry"
	"I would (talk to others about the experience). Yes definitely. I think it is very interesting"
Connecting to other people's skills	"This is the best tactile I have ever worked with. It is simplistic and it would be particularly useful for blind children"
	"I thought it was interesting to actually feel it and understand how blind people can determine what they are like"

Participants regularly mentioned the idea of skills. Their responses detail a set of subthemes as presented in Table 5. Some people found it easy to deploy many senses, while others found it challenging. One participant noted that the tactile exploration was a "new venture". As for communicating the experience, some people felt confident in explaining what had happened, while others not. Particularly interesting was the fact that some participants associated the exploration with other people's skills. One blind participant suggested that the relief would be useful for blind children. Another partially sighted user felt connected to blind people in a sense of understanding their experience of the world.

The **behavioural** outcome of the experience highlights people's actions, life-changes and progress connected to skill acquisition and learning. Behavioural data are closely related to skills and engagement/interest. The main subthemes regarding behaviours are presented in Table 6. Here, the analysis emphasises the importance of trialling and developing the idea of using replicas to assist visually impaired visitors. It also reflects some scepticism about the technology. However, accessing artefacts with the support of replicas is considered a positive action benefiting organisations and visually impaired visitors. Some participants also expressed a desire for learning which could be connected to future choices and actions, while another one related the experience to other people's actions.

Table 6. Behaviours related to the experience.

Subthemes	Quotes
Future trialling and development	"I would like to see how could it be developed further to be much more accessible for people like myself"
Change in accessing information and CH organisations	"I would also like to see people who have lost their sight as adults not to sit around at home, but to be able actually to do the things they used to do when they had sight and still be able to enjoy them and be able to access and therefore find that love back again"
	"... would not only improve, but it would make the experience more realistic"
Change in professional practices	"Very good. I would save me having to take things out of the stores (he means for handling sessions)"
Participation	"Totally encourages people to visit a museum, but also to be part of it"
Learning desire or progression	"Yes, well I'm always trying to learn something new"
	"I am fascinated by the 3D printer. I'd like to get my hands on it..."
Action as result of the experience	"My daughter is bringing her grandson just for a week from Worthing. I will definitely recommend that she brings him here"

One user, who had previous experience working in CH settings, noted that having replicas to handle would change professional practices.

Other Themes. Apart from the findings that have been analysed, there are some further aspects of the experience that deserve special attention. The first one is about the importance of **guidance**, which is a key component for a meaningful experience. Guidance pertains to clear instructions to visually impaired visitors whenever a replica is deployed, but also refers to clearly structured material, in case there is an audio (or other) description. Another interesting idea is that of **realism**. Some participants expressed their desire for realistic representations of feathers and plants. Until now digital fabrication does not address adequately the need for realistic organic material representations. Further research about materials or alternative representations could provide better solutions to fulfill users' needs. Realism is also associated with the provision of full 3D replicas when that is possible. One last theme concerns the **fragile nature** of replicas. In some instances, both officers and visitors behaved as having a valuable, fragile object in their hands when handling a replica. Such remark, might highlight a general perception about the products of digital fabrication, which in some cases seem to inherit the non-touchable features of their original "ancestors".

4   Discussion and Conclusions

This paper discussed the evaluation of an experience where visually impaired users interacted with a 3D printed relief representing a Victorian diorama with the support of a context-aware mobile application. The potential of these types of experiences is that: they can facilitate learning and enjoyment of CH for a wide range of audiences through customisation in order to satisfy users' particular needs [26]; they can further contribute towards the "Design for All" principles [8]; and they provide a more democratised access to CH [17]. It is also important to understand that such physical-digital negotiations move beyond the digital world and place visitor's experience as the main point of interest. They also comply with the postdigital character of museums [20], while improving their relevance to society.

The results of our study demonstrate how unique an experience can be and the great perceptual variation with respect to learning, engagement, enjoyment and personal development that such experience might have as an effect. People's comments indicate that it is possible to design satisfactory experiences with the use of replicas. To achieve, though, the best possible outcome, CH professionals will have to design a holistic experience and integrate as many elements the users have positively highlighted about the physical nature of replicas and their contribution at a physical, cognitive, attitudinal and emotional level.

Future work for the research involves the enrichment of data from more users as well as the development of other studies to address questions around the physical aspect of replicas and their meaning-making implications. By doing this, a set of principles can be proposed to assist CH professionals when designing experiential frameworks and making decisions about the incorporation of digitally fabricated artefacts in CH settings and events. Such principles, could also be further developed through co-design processes when planning interpretative resources involving replicas for diverse audience groups.

References

1. Anagnostakis, G., Antoniou, M.: Accessible museum collections for the visually impaired: combining tactile exploration, audio descriptions and mobile gestures. In: Proceedings of the 18th International Conference on Human-Computer Interaction with Mobile Devices and Services Adjunct, Italy, pp. 1021–1025 (2016)
2. Arts Council England: Inspiring Learning for All (2014). http://www.artscouncil.org.uk/advice-and-guidance
3. Balletti, C., Ballarin, M., Guerra, F.: 3D printing: state of the art and future perspectives. J. Cult. Herit. **26**, 172–182 (2017)
4. Candlin, F.: Museums, modernity and the class politics of touching objects. In: Chatterjee, H.J. (ed.) Touch in Museums: Policy and Practice in Object Handling. Berg, Oxford (2008)

5. Carfagni, M., Furferi, R., Governi, L., Volpe, Y., Tennirelli, G.: Tactile representation of paintings: an early assessment of possible computer based strategies. In: Ioannides, M., Fritsch, D., Leissner, J., Davies, R., Remondino, F., Caffo, R. (eds.) EuroMed 2012. LNCS, vol. 7616, pp. 261–270. Springer, Heidelberg (2012). https://doi.org/10.1007/978-3-642-34234-9_26

6. Chen, G., Zhang, Y., Chen, N.S., Fan, Z.: Context-aware ubiquitous learning in science museum with ibeacon technology. In: Spector, M., Lockee, B., Childress, M. (eds.) Learning, Design, and Technology, pp. 1–24. Springer, Cham (2016). https://doi.org/10.1007/978-3-319-17727-4_5-1

7. Chou, S.c., et al.: Semantic web technologies for context-aware museum tour guide applications, pp. 2–7 (2015)

8. Design for All Foundation: Design for All Foundation. http://designforall.org/

9. Diamond, J., Horn, M., Uttal, D.H.: Practical Evaluation Guide: Tools for Museums and Other Informal Educational Settings. Rowman & Littlefield Publishers, Lanham (2016)

10. Economou, M.: Heritage in the digital age. In: Logan, W., Craith, M.N., Kockel, U. (eds.) A Companion to Heritage Studies, Chap. 15. Wiley, Hoboken (2016)

11. Falk, J.: Museum audiences: a visitor-centered perspective. Loisir et Societe **39**(3), 357–370 (2016)

12. Falk, J.H., Dierking, L.D.: The Museum Experience, 1st edn. Whalesback Books, Washington, D.C. (1992)

13. Falk, J.H., Dierking, L.D.: The Museum Experience Revisited, 1st edn. Left Coast Press Inc., Walnit Creek (2013)

14. Falk, J.H., Moussouri, T., Coulson, D.: The effect of visitors agendas on museum learning. Curator Mus. J. **41**(2), 107–120 (1998)

15. Hein, G.E.: John dewey and museum education. Curator Mus. J. **47**(4), 413–427 (2004)

16. MacDonald, S.: Exploring the role of touch in connoisseurship and the identification of objects. In: Pye, E. (ed.) The Power of Touch: Handling Objects in Museum and Heritage Contexts. Left Coast Press Inc., California (2007)

17. Mota, C.: The rise of personal fabrication. In: Proceedings of the 8th ACM Conference on Creativity and Cognition, C&C 2011, p. 279 (2011)

18. Neely, L., Langer, M.: Please feel the museum: the emergence of 3D printing and scanning. museums and the web 2013 (2013). http://mw2013.museumsandtheweb.com/paper/please-feel-the-museum-the-emergence-of-3d-printing-and-scanning/

19. Neumüller, M., Reichinger, A., Rist, F., Kern, C.: 3D printing for cultural heritage: preservation, accessibility, research and education. In: Ioannides, M., Quak, E. (eds.) 3D Research Challenges in Cultural Heritage. LNCS, vol. 8355, pp. 119–134. Springer, Heidelberg (2014). https://doi.org/10.1007/978-3-662-44630-0_9

20. Parry, R.: The end of the beginning: normativity in the postdigital museum. Mus. Worlds **1**, 24–39 (2013)

21. Reichinger, A., Fuhrmann, A., Maierhofer, S., Purgathofer, W.: Gesture-based interactive audio guide on tactile reliefs. In: Proceedings of the 18th International ACM SIGACCESS Conference on Computers and Accessibility - ASSETS 2016. pp. 91–100 (2016)

22. Reichinger, A., Maierhofer, S., Purgathofer, W.: High-quality tactile paintings. J. Comput. Cult. Herit. (JOCCH) **4**(2), 1–13 (2011)

23. Reichinger, A., Schröder, S., Löw, C., Sportun, S., Reichl, P., Purgathofer, W.: Spaghetti, sink and sarcophagus: design explorations of tactile artworks for visually impaired people. In: Proceedings of the 9th Nordic Conference on Human-Computer Interaction - NordiCHI 2016, pp. 1–6 (2016)
24. Royal Pavilion & Museums: Mr Booth and his Museum (2012). https://brightonmuseums.org.uk/discover/2012/11/07/
25. Samaroudi, M., Echavarria, K.R., Song, R., Evans, R.: The fabricated diorama: Tactile relief and context-aware technology for visually impaired audiences. In: Eurographics Workshop on Graphics and Cultural Heritage. The Eurographics Association, Graz (2017)
26. Scopigno, R., Cignoni, P., Pietroni, N., Callieri, M., Dellepiane, M.: Digital fabrication technologies for cultural heritage (STAR). In: Santos, P., Klein, R. (eds.) 12th Eurographics Workshops on Graphics and Cultural Heritage (EG GCH 2014), pp. 75–85. Eurographics Association (2014)
27. Scopigno, R., Cignoni, P., Pietroni, N., Callieri, M., Dellepiane, M.: Digital fabrication technologies for cultural heritage: a survey. Comput. Graph. Forum **36**(1), 1–17 (2015)
28. Wonders, K.: Habitat dioramas as ecological theatre. Eur. Rev. **1**(3), 285–300 (1993)

Disciplinary Applications: History

Time Travel as a Visitor Experience: A Virtual Reality Exhibit Template for Historical Exploration

Catherine Anne Cassidy$^{(\boxtimes)}$, Adeola Fabola, Iain Oliver,
and Alan Miller

School of Computer Science, University of St Andrews, St Andrews, UK
{cc274,aef6,iao,alan.miller}@st-andrews.ac.uk,
http://www.cs.st-andrews.ac.uk/

Abstract. Developments in digital infrastructures and expanding digital literacies lower barriers for museums and visitor centres to provide new interactive experiences with their collections and heritage. With virtual reality more accessible, heritage institutions are eager to find out how this technology can create new methods in interpretation, learning and visualisation. This paper reviews a virtual reality framework implemented into exhibits in three cultural heritage centres. By taking advantage of existing visitor digital literacies, the exhibits provided accessible immersive exploratory experiences for inter-generational audiences. The digital framework developed is a template for virtual reality content interaction that is both intuitive and powerful. The exhibits include digital reconstructions of physical scenes using game engines for a convincing visual experience. We contextualise the logic behind a virtual reality setup for the separate institutions, how they assisted with the narrative as well as if an immersive digital environment provided a more profound response in users. Our aim is to communicate approaches, methodologies and content used to overcome the challenge of presenting a period in history to a modern audience, while using emergent technology to build connections and disseminate knowledge that is memorable and profound.

Keywords: Virtual reality · Cultural heritage · Museum exhibits

1 Introduction

Opportunities presented by advancing technology can be used to enrich and connect museum visitors to archaeological and historical research in ways which provide an authentic experience [1]. This paper suggests a framework for virtual reality (VR) exhibits located within cultural heritage visitor centres and museums. It draws upon experience developing and deploying VR interactives for museums.

The application of emergent technologies to cultural heritage offers the opportunity to: widen participation in its construction, deepen understanding through holistic interpretation, connect researchers and communities, communicate knowledge in engaging and accessible ways, and stimulate debate leading to further research. For these opportunities to be realized in the context of the museum, there are specific

© Springer Nature Switzerland AG 2019
D. Beck et al. (Eds.): iLRN 2019, CCIS 1044, pp. 103–116, 2019.
https://doi.org/10.1007/978-3-030-23089-0_8

challenges that need to be met. These challenges are authenticity of content, motivation for continued learning (connecting with the subject and museum), ease of use and navigation, adaptability, low maintenance, and value for money. These considerations mean VR systems designed for home gameplay should not be directly inserted into a museum without modification. This motivates the idea of a VR template which address all the above issues whilst enabling specific content to be added for exhibits.

Our approach is to support creation of VR exhibits which enable users to immerse themselves in historical content. Physical requirement consists of a screen or projection which can be viewed by multiple visitors at once, a VR headset and controller, with its view mirrored on the screen, and built around a graphically-capable commodity computer. An introductory video is looped on the screen while the VR headset is not in use. The exhibit can contain virtually constructed environments in large landscapes with the ability to free roam or tour between viewpoints, spherical media (360°), 3D object galleries and a virtual cinema.

Our procedural methods for digital cultural and natural heritage projects are practice-based. This enables us to identify real world issues and creatively address them, while meeting the immediate challenges provided as well as contributing to more general solutions, such as ensuring the technology works reliably without human intervention.

This paper looks first at the context for the work; developing a conceptual framework, the Virtual Reality Exhibit Template (VRET), and placing VR exhibits in the context of mainstream media, such as movies and games, while satisfying the needs of the museum. Next, we consider a practice-based methodology and workflows used for creating VR exhibits. This is followed by discussion and evaluation of two exhibits. We then discuss a framework for creating exhibits that is based upon this experience and discuss the final exhibit developed using the template.

2 Context

Museums, as defined by UNESCO, are the guardians of tangible and intangible heritage, and are responsible for their "preservation and promotion" [2]. The ways in which museums and other heritage institutions have 'preserved and promoted' their own narratives have evolved from simple displays to investing in the visitor experience [3]. Museums have also established themselves as modern cultural and community hubs, not just forums for knowledge transfer, enabling community members to contribute, express views, and tackle issues that are pertinent to society [4]. This evolution allows for greater visitor participation and deepens ties between community and its heritage [5].

Popular media has had an interest in presenting the past for over a century; from silent films to period video games. Historical narratives drive multiple gaming franchises such as Assassins Creed, based in an open world environment, and simulation games such as Total War and Age of Empires. Successful commercial games use elements of learning theory, which attributes to user engagement [6]. Since history-based video game popularity has proven the medium is engaging and immersive, institutions such as museums have begun to follow suit by exploring possibilities with emergent technologies.

VR offers the possibility of combining the visual power of films with the interaction of games in an immersive setting that transports users to locations remote in time or space. This immersion can include full scale VR room set ups [8], interactive projections [7] or headsets which can lead to transformative experiences. The continuous research and development of VR along with increasing digital literacies implies that it is possible to deliver large scale VR scenes in museum exhibitions that are accessible and comprehensible to most visitors. This in turn allows for intensive dissemination that connects a user with the narrative of the exhibit, strengthening the relationship between themselves, heritage and the exhibit's message.

Previous projects that lay the foundations for the VR exhibits we examine are based in Scotland; the Virtual Museum of Caen, The Bannockburn Visitor Centre, the Picts & Pixels Exhibition at the Perth Museum and Art Gallery and the Curing Yard. Collaboration between the research team and Timespan Museum and Art Gallery developed digital representation of Caen, a pre-clearances Highland village in the Strath of Kildonan [8]. This included a VR room where visitors controlled an avatar using an Xbox Kinect to explore a reconstruction of the village. The Bannockburn Visitor Centre allowed visitors to fight the Battle of Bannockburn themselves, changing the outcome based on the user's decisions. The Picts & Pixels exhibition adopted a mixed reality approach in which physical objects and digital exhibits were displayed in parallel and complementary to one another [7]. Interactive photospheres, digitised models and a VR headset facilitated multimodal interaction with the world of the Scottish Picts. The Curing Yard was a second collaboration with Timespan Museum, which included an immersive controller-free VR headset exhibit of a curing yard, historically represented in the exact location of the install within the museum [9].

3   Design and Development

Implementation of the VRET was made when the projects were in early stages of development. Each collaboration had a wealth of resources and materials that would supplement their chosen narrative and wished to experiment with latest technologies. Digital reconstructions were to be in each project as a base of work, along with a combination of provided and newly generated content.

Stakeholders worked in collaboration throughout the development of the exhibits; the majority were experts in the related subjects, such as archaeologists, historians, archivists and museum professionals. Scenes to be digitally reconstructed were discussed with the research team and those affiliated; decisions and adjustments occurred throughout the entirety of the builds. Selection of objects to be digitised, sites for aerial and spherical capture and narratives were chosen early in the creation process. Content varied between exhibits, based on what was available to the team and the level of importance to the overall narrative.

Further development of the technology and interpretation for use in museums, the framework has the possibility of connecting ourselves and our work with institutions as well as their network of organisations. This offers the opportunity for bilateral knowledge exchange. In each project we arranged workshops and discussions with local partners, to better understand the needs of the organisations and to deepen local understanding of both the historical research and technology which shapes the exhibit.

3.1   Workflow for Creating Virtual Reality Exhibits

The workflow for VR exhibit creation is a multistep process. The first phase is to identify the subject and possible narratives to be used to tell relevant stories. This is followed by identification of digital resources to be used in the project, pulling from an inventory of existing resources or media to be created. Digital resources often consist of terrain, models, photospheres, aerial footage, video, audio and historical photos. Finally, an investigation into best methods for navigation of media and narratives, which includes interpretation and interaction, is included into the system design.

Landscapes and Terrain. Illustrated through "A Boy and his Kite" demo [10], now called the Open World Demo Collection [11], Unreal Engine 4 (UE4) is capable of supporting landscapes that are hundreds of square miles in size using commodity hardware. This offers the opportunity of providing landscapes within the virtual environment that give context to the subject of the exhibit. In the context of a heritage exhibit, it is desirable for landscapes to accurately represent the real world, seen in Fig. 1. The following procedures can be used to create digital landscapes based upon survey data.

Fig. 1.   Large scale terrain created for Tomintoul exhibit.

Terrain data acquired from appropriate sources, such as Ordnance Survey (OS) data or LIDAR data, are often dictated by region. Data is combined from the supplied tiles into a single GeoTiff file using QGIS* (open source geometric information system). An OpenStreetMap layer is required as well as a shape file with polygons for the extent of the terrain. A print layout is necessary from the supplied data and layers to import the terrain into UE4.

The information is imported into World Machine, a 3D terrain generator, to a file with existing set of nodes. The heights of the terrain are programmed into the project properties and extents for desired map locations are created. By selecting extent and output nodes, processing results in a PNG file that are used to create a terrain in UE4.

The terrain material is copied to a new project in UE4. A new level is required to host the terrain and relevant files. A spreadsheet is used to calculate the location and scale values for the terrain.

System Design and Implementation. The VRET framework is built around UE4 but adds functionality that is required for the game engine to be used effectively as a public exhibit though a bespoke Chimera system, answering a challenge realized early in development. This includes managing idle screens and video overlays as well as allowing pop up screens for interpretation and automating management functions, such as start of day startup and end of day shutdown. It also enables error detection and correction as well as remote access for content updates.

The system interactions are shown in the diagram Fig. 2. UE4 and Chimera communicate over a network connection using a plugin to UE4 which was purpose created. This plugin allows the developer to send and receive messages in a text format between UE4 and Chimera.

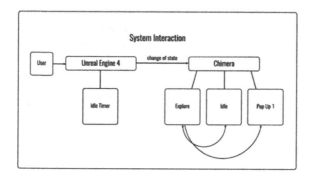

Fig. 2. System interaction with the user.

In the VR exhibits, the UE4 executable drives the interaction by taking input from the user and signaling to Chimera to change state in order to display information to observers. The UE4 game consists of a single persistent level and several streaming levels which are loaded when needed, seen in Fig. 3. When the user starts interacting with the system, they see a menu system in the Start level which is loaded when the system starts or returns from the idle state. The menu provides 3 or 4 buttons to the user. To select these buttons the user looks at them and then presses the center navigational button. This action fire an "event" which is handled by UE4's blueprint system. This allows event-based programming to be used to control the virtual environment and actors within it.

The system registers when the idle count reaches the specified value and transitions to the idle state by sending a message to the Chimera to display the idle video. Chimera does this by changing to an internal state where it displays a video, seen in Fig. 4. When a user then interacts with the system by picking up the headset, UE4 signals Chimera to return to the main play state, which removes the video from the screen.

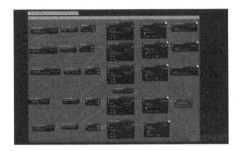
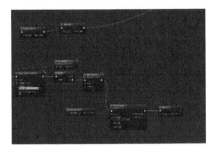

Fig. 3. Blueprint structure of persistent and streaming levels in UE4. The visual code unloads the current level and loads the menu level.

Fig. 4. Blueprint code structure that sends a signal to Chimera that it should enter or leave idle state in UE4.

The exhibit has a purpose-built startup script which initiates the programme and creates a connection to a server using an SSH server setup which is used to log in to the remote machine. A VNC server runs on the remote machine which allows remote access to the desktop without required a fixed IP address. All VR exhibit have the aforementioned capabilities, allowing for automatic start up and remote access for addressing system issues.

4   The Illicit Still Experience (Tomintoul & Glenlivet Discovery Centre)

The Tomintoul & Glenlivet Discovery Centre (TGDC) is in the highland village of Tomintoul surrounded by the Glenlivet estate. Whisky has played an important role in the area's history, taking advantage of the surrounding landscape and continues to be a crucial part of the local and Scottish economy. With the HLF and LEADER funded redevelopment of the Discovery Centre in 2017, the Tomintoul & Glenlivet Development Trust (TGDT) and Tomintoul & Glenlivet Landscape Partnership (TGLP) were interested in using HIE Year of History and Heritage funding to install an immersive interactive exhibit that could accomplish the following goals: (1) communicate the connection between the natural and cultural heritage of the area (2) compliment other whisky displays in local distilleries with historical beginnings of the industry (3) show the landscape and archaeological sites as historically accurate as possible in the 18th century (4) invest in emergent technology that would be best suited for visually telling their narrative, interest visitors who may not have used the technology before and facilitate new experiences in the future (5) generate enthusiasm for visitors to explore the sites themselves (6) allow accessibility to sites if visitors could not physically do visit.

Elements of the VRET for Tomintoul were based off design and functionality changes after the VR installation in the Picts & Pixels exhibition. This included a single button design as opposed to a controller-based design which simplified user interaction. The exhibit featured similar components such as a VR Oculus headset, a screen, spherical images and 3D reconstructed environments. The exhibit comprised of a digital reconstruction of Ballanloan, an 18th century settlement of cottages and kilns, an illicit still hidden in a cave next to a stream and barley fields. Historical and landscape evidence were provided by OS data. Content included the digital reconstruction implemented as both a descriptive photosphere tour and as an environment for open world exploration as well as a real-world photosphere tour, shown in Fig. 5. As a request, a virtual theatre option was developed to show videos of both the digital reconstruction and real-world aerial footage within the headset.

Fig. 5. Example of real content in photosphere tour, Glenlivet Distillery.

5   Skriðuklaustur Monastery (Skriðuklaustur Cultural Center & Historical Site)

Skriðuklaustur is in the east of Iceland where a Catholic monastery and a consecrated church were found to be inhabited during the 1500's. An archaeological excavation began in 2002 at the site and continued for a decade after. The excavation uncovered the building foundations, information about the building materials used and unique artefacts [12]. Ongoing projects have been exploring the site through technology; a previous reconstruction of the monastery, aerial footage shot along a proposed route to the monastery over a glacier, and digitisation of objects from the excavation. Continuation with the newest iteration of the reconstruction led both researchers and Skriðuklaustur to choose the VRET as an appropriate method of content interaction. The interactive's goals were: (1) to offer an updated visual representation of the monastastic ruins (2) create an immersive experience by allowing visitors to explore the ruins inside and out (3) allow accessibility for visitors who cannot visit the site or when weather restricts access (4) use emergent technology that grants full immersion into a period in Iceland's history (5) an attraction for visitors to visit the remote museum.

Skriðuklaustur was the next evolution in the VRET design and functionality after its installation in Tomintoul. The single button was kept for simplicity as the remote encouraged use. The exhibit features an Oculus headset, a screen, photospheres, digital reconstructions and 3D objects added into the reconstruction. The updated reconstruction of the monastery and the surrounding landscape was included, as well as the interiors of the church. 3D digitised objects were placed back into the reconstruction as they would have been found during that time. The digital landscape was built from terrain data provided by the National Land Survey of Iceland. Content levels includeda descriptive photosphere tour, a 3D object gallery to interrogate artefacts and a video theatre for real world and virtual footage.

6 Evaluation and Evolution of Design

All exhibits used for cultural and natural heritage dissemination go through multiple assessments before, during and after installation. The systems are evaluated from the following perspectives: (1) community (2) museum (3) non-community visitors (4) field specialists, as well assessing the following aspects of the system: (1) usability (2) responsiveness (3) enjoyment (4) engagement (5) learning (6) motivation for further learning.

The exhibitions were well received and collected feedback: "*A fantastic museum and resource for our school trip! Excellent activities for the students and informative exhibits about local history. We particularly enjoyed the 'den', VR and making poppies! Thank you!*", "*Excellent visitor centre – do try the 3-D experience in the corner!!*", "*Wow what a different the place looks amazing, all the new tech is great, good how it's been brought up to date...*", "*The best museum ever and the best VR reality*". Whilst the feedback is positive, it also illustrates that visitors see the VR exhibit as an integrated part of the museum and that visitors with a historical interest in the museum view new technology in a positive light.

Laboratory research and evaluation has been ongoing since the creation of the VR exhibit framework; originally with the Curing Yard, a single level exhibit for Timespan museum, and then a multi-level exhibit for the Picts & Pixels exhibit in Perth Museum & Art Gallery summer 2017. Evaluation from the first exhibits evolved design and system methods to implement changes for the next exhibit, the Illicit Still Experience for TGDC. Exhibits included in this publication have developed from installation, use and evaluation of the previous, leading to dynamic and effective framework.

Based on user evaluation at an open day event for the Picts & Pixels exhibition, users reported the Xbox controller was hard to use as the VR headset occluded the user field of vision [7]. If the user did not have video game experience nor read the instructions before wearing the headset, they had trouble associating directions navigators to the buttons associated on the controller. User evaluation from the Curing Yard showed the benefits from a hands-free system but lacked navigational ability for multiple levels [9]. Due to this response, the Oculus controller was adapted for future use as it was more functional and efficient than controller-free design yet less complex than a multi-button game controller. Skriðuklaustur retains the Xbox controller due to an initial supply issue but is due to switch over to the Oculus remote in the future.

An internal assessment of the look and feel and usability of user interfaces within the levels, along with informal user evaluation in the field, confirmed that the descriptive photosphere tour was not intuitive and had issues with textual display. After installation in Tomintoul, its design evolved for Skriðuklaustur but was completely redesigned for Finlaggan. It was decided to combine the photosphere tour with the open world exploration level, allowing for a narrative along with open environment exploration.

6.1 Organisational Evaluation - Tomintoul

Museum staff at TGDC have recorded informal evaluations since the installation of the exhibit in spring 2018. Evaluations in this publication include interaction and mode of engagement, while written assessment has been recorded in visitor log books. Future plans include VR and exhibit elements taught in workshops at TGDC and formal evaluations of visitors and attendees.

Interaction. TGDC caters to a wide variety of visitors while it is open to the public during the peak tourist months of April through October. The centre opens for events and groups during the winter months, allowing year-round engagement with the VR exhibit. By October 2018, 10,000 visitors had gone through the centre, a 20% increase from 2016 and 50% increase from 2014 [13]. The redevelopment of the centre and its use of VR received national recognition from First Minister Nicola Sturgeon when she toured in August 2018.

Dedicated staff do not supervise the exhibit but are stationed nearby at a front desk for any needed guidance and support. Thus far, there has been a wide age demographic of users with varying level of technical skill. As a result, staff have been able to observe diverse interactions and trends with the exhibit. Users tend to investigate the open world exploration level for the longest period of time, likely due to the explorative nature of the level itself; gameplay length is largely dictated by presumed comprehensive completion of the environment. Details in the open world environment such as the farm animals have been of interest to younger users.

A spinning office chair is in place for mandatory use for those using the VR exhibit to limit wandering and accidents, while encouraging freedom to explore the entire 360-degree space. This has sometimes become difficult with the hardwired Oculus Rift and gets caught if users spin in a complete circle. Staff have concluded that though entanglement occurs occasionally, the chair relieves users from too much disorientation, granting staff at the front of house the ability to concentrate elsewhere.

Modes of Engagement. In TGDC, the exhibit is installed in a corner of the main room, where visitors enter and move on to explore the traditional exhibition or the digital library area. As a room where visitors begin their tour, groups of people can accumulate, limiting the direct use of the VR headset. This demonstrates the use of the screen as an important type of engagement, as the exhibit can be a social activity for a large group as well as self-promoting itself for later use if there is a queue. This type of engagement has received positive response by visitors as an unexpected aspect to the exhibit.

6.2 Organisational Evaluation - Skriðuklaustur

Museum staff have recorded informal user evaluations since the exhibit's installation, including interactions at external events. The installation has been on display at the museum since August 2018. Evaluations have included ease of use, interaction, type of engagement from visitors, and reactions to supplementary content.

External events included Tæknidagur fjölskyldunnar (Technology Day for Family) with over 1,700 attendees and Að heiman og heim – náms og atvinnulífssýning Austurlands (education and work opportunity event in East Iceland) with over 200 people who used the exhibit. Scholarly users at the museum have included archaeologists, authorities involved with archaeological sites and excavations, game developers and museum professionals.

Interaction. Museum staff are posted in the room hosting the VR exhibit in order to help guests and navigate them through the levels. Most guests have limited VR experience and often require guidance with the headset and Xbox controller. The Oculus Rift 'guardian' feature enables users to find the sensor tracking boundaries, but restricting movement further deters wandering and accidents. The addition of knowledgeable staff alongside the VR increases the depth of experience for a user. The visualisation of VR and the included media constructs a connection that encourages understanding of contextual data, such as from an archaeological excavation. Users reacted when told the height of a ceiling by leaning back and looking, just as most would in the reality.

When taken out to events, staff reported that a younger age demographic tend to approach and use the exhibit, as opposed to a wider age demographic found at the museum. User at the external events tend to have used VR or video games before, so functionality of the VR exhibit and operability of the navigation through the Xbox controller requires less explanation.

Users have found the headset occludes a user's view of the controller, navigation through a multi-button layout is challenging if there is no prior gaming knowledge [7]. The installation retained the current controller layout as an Oculus remote did not arrive on time for installation but will be switched over in the near future.

When visitors use the exhibit in VR mode with the headset, the experience has been reported to be different than those who watch on the screen. The functionalities of the exhibit are realised when using the VR headset and controller, and elements of those capabilities do not completely transmit to passive engagement. Users reported to enjoy "zooming in" on objects in VR while in the 3D gallery, utilising body movement to enhance their experience.

Modes of Engagement. The dual set up of the headset and screen have allowed for both active and passive engagement, but staff have encouraged visitors to engage with the headset even when first reluctant. The assumption that the passive engagement of watching the screen is identical or similar enough to the interaction with the headset. The distinction between the two types of engagement has been noted by visitors that try both to be significantly different in how they interact with the content.

Large tourist groups are frequent visitors to the museum and often stay in groups through the galleries and rooms. The passive engagement offered by the screen satisfies visitors when in a group situation, as one user engages with the headset, the remaining watch their actions. Staff that assist with the VR exhibit explain what is shown on the screen to the group as well directing the user to different parts of the exhibit.

7   VR Exhibit Template (VRET)

To facilitate both an individual user and groups, the exhibit consisted of (1) Oculus VR headset (2) a sensor for tracking headset movement (3) navigational controller (4) large screen for mirroring actions within the headset. Each exhibit is in a central point in the museum or centre to maximise its discovery and use by visitors. This also allowed large groups to engage with the exhibit passively through the mirrored screen; turning the exhibit into a social activity, as well as provide direct intellectual stimulation to the active user.

VRET can incorporate several types of levels, all chosen from a menu system, showing in Fig. 6. These include (1) an open world environment (2) photosphere tours, either real or virtual content (3) 3D model gallery for interrogating digitised objects (4) video theatre and (5) adapted open world tour.

Fig. 6. Menu system in VRET.

The goal for navigation was to make it intuitive and consistent across levels. Working within the Oculus ecosystem, a straight forward button system was applied. Controller-based interaction draws from digital literacies, specifically games proficiencies and familiarities. This is useful because a significant portion of the population play video games and these games offer benefits for learning and social interaction, hence by gamification of exhibits, museums can deliver interactive experiences to visitors using familiar technologies and devices [14]. Movement through an environment was achieved by pushing a button, then the viewpoint would move forward in the direction that the user was looking. Menu selection was achieved by the user looking at the level selection buttons, then clicking the main selection button when their desired button was highlighted. Progression through tours was through the navigation buttons designed on a circle for non-visual prompting. When the exhibit is not in use, an idle video plays on a loop. When the user puts on the headset, the video is interrupted, and the menu appears for level selection.

Interaction is triggered through location and through focus on interaction points. The interpretation can be displayed in world or through a heads-up display. A user can click on a hotspot that will bring up a 3D artefact, created through photogrammetry or laser scanning techniques. This enables integration of digital and physical content within the exhibit.

A gallery-like 3D environment is used to house digital artefacts. The 3D gallery is designed to place less emphasis on the level of detail in the virtual environment, and more emphasis on the 3D objects. Interaction is built into the gallery so that users rotate artefacts around multiple axes, zoom in/out and move around the centrepiece. Users can switch between artefacts in a manner that is similar to navigating through images in a photo gallery. The framework also supports the simple virtual environment to switch to a real or virtual photosphere, giving the object its original context.

As part of further education and development, components of the framework have been made freely available in guides and downloadable templates for community members and heritage practitioners with basic UE4 experience [15]. Users can combine assets and functionality templates into game engine levels, populate levels with their content and package them to create immersive museum installations.

8   Lord of the Isles

Finlaggan was a seat of power for the Lord of the Isles and Clan Donald, who ruled over parts of mainland Scotland, the Hebrides, and Ulster. The site was used for council meetings, ceremonies and entertaining, and is located on the Scottish island of Islay, now famous for whisky distilleries. The visitor centre is located at the site and care for the ruins and has had a redevelopment. Archaeological excavations have occurred since 1990 which uncovered various buildings, tombstones and artefacts. Work is still ongoing, with further digitisation of objects for the exhibit's official opening in April 2019. Other sites around the island were documented through photospheres and aerial footage. The VRET was chosen as a platform for interaction due to the following reasons: (1) visually represent the numerous buildings, paths and boundaries from the site (2) allow visitors to explore inside many of the structures as well as the grounds around them, to further understand Medieval Scottish royal life (3) give the visitor centre a different platform to inform audiences of the narrative of the site (4) connect other sites on the island that are associated with Finlaggan to be viewed all from one location.

The edition of VRET that was used in Finlaggan has been the latest design to be installed and has gone through significant development. The exhibit includes a reconstruction of multiple buildings, key building interiors and the surrounding landscape. Based on evaluations from both Tomintoul and Skriðuklaustur, along with laboratory research for more efficient exploration, the descriptive photosphere tour and open world environment were combined to create an open world tour. The physical exhibit included an Oculus headset, an Oculus remote, and a screen for passive and group engagement. Exhibit levels include the open world tour, a video theatre and a 3D object gallery. The landscape was built using OS data and corroborated with modern drone footage.

The adapted open world tour created specifically for the Finlaggan exhibit offers two avenues of investigation. The initial drop point in the tour displays text to give context to the scene and times out or disappears after a click on the controller. This specifically engineered system consists of descriptions of the parts of the reconstruction which are displayed to the user on the headset overlay and to the observers using the

Chimera overlay for that location. This involves a state created for each location. The setup allows information to be formatted differently for the user and to observers. The user can navigate through the environment by pressing the main controller button and looking in the direction they want to move in or by pressing the left and right buttons which will take them to next information point, which displays more information about that point.

9   Conclusion

In conclusion we have presented experiences in developing VR exhibits for small to medium sized visitor centres and museums. From these experiences we have developed both a software template for VR exhibits that can be widely used in museums and visitor centres globally. We have also developed workflows for the creation of content for VR experiences.

We have found that the aforementioned is of value for the following reasons: (1) it makes heritage available to audiences in new engaging ways, (2) it acts a stimulus for an holistic approach to historic research and as a platform for stimulating controversy and discussion, (3) it engages local communities in the understanding and construction of heritage, (4) through enhancing the visitor experience the potential exists to stimulate the local and national economies.

Furthermore, we have resolved issues of specific relevance to museums using VR technology, specifically: (1) the need to address ease of use; users will not expect to invest time required in learning to play a computer game. This has guided our approach to interaction and movement, (2) the requirement to make the system robust to minimise the need for input from museum staff and to maximise uptime, (3) flexibility to integrate different types of content together with the ability to connect digital artefacts with digital scenes, (4) to facilitate users in discovering points of interest, through direction, whilst providing the freedom to explore the environment and its content.

We perceive the VRET as one approach to applying digital and VR within the context of a museum. It collects together multiple forms of digital content and creates a connection to current archaeological and historical research while ensuring a worthwhile visitor experience.

References

1. Kalay, Y., Kyan, T., Affleck, J.: New Heritage: New Media and Cultural Heritage, 1st edn. Routledge, Abingdon (2007)
2. Recommendation concerning the protection and promotion of museums and collections, their diversity and their role in society (2015). http://unesdoc.unesco.org/images/0024/002463/246331m.pdf. Accessed 22 Nov 2018
3. Vermeeren, A., Calvi, L., Sabiescu, A. (eds.): Museum Experience Design. SSCC. Springer, Cham (2018). https://doi.org/10.1007/978-3-319-58550-5
4. Cassidy, C.A., et al.: Digital pathways in community museums. Mus. Int. **70**(1–2), 126–139 (2018)
5. Simone, N.: The Participatory Museum. Museum 2.0, Santa Cruz (2010)

6. McCall, J.: Gaming the Past: Using Video Games to Teach Secondary History. Taylor and Francis, Florence (2013)

7. Cassidy, C.A., Fabola, A., Rhodes, E., Miller, A.: The making and evaluation of picts and pixels: mixed exhibiting in the real and the unreal. In: Beck, D., et al. (eds.) iLRN 2018. CCIS, vol. 840, pp. 97–112. Springer, Cham (2018). https://doi.org/10.1007/978-3-319-93596-6_7

8. Miller, A., Vermehren, A., Fabola, A.E.: The virtual museums of Caen: a case study on modes of representation of digital historical content. In: Guidi, G., Scopigno, R., Torries, J. C., Graf, H. (eds.) Proceedings of the Digital Heritage International Congress: Analysis & Interpretation Theory, Preservation & Standards, Digital Heritage Projects & Applications, vol. 2, pp. 541–548. IEEE (2015)

9. Fabola, A., et al.: A virtual museum installation for time travel. In: Beck, D., et al. (eds.) iLRN 2017. CCIS, vol. 725, pp. 255–270. Springer, Cham (2017). https://doi.org/10.1007/978-3-319-60633-0_21

10. A Boy & His Kite: Annotated Features - Feature Highlight - Unreal Engine, YouTube (2015). https://www.youtube.com/watch?v=JNgsbNvkNjE. Accessed 15 Apr 2019

11. Open world demo collection by epic games in epic showcase, environments - UE4 marketplace, Unrealengine.com (2015). https://www.unrealengine.com/marketplace/en-US/slug/open-world-demo-collection. Accessed 15 Apr 2019

12. East Iceland archaeological site unveils 3D tour, guide to Iceland now (2018). https://now.guidetoiceland.is/2018/09/21/news/east-iceland-archaeological-site-unveils-3d-tour/. Accessed 27 Feb 2019

13. New discovery centre proves a hit with visitors – Tomintoul and Glenlivet (2018). http://tgdt.org.uk/new-discovery-centre-proves-a-hit-with-visitors/?fbclid=IwAR2p7EOVjTam-fX2Wwnlm_39srbJ8lOBR-dOS7eekdflHGSBmXR7svh6WqA. Accessed 23 Feb 2019

14. Lofgren, K.: 2017 Video game trends and statistics – who's playing what and why? - big fish blog, big fish games (2017). https://www.bigfishgames.com/blog/2017-video-game-trends-and-statistics-whos-playing-what-and-why/. Accessed 23 Feb 2019

15. VR Exhibit – Toolkits, Cineg.org (2018). https://cineg.org/wordpress/toolkits/3d-exhibits/. Accessed 27 Feb 2019

Viewing the Past: Virtual Time Binoculars and the Edinburgh 1544 Reconstruction

Elizabeth Rhodes$^{(\boxtimes)}$, Alan Miller, Christopher Davies, Iain Oliver, and Sarah Kennedy

University of St Andrews, St Andrews, Fife, UK
egsr@st-andrews.ac.uk

Abstract. This paper discusses how a digital reconstruction of the Scottish capital of Edinburgh around the year 1544 was created and communicated to the public. It explores the development and reception of the Virtual Time Binoculars platform – a system for delivering virtual reality heritage apps suitable for use on most smartphones. The Virtual Time Binoculars system is placed in the context of earlier research into mobile heritage experiences, including Situated Simulations (Liestøl [3]) and the Mirrorshades Project (Davies et al. [4]). The eventual virtual reality app is compared with other means of viewing the historic reconstruction, including online videos and an interactive museum and educational exhibit. It outlines the historical and technical challenges of modelling Edinburgh's sixteenth-century cityscape, and of distributing the eventual reconstruction in an immersive fashion that works safely and effectively on smartphones on the streets of the modern city. Finally, it considers the implications of this project for future developments in mobile exploration of historic scenes.

Keywords: Historical reconstruction · Virtual reality · Mobile devices

1 Introduction

Twenty-first-century cities are shaped by the priorities and planning decisions of previous generations. Yet many modern urban residents and tourists have only a vague awareness of the relationship between past and present cityscapes. One way to improve understanding of the evolution of our urban spaces is via reconstructions of historic scenes. Traditionally, reconstructions were either still pictures or hand-made models, typically printed in books or displayed as part of the interpretation at museums and heritage sites [1]. However, these methods of communicating with the public have major limitations. Most history books do not have vast sales, while conventional museum displays and information panels are inevitably fixed in specific locations (often some distance from the historic site they are representing).

Over the last twenty years digital technologies have revolutionised how reconstructions of historic sites are made and (potentially) experienced. Digital representations of past scenes involving interactivity, movement, and complex sound effects are now possible. Lately, major developments in virtual reality have improved the immersiveness of simulated environments. Yet the contexts in which these digital

© Springer Nature Switzerland AG 2019
D. Beck et al. (Eds.): iLRN 2019, CCIS 1044, pp. 117–128, 2019.
https://doi.org/10.1007/978-3-030-23089-0_9

representations are viewed by the public have remained relatively traditional. Digital reconstructions tend to be shown as part of fixed museum installations, or are brief video clips included in documentaries or embedded in conventional websites. On occasions digitally created reconstruction images are even published as illustrations in conventional books [2]. In short, it is still assumed that people will primarily engage with reconstructions in indoor settings – either in the comfort of their own homes and workplaces, or in museums.

The mass adoption of smart phones has the potential to change this situation. People have become used to carrying complex digital devices in their handbags and pockets – providing new possibilities for portable digital interpretation of historic cityscapes. It is now technologically possible for users to view a digital reconstruction of a historic scene on a mobile device, at the same time as exploring those same spaces in reality today. The past and present appearance of a street can be experienced in tandem. However, currently, both heritage experts and digital developers have only begun to respond to these exciting opportunities.

This paper discusses how a recent reconstruction of the Scottish capital of Edinburgh in the 1540s was created and communicated to the public, and the efforts which were made to foster an immersive, yet portable, user experience. It will outline the historical and technological challenges of modelling a cityscape which can be accessed on mobile devices out of doors, and the development of the so-called Virtual Time Binoculars – a framework for delivering simple virtual reality apps suitable for most mainstream smart phones. Additional ways in which the reconstruction could be viewed (including online videos and an immersive museum exhibit) will also be discussed. Finally, it will consider the overall reception and use of the reconstruction, and possibilities for future development.

2 Technical Background

The Edinburgh 1544 reconstruction, and the associated Virtual Time Binoculars framework, were deliberately designed to be used out of doors and on the street (as well as in more controlled indoor settings). Accessing a digital reconstruction in an outside urban space raises certain challenges. Firstly, it is essential that on-street users can enjoyably engage with the virtual scene, while remaining safe in the actual twenty-first-century world which surrounds them. Secondly, there is the question of ensuring the virtual experience functions efficiently on ordinary smartphones, without asking too much of a mobile device's processing power, storage space, and battery consumption. In order to address these complications, the Virtual Time Binoculars framework drew on nearly a decade of research into how people interact with augmented reality, virtual reality, and smartphones.

As far back as 2009, Gunnar Liestøl and his colleagues at the University of Oslo developed the concept of Situated Simulations (or sitsim), using powerful location and orientation-aware smartphones and tablets to render a 3D virtual environment, which was then navigated through the user's position in the real world [3]. Users of sitsim were intended to view reconstructions via phone and tablet screens (rather than by headsets), and to travel around the virtual model by really walking about a heritage site.

Liestøl's pioneering work demonstrated the outstanding possibilities of smartphones for presentating portable virtual reconstructions. However, the sitsim approach does have its limitations. There are practical problems associated with using real world movement to navigate a virtual environment in an uncontrolled space such as a city street. It frequently is not safe for a user to stand in the middle of a busy road holding up a smartphone in order to experience the perfect view of a historic scene. Additionally, the small screen of a mobile phone does not provide users with a particularly immersive experience, and can have significant problems with reflection when used out of doors in fine weather.

Between 2013 and 2015 researchers at the University of St Andrews worked on the Mirrorshades project [4]. This further examined the concept of seeing a real environment in tandem with a virtual representation of the same location. Yet, rather than showing reconstructions on a tablet or smartphone screen, the Mirrorshades project used a virtual reality (VR) headset equipped with stereo passthrough video cameras, and a magnetic indoor positioning system, providing a more immersive exploration of the reconstruction [5]. By using a VR headset that completely encompassed the user's view, the experience of the Mirrorshades parallel reality system was of shifting between two distinct and fully immersive environments, rather than only having a small 'window' onto the virtual environment as provided by a smartphone screen in the sitsim scenario (Fig. 1).

Fig. 1. The Mirrorshades parallel reality platform in use at the fifteenth-century St Salvator's Chapel. Still from youtube video [6].

Critically the Mirrorshades project logged experimental participants' walking behaviour, head movements, and viewing modes – which provided valuable information for the development of the Virtual Time Binoculars framework. Analysis of user studies within the Mirrorshades platform revealed that engagement with the virtual environment was predominantly performed while people were stationary. Users typically looked at their real world view while walking between perceived locations of interest, at which point they would stand still and look fully at the virtual environment. The users' behaviour can probably be explained by the fact that successful ambulation around a space is dependent on avoiding actual obstacles in the real world, causing viewers to focus on reality rather than any equivalent virtual environment. This acquires a particular importance when real and virtual environments do not share precisely the same layout, if the registration and position tracking between the two environments is imperfect, or if the real world situation is potentially hazardous (as is the case with a city street) (Fig. 2).

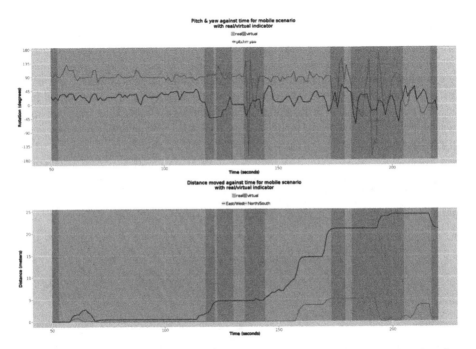

Fig. 2. Mirrorshades participants' walking behaviour and head movements contrasted against real and virtual visuals.

The Mirrorshades behavioural observation raises questions about whether systems which allow users to explore real and virtual environments always need to provide a full 3D reconstruction. This is a important consideration as hosting a full 3D reconstruction places considerable demands on a smartphone in terms of processing power, download size, storage space, and battery life. The Mirrorshades project suggested that an experientially similar virtual reality platform might be achieved by using a combination of still 360° images, and videos captured from a 3D reconstruction. Rather than the user having to move to a new location to obtain a new view, movement becomes an intrinsic part of the media loaded into the virtual reality experience. Such a change promises significant benefits in outdoor virtual reality experiences. The smaller footprint of an app which uses a combination of 360° images and short looping videos (instead of a full interactive 3D reconstruction) is a substantial boon for users, given the patchy nature of 3G/4G data services in the United Kingdom, and the fact that many international visitors have prohibitively expensive or non-existent mobile data plans. Meanwhile, the fact that walking around the virtual reconstruction is no longer dependent on actual physical movement has substantial health and safety benefits in the context of a busy urban space.

This thinking heavily influenced decisions regarding the functionality of the Virtual Time Binoculars system. As a result of the Mirrorshades research it was determined that the Virtual Time Binoculars:

1. Did not need to provide users with a completely free-roaming exploration of a 3D reconstruction. Instead a more focused 'guided tour' approach would fit with most users' tendency to concentrate on locations of perceived interest.
2. Movement between locations in the reconstruction should not be dictated by the users' actual movements in the real world (a feature that raises considerable safety issues in a busy urban space).
3. Users should be able to switch easily between a screen view and a headset view, allowing them to combine a highly immersive virtual reality experience, with a more 'window-like' screen based experience (which might be preferable in some urban spaces).

3   Identifying 1540s Edinburgh as a Place to Reconstruct

The Virtual Time Binoculars framework was initially launched for use with a 3D model of Edinburgh in the 1540s. Sixteenth-century Edinburgh was selected as a suitable site to reconstruct for a variety of reasons. First and foremost, as the capital of Scotland and a world heritage site, Edinburgh is a site of international importance [7]. Yet heritage interpretation for its sixteenth-century history is patchy at best. Indeed, before the Edinburgh 1544 project, there were no publicly available digital reconstructions of the sixteenth-century cityscape. This gap is surprising as before 1603 Edinburgh was the capital of an independent kingdom, and dominated Scottish trade and politics.

The year 1544 was specifically focused on, as both a tumultuous time in the city's history, and because of the existence of an early bird's-eye view plan from this time. In May 1544 the Scottish capital was attacked by an English army with instructions to 'burn Edinburgh town' leaving it 'so razed and defaced…that there may remain forever a perpetual memory of the vengeance of God' [8]. In fact, the eventual outcome was slightly less cataclysmic. The English failed to take Edinburgh Castle, and departed after burning sections of the capital, and sacking the Abbey and Palace of Holyrood [9].

Among the English forces in May 1544 there was a military engineer named Richard Lee, who created a remarkable aerial view of how Edinburgh appeared during the English attack. The bird's-eye plan was probably intended to inform Henry VIII and his advisors about how the English operations unfolded [10]. Lee's drawing is now in the British Library, and is the oldest (relatively) realistic representation of the

Scottish capital [11]. The Lee plan formed the inspiration for the Edinburgh 1544 reconstruction. Evidence from Lee's drawing was supplemented with information from archaeological reports, sixteenth-century written descriptions of Edinburgh, and other early visual depictions – notably James Gordon of Rothiemay's seventeenth-century engravings of the capital and William Edgar's mid-eighteenth-century maps [12].

4 Creating the Reconstruction

Like most cities, Edinburgh was smaller in the sixteenth century than today, being focused on the quarter now known as the Old Town. In 1544 the built-up area spanned about 2 km from east to west, and about 0.5 km from north to south at its widest points. Although diminutive in terms of twenty-first-century cities, this is a relatively large area to reconstruct digitally. Creating a reconstruction of the whole of sixteenth-century Edinburgh (including the associated suburb of the Canongate) was an ambitious undertaking, which posed challenges regarding historical research, modelling time, and ensuring that the eventual digital output was not unduly large for use on mobile devices.

The underlying terrain for the reconstruction was created with World Machine and was informed by modern OS map data [13]. Some adjustments were made to take into account changes in Edinburgh's geography – notably the disappearance of the large stretch of water known as the Nor Loch (formerly located where Waverley Station now stands). The landscape was then imported into the gaming engine Unreal Engine 4, and modern and historic maps were overlaid on the 3D terrain, providing a guide for the layout of the historic street plan [14].

Unfortunately none of the sixteenth or seventeenth images of Edinburgh were sufficiently geographically accurate to be used as the base for the reconstruction's street plan without major distortion. The oldest plan which successfully layered onto the 3D terrain was William Edgar's map from about 1765 [15]. The Edgar plan pre-dates the main eighteenth-century redevelopment of Edinburgh. However, some boundaries did shift between the sixteenth and mid-eighteenth centuries. In particular the frontages of buildings had a tendency to encroach onto the streets. Using the eighteenth-century street plan as a base layer therefore almost certainly introduced elements of inaccuracy into the reconstruction.

The sixteenth-century buildings were initially modelled in SketchUp and then imported into Unreal [16]. Major sites (such as Holyrood Palace, St Giles' Kirk, the Netherbow, and Trinity College) were based on detailed historical research. However, a combination of time constraints and gaps in the historical sources meant that many of the ordinary urban residences were generic buildings, located approximately according to historic property boundaries [17]. The reconstruction process highlighted the numerous lacunae in our understanding of Edinburgh's early sixteenth century domestic architecture (in particular the design of vernacular timber structures) – and it is to be hoped that the Edinburgh 1544 project will trigger further discussion and research on this topic (Fig. 3).

Fig. 3. Reconstruction of the Netherbow from the Edinburgh 1544 project. This was one of the most important gateways to Edinburgh in the sixteenth century (and the focus of significant fighting in 1544). However, the structure was completely demolished in the eighteenth century as it was obstructing traffic.

5 Communicating the Reconstruction

A major advantage of digital reconstructions (as against traditional drawings or physical models) is the variety of media that can be generated from one model. A range of digital outputs were created from the Edinburgh 1544 model in Unreal Engine 4. The core output was of course the content included in the Edinburgh 1544 Virtual Time Binoculars app. However, additional videos and spherical media were generated for embedding in web-resources and sharing on social media. A full 3D reconstruction which allows users to roam freely about the virtual historic city was also developed for use in museum exhibits and educational contexts.

5.1 The Virtual Time Binoculars

The Edinburgh 1544 Virtual Time Binoculars app provides a tour through the 3D reconstruction of Scotland's early sixteenth-century capital [18]. Following a brief introductory video there is an interactive historic map, with a marker indicating the user's current location, and buttons to select a range of key sites. Some of these historic sites exist today in a modified form (like St Giles' Kirk), while others have been completely demolished (such as the Netherbow). Selecting a site starts a video of a relevant section of the 3D reconstruction (for instance the journey along a particular street), providing users with a sense of movement and discovery in their experience of the model. Upon the completion of the video users reach a 360° virtual historic scene, which can be explored either via a mobile device's touch-screen, or through a simple virtual reality headset of the Google Cardboard or Google Daydream type [19]. Users can switch between touch-screen and headset mode through an icon in the corner of the screen. Interactive information points are located within the 360 view, which can be selected to access brief factual information about a site's history and to view early images of the location(such as paintings or engravings), giving users a hint of the actual historical sources which informed the reconstruction process. This presentation of the 3D reconstruction was devised with the intention of creating a package which is not unduly large for use on standard smartphones, can be used in outdoor and indoor environments, but which nevertheless provides a degree of immersiveness, and does not significantly restrict how a large proportion of people tend to interact with virtual reality experiences.

Virtual Time Binoculars apps are designed for use on Android and Apple devices in conjunction with Google Cardboard type viewers, or as an extended android app for use with Google Daydream. The Virtual Time Binoculars platform consists of three parts: the package creation system, the package management system, and the app framework. The system is designed to enable the easy creation of virtual reality tour apps. The tours can contain a variety of types of media files including 360 photo-spheres, video spheres, videos, still images, and audio. All the visual media can be displayed stereoscopically. Tours can be set up to be linear or involve navigation via a map system. The packages consist of an XML file describing the tour and the relevant media files in a zip file.

Currently, package creation is undertaken using an Omeka plug-in. Omeka is a content management system for online digital collections [20]. It provides Dublin core metadata and is easily extendable. The plug-in creates a private online exhibit of the contents of the app. This allows the alignment of the hotspots to be checked. All of the elements of the tours are items in Omeka and nodes in the exhibit. The package system creates an XML file with URLs referring to the media files. When the package is exported to the package management system the XML file is sent to the package management system which copies files to a local location, adds them to a zip file, and makes the media references local to the zip.

The package management system controls the relationship between packages and their content and apps. It stores the packages and is used to create lists of packages for apps. These lists contain metadata about the packages including a thumbnail and when they were last updated.

The app framework is a system which takes a list of packages, downloads them, and renders the packages. There are three implementations of the app framework, namely for Android (Google Cardboard), Extended Android (Google Daydream), and Apple (Google Cardboard). The three frameworks are configured with a number of parameters including the package list URL, and whether there are to be multiple packages or just one. Single package apps start by downloading the single package and unpacking it. The package list tells the app whether it is to be downloaded automatically, or it will require the user to request download.

The apps allow two modes of interaction, virtual reality mode or wide screen mode. In VR mode any flat media is rendered onto a plane in front of the user, while spherical media is rendered on the inside of a sphere. In Cardboard VR versions users focus their gaze on a hotspot in order to select it. The Daydream app uses the hand-held controller to select points. When the Cardboard app is in wide screen mode the flat media is rendered on an overlay layer, though spherical media is still rendered on the inside of a sphere. In wide screen mode hotspots are selected by touching them.

The apps use OpenGL to render the media which allows them to also include 3D artefacts. To use the virtual reality mode a mobile device must have a gyroscope sensor to track its orientation. This means that on Apple devices the virtual reality mode only works on iPhone 4 or subsequent models. All Daydream compatible phones have gyroscope sensors, but not all older Android phones have this feature.

5.2 Website, Social Media, and Interactive Exhibit

In addition to the Virtual Time Binoculars app, an Edinburgh 1544 website was created. This serves the dual purpose of publicising the app, and provider greater context on the reconstruction [21]. Videos from the reconstruction were also posted on the Vimeo video sharing site, and photospheres were uploaded to Roundme [22]. It was felt that it was important to provide a range of ways in which people could access the reconstruction, not of all which should involve having to install an app on a mobile device (a relevant consideration as 49% of people aged over 55 still do not have a smartphone) [23]. Having video content on Vimeo also facilitated sharing on social media and via traditional media outlets.

An interactive exhibit, which allows users to explore freely the full 3D reconstruction of Edinburgh in 1544, was also developed for use in museums and educational contexts. This was exhibited at public events at the Museum of Edinburgh, and at Riddle's Court (where it was one of the attractions for the Edinburgh Doors Open Day). It has also been used in educational contexts including local schools and the Curiosity Live science festival in Glasgow. This exhibit can be used either with a traditional flat screen, or an Oculus Rift virtual reality headset [24]. It has not, as yet, been generally released to the public, partly because the current version requires considerable processing power and a high-quality graphics card in order to function quickly. All of the fully released content, both the Edinburgh 1544 Virtual Time Binoculars app and the online videos and photospheres, are available free of charge.

6   Reception and Use of the Reconstruction

The online videos on Vimeo have proved to be by far the most heavily used of the Edinburgh 1544 project outputs. The most popular of these videos has over 61,000 views, while another has in excess of 33,000 views [25]. To put these figures in context, it has been claimed that an average academic monograph on a historical topic sells in the region of 200 copies [26]. Clearly, making content freely available online can enable historical research to reach much wider audiences than traditional academic publishing.

When compared with the number of video views, the Edinburgh 1544 Virtual Time Binoculars apps have had significantly fewer downloads. The relative popularity of the videos is probably attributable to a range of reasons, including the fact the videos were linked to by major media organisations. It also perhaps reflects people's familiarity with watching online video content, the ease with which videos can be shared, and the slightly lesser time and commitment involved in clicking on an online video as against downloading and starting to use an app. That being said, the app has fulfilled its aim of enabling people to take a reconstruction out onto the street. It has been used by tour guides, and has generally received positive feedback. The app also generated considerable media interest around the time of its launch, leading to reporting in print editions of *The Times*, the *Daily Express*, the *i*, *The Scotsman*, and *The Herald* [27]. The BBC also subsequently approached the app creation team to discuss Edinburgh's experiences in 1544 for a Newsnight report – arguably indicating that the app succeeded in its overall aim of raising the profile of an under-appreciated moment in Edinburgh's history [28].

7   Considerations for Future Development

At the heart of the Edinburgh 1544 project lay the creation of a full 3D digital reconstruction of a sixteenth-century cityscape. The project clearly demonstrated that modern modelling software and gaming engines can readily handle reconstructions on the scale of an entire urban community. From the perspective of historical reconstruction the key limitations in creating city-wide representations now lie in the amount of preliminary historical research required and the man-hours it takes to model the virtual cityscape – which are still significant considerations.

The Edinburgh 1544 project further demonstrated the viability of creating an app which provided an immersive experience of a pre-modern cityscape, while being of a size to work effectively on ordinary smartphones. The Virtual Time Binoculars framework is now being tested on other reconstructions, with satisfactory initial results. The project arguably also highlighted the importance of accompanying new apps with videos and other content placed on social media and other media sharing platforms which people are already familiar with. Apps have tremendous potential for on street heritage interpretation experiences, but they should not be the sole focus of future development. Moving forward, the project team would like to introduce into the Virtual Time Binoculars apps (and potentially other resources) more information on the historical sources behind the reconstructions. In so doing they aim to achieve a state where the evidence from the past, the visualization of the past, and experience of the present seamlessly integrate – encouraging users to embark on their own research journeys into the spaces and buildings of earlier generations.

References

1. Davison, B.: Picturing the Past Through the Eyes of Reconstruction Artists. English Heritage, Stroud (1997)

2. Gorski, J., Packer, J.: The Roman Forum: A Reconstruction and Architectural Guide. Cambridge University Press, New York (2015)
3. Liestøl, G.: Augmented reality and digital genre design - situated simulations on the iPhone. In: Proceedings of ISMAR 2009 IEEE International Symposium on Mixed and Augmented Reality - Arts, Media and Humanities, Orlando, pp. 29–34. IEEE, (2009). http://sitsim.no/. Accessed 27 Feb 2019
4. Davies, C., Miller, A., Allison, C.: A view from the hill: where cross reality meets virtual worlds. In: Proceedings of the 20th ACM Symposium on Virtual Reality Software and Technology, p. 213. ACM, Edinburgh (2014)
5. Davies, C.: PhD thesis at the University of St Andrews. http://hdl.handle.net/10023/8098. Accessed 26 Feb 2019
6. Youtube video. https://www.youtube.com/watch?v=UsDRPjDwr8A,last. Accessed 26 Feb 2019
7. UNESCO World Heritage List, Entry for the Old and New Towns of Edinburgh. https://whc.unesco.org/en/list/728. Accessed 26 Feb 2019
8. Bain, J.: The Hamilton Papers: Letters and Papers Illustrating the Political Relations of England and Scotland in the XVIth Century, vol. 2, p. 326. Edinburgh, General Register House (1892)
9. Bain, J.: The Hamilton Papers: Letters and Papers Illustrating the Political Relations of England and Scotland in the XVIth Century, vol. 2, p. 369. Edinburgh, General Register House (1892)
10. Bain, J.: The Hamilton Papers: Letters and Papers Illustrating the Political Relations of England and Scotland in the XVIth Century, vol. 2, p. 384. Edinburgh, General Register House (1892)
11. British Library Online Gallery. http://www.bl.uk/onlinegallery/onlineex/unvbrit/a/001cotaugi00002u00056000.html. Accessed 5 Jan 2019
12. National Library of Scotland Digital Image of James Gordon of Rothiemay's Edinodunensis Tabulam. http://maps.nls.uk/view/74475427. Accessed 5 Jan 2019. National Library of Scotland Digital Image of William Edgar's Plan of the City and Castle of Edinburgh. http://maps.nls.uk/view/74400010. Accessed 5 Jan 2019
13. World Machine. https://www.world-machine.com. Accessed 2 Feb 2019
14. Unreal Engine 4. https://www.unrealengine.com/en-US/what-is-unreal-engine-4. Accessed 5 Jan 2019
15. National Library of Scotland Digital Image of William Edgar's Plan of the City and Castle of Edinburgh. http://maps.nls.uk/view/74400010. Accessed 5 Jan 2019
16. SketchUp. https://www.sketchup.com. Accessed 5 Jan 2019
17. Tait, R.: Configuration and dimensions of burgage plots in the burgh of Edinburgh. In: Proceedings of the Society of Antiquaries of Scotland, vol. 136, pp. 297–310 (2006)
18. Edinburgh 1544 Virtual Time Binoculars App. https://www.smarthistory.co.uk/Edinburgh1544/download.html. Accessed 24 Feb 2019
19. Homepage for Google Cardboard. https://vr.google.com/cardboard/. Accessed 24 Feb 2019. Homepage for Google Daydream. https://vr.google.com/daydream/. Accessed 24 Feb 2019
20. Homepage for Omeka. https://omeka.org/. Accessed 24 Feb 2019
21. Homepage for Edinburgh 1544. https://www.smarthistory.co.uk/Edinburgh1544/. Accessed 27 Feb 2019
22. Vimeo introductory video for Edinburgh 1544. https://vimeo.com/208677167. Accessed 27 Feb 2019. Photosphere of St Giles' Kirk. https://roundme.com/tour/171650/view/439692/. Accessed 27 Feb 2019
23. Ofcom Communications Market Report for 2018. https://www.ofcom.org.uk/__data/assets/pdf_file/0022/117256/CMR-2018-narrative-report.pdf. Accessed 27 Feb 2019

24. Homepage for Oculus Rift. https://www.oculus.com/rift/. Accessed 27 Feb 2019
25. Edinburgh 1544 Introductory video https://vimeo.com/224189702 and Edinburgh 1544 Townscape video https://vimeo.com/208677167. Accessed 27 Feb 2019
26. Dalton, M.: The publishing experiences of historians. J. Sch. Publishing **39**(3), 197–240 (2008)
27. Mair, G.: Edinburgh re-emerges from past. The Times, 18 March 2017. Milmo, C.: The really Old Town: 16th-century Edinburgh is brought back to life. i, 18 March 2017. Christison, G.: New virtual view of very Auld Reekie. Daily Express, 18 March 2017. O'Leary, D.: Step back in time as app visits capital in 1544. The Herald, 18 March 2017. Pringle, F.: Old, lost Edinburgh digitally recreated. The Scotsman, 18 March 2017
28. BBC Newsnight report on the Rough Wooing. https://www.youtube.com/watch?reload=9&v=nqbdSVZ5ZME&list=PLJxnQXiytA_Qc0B57aViue2G3DPet1Z0L&index=1. Accessed 6 April 2017

Pedagogical Strategies

Social Organisation and Cooperative Learning: Identification and Categorisation of Groups and Sub-Groups in Non-Cooperative Games

Edward Longford[(✉)], Michael Gardner, and Victor Callaghan

University of Essex, Colchester, UK
{elongf,mgardner,vic}@essex.ac.uk

Abstract. This paper outlines the results of a Modified SYMLOG (Mod-SYMLOG) analysis for group formation, structure and interactions. While collaborative working has been an established working methodology for Education and Computer Science researchers alike, there has been a lack of focus in the latter as to what a group actually is within psychologically complex human communities. Here we discuss why groups can be beneficial to student learning in education, but also how misusing groups has negative effects. This paper presents the results of two board game based experiments. The first experiment used the classic SYMLOG model to show validity of the scenario in data collection and the second testing our Mod-SYMLOG. Results showed that Mod-SYMLOG was effective in capturing group dynamics, with indications of group structure.

Keywords: Collaborative learning ·
Computer-supported collaborative learning

1 Introduction

This paper will outline work completed on the designing of Group Model for monitoring student group formation within a classroom environment. In our previous submission we highlighted the issues caused by increased classroom sizes in UK secondary schools and outlined the Intelligent Classroom Tutoring System (ICTS) [17], as direction of research to address this issue. The ICTS attempted to extend the Intelligent Tutoring System (ITS) model from a single learner to a group of learners and supplement human teachers within a traditional classroom environment via the use of Psychological theories of Intra- and Inter-group dynamics and monitoring tools within an immersive or virtual classroom. We shall cover the completed experimental work for the creation of a the Group Model, beginning with a review of SYstem for the Multiple Level Observation of Groups (SYMLOG) methodology from psychology as a starting point for understanding group behaviour. We then modified the SYMLOG (Mod-SYMLOG) classification system, and experimental results for both methodologies.

© Springer Nature Switzerland AG 2019
D. Beck et al. (Eds.): iLRN 2019, CCIS 1044, pp. 131–143, 2019.
https://doi.org/10.1007/978-3-030-23089-0_10

1.1   Intelligent Classroom Tutoring System

The ICTS framework is designed to assist a human teacher within either a physical or virtual classroom setting, augmented with additional technology for monitoring and interacting with the students and teacher. Our model is divided into two components, the individual ITS component, traditionally split into four modules Domain, Student, Pedagogy and Communication [21], and our group component. The feedback loops within the ITS and this ICTS model, which is where the learner, individually and/or as part of a group, is instructed through a series of teaching techniques transferring the domain knowledge via a communication interface and updating the learner model. See Fig. 1 for a functional illustration of the proposed framework. It is envisioned that he status of a class, would be relayed back to the human and AI teachers, providing details of both individual and group behaviour in real time. This information would then be used to calculate what time of intervention is needed and whether that is delivered from an AI agent or the human teacher. Intervention could be deployed in the form of human interaction or augmenting the classroom.

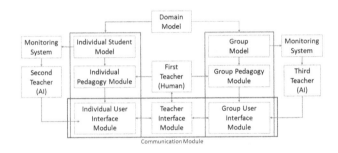

Fig. 1. Intelligent classroom tutoring system framework [17]

1.2   Understanding the Group and it's Importance to Learning and Development

Educational researchers have tended to agree that group learning is superior to individual learning, both in terms of academic performance and improvement in social skills [13]. However this does come with a caveat, the individuals reaction to working within a group. Studies from Educational Psychology have shown when group based learning was viewed as a positive event, this tends to lead to greater socio-emotional skills in forming personal relationship, improved relationship with learning, and improved academic outcome [2,6,13,23].

Unfortunately, other studies have found that group learning does not always produce a better outcomes than individual learning. A negative group interaction can lead to members associating both learning and social interaction with negative experiences and withdraw from both, potentially even permanently [4]. If the task is not sufficiently defined and structured [2], the individual efforts of learners are not rewarded, and free-riders not penalised [6] then group learning can have a negative impact on learning and social development [6, 13].

Negative groups tend to not appear in human experiments as they rely on volunteers, which can lead to a Volunteer Bias, which is a subset of the more general Sampling Bias [22, 27]. Volunteers, when compared to non-volunteers, tend to score lower for Neuroticism and higher in Conscientiousness, Agreeableness, Extraversion on psychological tests and, perhaps, have a higher need for social approval [18]. These individuals have a tendency of wanting to please the experimenter or be liked by others. This results in positive feedback between group members which can lead to validity problems when applied to real world scenarios where different personality types interact [18]. The importance of identifying "positive" and "negative" groups, or disruptive individuals within a group, and resolving issues before students develop a resistant attitude towards education, social-interaction or both, cannot be understated [4].

By utilising the mechanics of a board game which encourages dynamic group formation (cooperation) and division (non-cooperation) through social interaction, rather than preassigned roles, we hope to observe and capture negative groups and their formation. If this is found to be possible, then future research can examine training an AI system to detect these patterns.

1.3   Computer Supported Collaborative Learning Research

A significant amount of research has been carried out on supporting group work within real world smart environments [11, 26], intelligent classrooms [7] digitising of group based educational techniques [14, 19] and feedback from members as metrics of satisfaction [9]. Less has been focused at the structure of the group itself. Attempts to capture groups as an entity include aggregating Bayesian Network based individual student models [25], similar to one of the approaches taken by Economists [16], however researchers in Psychology have shown groups out perform what aggregate methods would suggest [8, 28].

Goodman et al. in a review of research between 1998 and 2016, posed 6 open research questions. The 3rd question posed stated that "[m]odeling of users takes on a different perspective in an intelligent CSCL. There are attributes of individual students (a 'student model') and of the whole group of human learners (a "group model") that need to be tracked to best drive the instructional support" [12]. The view that there is a group and that it is under examined within the research is supported by Stahl, where he states "...it is proposed that CSCL research should focus on the analysis of group processes and practices, and that the analysis at this level should be considered foundational for LS" [24].

It is here, alongside current research, that the authors wish to include a group model. The identification of positive and negative groups, the dynamic relationships that exist between individuals, and changes due to intervention, it is believed, will achieve a more inclusive and positive learning experience.

2   Methodology

For both sets of experiments, the participants played a board game known as Diplomacy. This first pilot experiment was designed to test the applicably of SYMLOG within the game set up and to run an initial analysis of results to provide a baseline for comparison for the Mod-SYMLOG methodology we have designed.

2.1   What is SYMLOG?

SYMLOG is an attempt to quantify group behaviour by categorising interactions between group members, with each interaction being rated externally, rather than self reflection [10]. I.E. if there is a conversation between two people (Person A and Person B) then Person A (or an external observer) would rate how they perceived Person B and Person B would rate how they perceived Person A. Rating of how individuals interact with a group is not one rating for the whole session, but one or more ratings per interaction (i.e. conversation) with one or more other people within the group [1,10,20]. Bales created a list of adjectives to rate these interactions between individuals within the group [1]. Each interaction can have one or more ratings assigned to it.

When these ratings are collected, groups can be assessed by how well the group is working together by examining the group itself rather than just the outputs from the group, e.g. task completion. This study hopes to establish that the Mod-SYMLOG can model the group evolving dynamically, before further research into automating the the Mod-SYMLOG process.

These ratings are then collated and a position within the group is assigned to each individual based on the net outcome of all there interactions (see Fig. 3 for visual examples).

These adjectives are assigned a combination of letters, based on a three dimensional scale of Up/Down (U/D), Positive/Negative (P/N) and Forward/ Backwards (F/B) and should be based on both verbal and non-verbal communication [10,15]. U/D is the measurement of a persons dominance or submissiveness to the group. P/N is a scale if a person's interactions are friendly or non-friendly within a group. And F/B is a measurement of how the person within the group is working either towards or against either the group goals or emotional status of the group. A few examples of the SYMLOG adjectives are listed below:

- U Individual financial success, personal prominence and power
- UPF Active teamwork toward common goals, organisational unity
- PF Responsible idealism, collaborative work
- N Self-protection, self-interest first, self-sufficiency
- DNB Admission of failure, withdrawal of effort

Adjectives ratings for each member of the group are collected and plotted onto a SYMLOG Field Diagram (SFD), which is a two dimensional axis of P/N and F/B, with U/D represented by the size of the plot point of each individual, i.e. the more dominate they were the larger the radius. Positions on the SFD can then be categorised into various group structures ranging from types of effective teamwork to opposition/destructive groups/group members (see Fig. 2).

For example, in Turn 1, Person A received a rating of "DPB" (Quiet contentment) from Person B and "UPF" from Person C. The U and D values cancel each other out (i.e. neutral), as does the F and B values. This leaves Person A with an overall rating of "P." Each axis on the graph was given a numeric range between 0 and 2. So here Person A receives a co-ordinate plot of (1, 2).

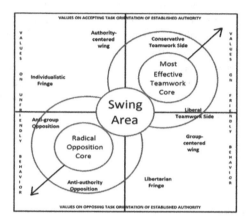

Fig. 2. SYMLOG field diagram [3]

2.2   Modifying SYMLOG

This modified SYMLOG (Mod-SYMLOG) replaces the adjective rating system with ratings based on the three axis points, U/D, P/N, and F/B. In this system, Person A would rate Person B on each of the following scales:

- U/_/D: Dominate, Neutral, or Submissive
- P/_/N: Positive, Neutral, or Negative
- F/_/B: Working towards group goals, Neutral, or working against group goals

So if a Person A though Person B was being Dominate they would record "U," the coordinates would resolve to (2, 1) If Person A thought Person B was being Positive at the same time, they would record "UP" (2, 2) Or if Person A thought that B was withdrawing from the group and being negative and activity working to disrupt the group, they would record "DNB" (0, 0).

Participants could also rate someone as being partially within these axis. For example if Person A thought that Person B was being submissive, but only slightly, and working towards the group goals they would record "DF, F" which would resolve to the coordinates (1.5, 1).

Participants could also rate someone as being partially within these axis. For example if Person A thought that Person B was being submissive, but only slightly, and working towards the group goals they would record "DF, F" which would resolve to the coordinates (1.5, 1).

3 SYMLOG Experimental Set up

Developed in the mid-late 1950s, Diplomacy is a turn based game where participants take the part of the "Great Powers" of Europe in 1900. Each game year consists of 2 phases (Spring and Autumn), each phase has a negotiation turn followed by a movement turn where all participants move simultaneously. At the end of the Autumn turn, participants either gain pieces or lose pieces depending on the outcome of the Spring and Autumn phases. The board is a map of Europe, divided into 52 land regions and 19 sea regions. 42 of the land regions are divided between the Great Powers at the start of the game, leaving 14 neutral land regions. All sea regions are considered neutral. 34 of land regions contain supply centres, 22 belonging to Great Powers, 12 in neutral land regions. Each supply centre provides the player with 1 unit (e.g. if a player controls 4 supply centres they can have 4 units on the board). The winner is the first to control 18 supply centres [5].

In the experimental set up, each participant was asked to fill out a Negotiation Log after each Negotiation turn. The Negotiation Log asked each participant to describe their current diplomatic status with other participants. Table 1 shows an example of the diplomatic status section of the Negotiation Log.

Table 1. Austro-Hungry diplomatic status

Alliance	None
Non-Aggression pact	None
Cooperative other	FRA, ENG
War	None

Participants would then fill in the number of interactions they have had with each other participant and the SYMLOG rating for each. SYMLOG ratings were provided to participants on a separate sheet of paper. An example of this can be seen in Table 2. This example, the Austrian Player rates England and France as "Active teamwork toward common goals, organisational unity" which is represented by the SYMLOG notation "UPF." Italy is rated as "Responsible idealism, collaborative work" (PF). Turkey is rated as both "Passive non-co-operation with authority" (DB) and "ejection of established procedures, rejection of conformity" (NB).

5 participants, out of a maximum of 7, took part in the experiment which ran for 3 hours on a Thursday evening. The subject group consisted of 3 males and 2 females, with 2 subjects of Arabic descent and the rest of a White British background. 3 participants were undertaking PhDs in Computer Science, 1 had

Table 2. Austro-Hungry SYMLOG

Country	SYMLOG rating
England	UPF
France	UPF
Russia	PF
Turkey	DB, NB

completed their PhD in Computer Science, and the final had just started a BSc in Mathematics. Due to the number of participants, the 5 player variant of Diplomacy was selected, meaning that Austro-Hungry, England, France, Russia, and Turkey would be taken by participants while Italy and Germany would remain neutral. Each country was randomly assigned a number between 1 and 5, then participants selected numbers from 1 to 5 from a hat to randomly assign a country to each person with minimal bias.

The participants, in conjunction with playing the game, filled out a negotiation log at the end of each negotiation phase, recording current and established agreements between participants and using the SYMLOG adjective rating system to score interactions they had with other participants.

3.1   Mod-SYMLOG Experimental Set Up

With the original SYMLOG experiment establishing Diplomacy as being a suitable analogue for cooperative and non-cooperative group interaction, we began a second phase of experimentation to test adjustments to the SYMLOG framework data collection and member position methodology. The Mod-SYMLOG experiments took place on two different evenings in January with two games played on each day. On the first day 5 participants took part in game 1, and 4 for game 2. The second day there were 7 players for game 3 and 6 for game 4. These were run with the same methodology as the pilot, with the only amendment being the new rating system. As with the pilot experiment, most of the participants were STEM PhD or MSc students. However the participants were significantly less diverse than the pilot. All groups were male and originated from the European continent.

4   Results

4.1   SYMLOG Results

Year 1 phase of SYMLOG Diplomacy tends to be fairly cooperative as players tend to avoid early conflict and agree on the division of neutral territory, participants followed this pattern and started as a cooperative group. Out of 13 recorded interactions between participants in Turn 1, 6 of the ratings were "UPF," 1 "PF," and 1 "F," meaning that 8/13 (61%) of the interactions were rated as positive. In turn 3 (Year 2 spring), 17 interactions were recorded of which 9 (53%) were negative. The position of each participant was calculated for each turn, based on the average rating received from all participants that recorded an interaction rating.

Once the results had been plotted, the participants were interviewed and asked if they felt that the SFDs accurately represented the group playing the game. Out of the 5 participants, 4 responded stating that the SFDs agreed with their own assessment of the group dynamics.

Figure 3 shows a sample of 2 SFDs from Turns 1 and 3. While all participants were in or near the effective teamwork sphere in Turn 1, the group is moving away from close cooperation by Turn 3, with Russia moving towards the disruptive area.

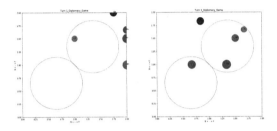

Fig. 3. Human Diplomacy SYMLOG Turns 1 & 3

More detail for the interaction between group members was captured and represented via node graphs. Interactions between participants were broadly defined as "Teamwork" and "Opposition" based on the location of these ratings when plotted within the classic SFD (Fig. 2). Teamwork rating fell within the "PF," "UPF," "UF," "P," "UNF," "UP," and "F" ranges, while Opposition ratings where "BD," "DB," "DN," "DNB," "DPB," "N," and "NB". The direction of opinion is noted by an arrow, for example the blue arrow in Turn 1 pointing from Turkey (T) to France (F) (Fig. 4) signifies that Turkey believes that France is being cooperative. These diagrams provide additional incite into how the group were interacting. We can see that Russia (R) is viewed, by Austria (A), as moving from working cooperatively to working against. This shift explains why Russia moves towards the disruptive area on the SDF.

4.2   Mod-SYMLOG

In all four games, Mod-SYMLOG recorded groups forming in cooperative and non-cooperative states. Similar patterns of behaviour were captured - the movement of the group from initial cooperation between all players to non-cooperation and/or formation of subgroups (see Fig. 5 for an example from game 3).

The results from Game 3 can provide indicators for sub-group formation. The node diagram in Fig. 6 shows negative interactions existing between Austria and

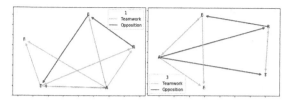

Fig. 4. Human node graphs Turns 1 & 3

Germany for turns 2 and 3. On turn 4, France moves from a cooperative state with Austria in turn 3, to a non-cooperative state, while maintaining a cooperative position with Germany. France has also been in a non-cooperative state with Italy, which maintained a cooperative state with Austria. This is the Potential forming of two sub-groups, where players seek cooperation against common non-cooperative players (France and Germany against Austria and Italy). The creation of these sub-groups transpires in turn 5 France and Germany are joined by England, while Austria and Italy and aligned with Russia. Turkey remains in a cooperative state with two to three members of each sub-group. Similar indicators of sub-group formation were seen in Games 1, 2, and 4. More detail how individual participants viewed other group members in Turn 5 can be seen in Table 3.

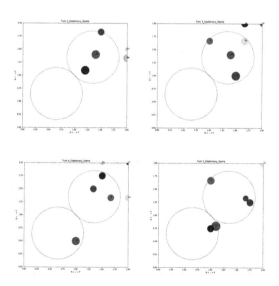

Fig. 5. Human Diplomacy game 3 Mod-SYMLOG Turns 2–5

Table 3. Game 3 Mod-SYMLOG ratings Turns 4 and 5

Player/Target	Turn	Ah	En	Fr	Ge	It	Ru	Tu
Ah	5					P	PF	PF
En	5			D,F,P	P,D			
Fr	5	UNB	DF		F	NF		
Ge	5	UB	DP	DPF			B	
It	5	PB	B	B	B		P	
Ru	5	UPF	NB		NB			PF
Tu	5	F, UNF				F	DPF	

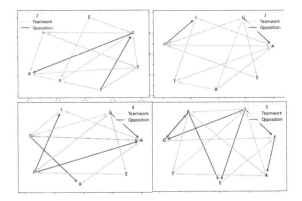

Fig. 6. Human Diplomacy game 3 Mod-SYMLOG Turns 2–5

5   Conclusion and Discussion

Both sets of experiments have shown the ability to capture the dynamics of group behaviour and how these interactions can be modelled.

Participants identified that categorisations of types of interaction as the most difficult part of the pilot experiment. For example, players found it difficult to distinguish between "UPF," "UF," and "UNF" during the negotiation phase. Mod-SYMLOG provided an easy to use alternative, with players asking fewer questions about how to encode ratings than in the pilot. Additionally, one of the experiment participants is an AI Games Lecturer, who expressed interest in using the Mod-SYMLOG system for a cooperative gaming AI, which aligns with the original intention that a simple triple axis would be easier for an AI to learn and model human behaviour from. This redesigned metric was intended for AI monitoring system, so feedback was beneficial over it's potential usefulness.

There is some indication that it is also possible to extract some group hierarchy from the data. In turns 4 and 5 Austria and Germany either viewed their respective cooperative partners as equal or submissive, or their partners saw them as dominate and positive (see Table 3). For example, in Turn 5 France viewed Germany as "F", while Germany viewed France as "DPF," suggesting some hierarchy. This concurs with observations from the game, where Austria and Germany were in clear leadership positions. Further experimental work would be required to establish the validity of detecting these hierarchies.

Active monitoring of students within the classroom, analysed through Mod-SYMLOG, could provide teachers with the ability to intervene and prevent negative groups from establishing a permanence through lessons or the school year.

6   Future Work

With experimental evidence that Mod-SYMLOG can capture group dynamics, it will be used to further the development of the ICTS. Our current intention is to apply the Mod-SYMLOG model of recording group interactions to a real classroom scenario and have the information fed back to a teacher.

AI agents for a digital version of Diplomacy, are to be created with a Mod-SYMLOG module to assist with decision making and AI-Human interaction. This could have potential applications in the creation of an AI monitoring system as part of the ICTS.

The next phase of research and development of the ICTS framework is the Group Pedagogy Module. Here the intent is to investigate various methods for selection for intervention methods within a classroom environment. Investigations towards modelling an N-Player Prisoner's Dilemma game. Results of intervention shall be measured not only by academic results of group work, but also the cooperative levels within the group as interpreted by Mod-SYMLOG data.

This will be followed by investigations of representing feedback gathered from the monitoring system to a teacher. Other methods under investigation Are 3 Dimensional SFD, heat maps of positive/negative interactions and assessing levels of detail the teacher requires.

References

1. Bales, R.F.: Interaction Process Analysis; A Method for the Study of Small Groups. Addison-Wesley, Oxford (1950)
2. Bartlett, R.L.: A flip of the coin-a roll of the die: an answer to the free-rider problem in economic instruction. J. Econ. Educ. **26**(2), 131–139 (1995)
3. Berdun, F., Armentano, M., Berdun, L., Cincunegui, M.: Building symlog profiles with an online collaborative game. Int. J. Hum. Comput. Stud. (2018). https://doi.org/10.1016/j.ijhcs.2018.07.002
4. Blumenfeld, P.C., Marx, R.W., Soloway, E., Krajcik, J.: Learning with peers: from small group cooperation to collaborative communities. Educ. Researcher **25**(8), 37–39 (1996)
5. Calhamer, A.B.: The Rules of Diplomacy (2000). https://www.wizards.com/avalonhill/rules/diplomacy.pdf
6. Cohen, E.G.: Restructuring the classroom: conditions for productive small groups. Rev. Educ. Res. **64**(1), 1–35 (1994)

7. Dooley, J., Callaghan, V., Hagras, H., Gardner, M., Ghanbaria, M., AlGhazzawi, D.: The intelligent classroom: beyond four walls. In: Proceedings of the Intelligent Campus Workshop (IC 2011) held at the 7th IEEE Intelligent Environments Conference (IE 2011), Nottingham (2011)

8. Engel, D., Woolley, A.W., Jing, L.X., Chabris, C.F., Malone, T.W.: Reading the mind in the eyes or reading between the lines? Theory of mind predicts collective intelligence equally well online and face-to-face. PLoS ONE **9**(12), e115212 (2014)

9. Felemban, S., Gardner, M., Callaghan, V.: Towards recognising learning evidence in collaborative virtual environments: a mixed agents approach. Computers **6**(3), 22 (2017)

10. Forsyth, D.R.: Group Dynamics **15**, (2014)

11. Gardner, M.R., Elliott, J.B.: The immersive education laboratory: understanding affordances, structuring experiences, and creating constructivist, collaborative processes, in mixed-reality smart environments. EAI Endorsed Trans. Future Intell. Educ. Environ. **1**(1), c6 (2014)

12. Goodman, B., Linton, F., Gaimari, R.: Encouraging student reflection and articulation using a learning companion: a commentary. Int. J. Artif. Intell. Educ. **26**(1), 474–488 (2016)

13. Gunderson, D.E., Moore, J.D.: Group learning pedagogy and group selection. Int. J. Constr. Educ. Res. **4**(1), 34–45 (2008)

14. Jambi, E., Gardner, M., Callaghan, V.: Supporting mixed-mode role-play activities in a virtual environment. In: 2017 9th Computer Science and Electronic Engineering Conference, CEEC 2017 - Proceedings, pp. 49–54. IEEE, September 2017

15. Keyton, J., Wall, V.D.J.: Research instrument SYMLOG theory and method for measuring group and organizational communication. Manage. Commun. Q. **2**(4), 544 (1989)

16. List, C.: Group knowledge and group rationality: a judgment aggregation perspective. Episteme **2**(01), 25–38 (2005)

17. Longford, E., Gardner, M.R., Callaghan, V.: Group immersion in classrooms: a framework for an intelligent group-based tutoring system of multiple learners. In: Beck, D., et al. (eds.) Workshop, Long and Short Paper, and Poster Proceedings from the Fourth Immersive Learning Research Network Conference (iLRN 2018 Montana), pp. 133–135 (2018). https://doi.org/10.3217/978-3-85125-609-3-20

18. Lonnqvist, J.E., Paunonen, S., Verkasalo, M., Leikas, S., Tuulio-Henriksson, A., Lonnqvist, J.: Personality characteristics of research volunteers. Eur. J. Pers. **21**(8), 1017–1030 (2007)

19. Olsen, Jennifer K., Belenky, Daniel M., Aleven, Vincent, Rummel, Nikol: Using an intelligent tutoring system to support collaborative as well as individual learning. In: Trausan-Matu, Stefan, Boyer, Kristy Elizabeth, Crosby, Martha, Panourgia, Kitty (eds.) ITS 2014. LNCS, vol. 8474, pp. 134–143. Springer, Cham (2014). https://doi.org/10.1007/978-3-319-07221-0_16

20. Palmgren-Neuvonen, L., Korkeamäki, R.L.: Group interaction of primary-aged students in the context of a learner-generated digital video production. Learn. Cult. Soc. Inter. **3**(1), 1–14 (2014)

21. Rrafzadeh, A., Alexander, S., Dadgostar, F., Fan, C., Bigdeli, A.: How do you know that I don't understand? A look at the future of intelligent tutoring systems. Comput. Hum. Behav. **24**(4), 1342–1363 (2008)

22. Salkind, N.: Encyclopedia of Research Design (2010)

23. Springer, L., Stanne, M.E., Donovan, S.S.: Effects of small-group learning on undergraduates in science, mathematics, engineering, and technology: a meta-analysis. Rev. Educ. Res. **69**(1), 21–51 (1999)

24. Stahl, G.: The group as paradigmatic unit of analysis: the contested relationship of CSCL to the learning sciences. Learn. Sci. Mapp. Terrain (2015)
25. Suebnukarn, S.: Intelligent tutoring system for medical problem-based learning. Prog. Educ. **18**(18), 233–302 (2010)
26. Walker, E., Rummel, N., Koedinger, K.R.: Designing automated adaptive support to improve student helping behaviors in a peer tutoring activity. Int. J. Comput. Support. Collaborative Learn. **6**(2), 279–306 (2011)
27. Wallin, P.: Volunteer subjects as a source of sampling bias. Am. J. Sociol. **54**(6), 539–544 (1949)
28. Woolley, A.W.: Evidence for a collective intelligence factor in the performance of human groups. Science **330**(6004), 683–686 (2010)

Adaptive Hypermedia Driven Serious Game Design and Cognitive Style in School Settings: An Exploratory Study

Alex Hadwen-Bennett[1(✉)] and Daphne Economou[2]

[1] School of Education, Communication and Society, King's College London, London, UK
alex.hadwen-bennett@kcl.ac.uk
[2] Department of Computer Science, Faculty of Science and Technology, University of Westminster, London, UK
d.economou@westminster.ac.uk

Abstract. The potential value of adaptive hypermedia and game based learning to education and training has long been recognised, numerous studies have been undertaken in both those areas investigating its potential to improve learner performance. In particular research has indicated that tailoring content to match the prior knowledge of the user has the power to increase the effectiveness of learning systems. Recent studies have begun to indicate that Adaptive Hypermedia Learning Systems (AHLS) based on cognitive styles have the power to improve learner performance. Recent examples of research exploring avenues for effectively incorporating serious games into AHLS indicated that integrating serious games into a personalized learning environment has the potential educational benefits of combining a personalized delivery with increased learner motivation. The exploratory study presented in this paper here developed an Adaptive Hypermedia Driven Serious Game (AHDSG) based around Pask's Holist-Serialist dimension of cognitive style. A prototype AHDSG was designed and developed to teach students about Sutton Hoo and archaeological methods. Sixty-six secondary school students participated in this study. Overall the findings of this study show that there was an improvement in performance among all participants. Although the participants that used the system which adapted to their preferred cognitive style achieved a higher mean gain score, the difference was not significant.

Keywords: Serious games · Adaptive hypermedia · Cognitive styles · Holist-serialist

1 Introduction

It has long been recognised that people learn and process information in different ways, however opinions regarding the validity of the numerous cognitive style theories vary greatly among academics in the field. Recent studies have begun to indicate that Adaptive Hypermedia Learning Systems (AHLS) based on cognitive styles have the power to improve learner performance [8]. An AHLS can be defined as an interactive training resource designed to personalise content and navigation based on the

© Springer Nature Switzerland AG 2019
D. Beck et al. (Eds.): iLRN 2019, CCIS 1044, pp. 144–157, 2019.
https://doi.org/10.1007/978-3-030-23089-0_11

individual characteristics of each user. Many of these systems have been developed to tailor content to match the prior knowledge or cognitive style of the user.

Although there are various cognitive style models, Witkin's Field Independence/Dependence model is one of the most widely studied within the context of AHLSs [16]. Witkin defines field-independent learners as those that work within an internal frame of reference and are able to structure their own learning, whereas field-dependent learners rely on an external frame of reference and require guidance from the instructor. Conceptual links have been identified between the Field Independence/Dependence model and Pask's Holist-Serialist model [12], however relatively few studies have investigated the merits of the later in relation to AHLS [2]. A study investigating the effects of an AHLS based on Pask's Holist/Serialist model on postgraduate students indicated an increase in learner performance [8].

Recent research stresses the benefits of Games[1] and Simulations[2], so called Serious Games[3](SG) [18, 24], in increasing learner motivation through: (a) increasing learner engagement achieved by a combination of education and entertainment, introducing fun into the learning process [19]; and (b) the adaptation of the interactive learning experience responding to the evolution of learners' needs and requirements [20]. Adding fun into the learning process makes learning not only more enjoyable and compelling, but more effective as well [25]. A game that is motivating makes learners become personally involved with playing it in an emotional and cognitive way. By engaging in a dual level, learner attention and motivation is increased [26]. However, depending on the topic which is being covered Games and Simulations may be more or less suitable depending on the topic or the user's cognitive style.

This project aims to broaden current research by examining the capacity of Holist/Serialist based Adaptive Hypermedia Driven Serious Game (AHDSG) to improve the performance of learners in Key Stage Three (KS3).

Educators are encouraged to adapt their style of delivery to accommodate the varied cognitive styles of their students, logistically and technically this can be hard to achieve as teachers need the technical expertise to produce resources that meet the needs of all students. The ever-increasing use of hypermedia within educational environments affords an opportunity to meet the individual needs of each learner leveraging the power of AHDSG.

2   Background

2.1   Adaptive Hypermedia

Hypertext and Hypermedia. The meanings of the terms hypertext and hypermedia vary considerably within the research community, Wardip-Fruin argues that a historical

---

[1] We recognise games as recreational activities whose main objective is the entertainment.

[2] Simulations are about trying to recreate a situation that occurs in real life through a game.

[3] Serious Games are characterised as games/interactive gamified applications having other purposes besides the element of entertainment, such as education or training.

approach can be employed to determine a common meaning. The terms hypertext and hypermedia were originally coined by Nelson in 1965 [10] and developed further in 1970 [11, 16]. Hypermedia take the form of branching presentations consisting of words and pictures, which the user can control and explore freely, whereas hypertext is a form of hypermedia which consists of discrete pieces of text that are connected by links [11].

The following section will discuss the limitations of ordinary hypermedia systems and how these may be addressed through the use of adaptive hypermedia systems.

Adaptive Hypermedia Systems. The non-sequential nature of standard hypermedia systems offers many advantages to the learner, allowing them to access and process the content in any order. On the other hand, they do have limitations; they are unable to cater for the diverse individual characteristics of the users, for instance goals, interests and knowledge [1]. Different users may require alternate navigational structures or alternate content. Adaptive hypermedia systems are designed to address this void by personalising the content and navigation based on the individual characteristics of each user.

Adaptive Hypermedia Driven Serious Games. The potential value of AH to education and training was quickly recognised, numerous studies have been undertaken investigating its potential benefits. For example, a range of studies have investigated the potential benefits of adapting learning experiences according to learning and cognitive styles [35]; focusing on factors such as learner performance, perceptions and satisfaction [17]. The Felder-Silverman learning style model [36] is most commonly applied to this field, however Truong [35] suggests that research focusing on different models is required. Cognitive styles, which are different to learning styles [15], have received less attention from researchers and it has been indicated that AHDSGs based on Pask's Holist/Serialist model of cognitive styles have the potential to increase learner performance [8]. Before investigating AHDSGs further it is necessary to gain an understanding of serious games (see Sect. 2.2) and cognitive styles (see Sect. 2.3).

2.2   Serious Games

Digital computer games have now been around for over three decades and the term games-based learning has been attributed to the use of computer games that are thought to have educational value, however there has been much debate surrounding this theory [27]. Research [22, 25, 28–32] indicated the educational benefits of serious games in assisting learning by providing an alternative way of presenting instructions and content on a supplementary level. Games and gamified environments can promote student motivation and interest in subject matter resulting in enhanced learning effectiveness. In recent years, a huge effort has been made towards the development of educational gaming experiences and the exploration of their advantages for learning by introducing a set of possible educational scenarios using leaderboards, badges, level-systems, geolocation services, achievements and rewards [33]. Wrzesien & Alcañiz

Raya [23], conducted a thorough literature of serious games during the last decade and identified three main reasons for their growing use in education:

- they use actions rather than explanations and create personal motivation and satisfaction;
- they accommodate multiple learning styles and abilities;
- they foster decision-making and problem-solving activities in a virtual setting.

Mayo [21] discusses that SG are becoming a recognized venue of creative attempts to develop students' skills and attributes in both formal and informal educational settings due to the potential benefits of their use in educational contexts like: massive reach; experiential learning; enquiry-based learning; self-efficacy; goal setting; cooperation; continuous feedback; enhanced brain chemistry; time on task.

The successful use of SG for learning is based on:

- adopting gamified elements that support increased motivation and engagements which are usually considered prerequisites that lead to learning;
- accommodate multiple learning styles and abilities;
- adapt to users/learners learning and cognitive style.

The next section will discuss the two dimensions of cognitive style theories (verbalizer-visualiser and wholist-analytic) that can be potentially integrated in AHDSG.

2.3   Cognitive Styles

The terms learning style and cognitive style are perceived by many to have similar meanings and are therefore often used interchangeably. However, studies have shown that these terms should be treated as separate constructs [15]. Cognitive styles have been defined as individual different preferences of organising and processing information and experience whereas learning styles are individual skills and preferences that affect how students perceive, gather and process learning materials. Cognitive styles are generally seen as stable characteristics and learning styles are seen as variable, dependent on the environment [9]. Numerous theories relating to identification cognitive styles have been put forward, Riding and Cheema [14] found that they could be grouped under two dimensions; Verbaliser-Visualiser and Wholist-Analytic. This section will now provide an overview of each dimension:

Theories, which fall within the verbaliser-imager dimension are used to describe the different modes and methods of thought among individuals, placing them into one of two categories. Imagers (also known as visualisers) tend to think in the form of mental pictures whereas verbalisers are more inclined to think in the form of words [14]. Table 1 on the following page outlines the three main measures used to assess the verbaliser-visualiser dimension.

The wholist-analytic dimension of cognitive style has particular relevance to the learning preferences of individuals. Research has indicated that analytic students prefer to learn sequentially, building understanding in a logical and guided manner. However,

Table 1. A summary of the theories grouped within the verbaliser-imager dimension by riding and Cheema (1991).

Individual difference questionnaire	Paivivo, 1971
Verbaliser-Visualiser	Richardson, 1977
Verbal-Imagery	Riding & Taylor, 1976

wholist learners need to start with an overview of a topic before drilling down to the fine details [14]. Table 2 outlines the five main theories grouped under the wholist-analytics umbrella:

Table 2. Summary of the main theories grouped within the wholist-analytic dimension by Riding and Cheema (1991).

Field dependence-Independence	Witkin, 1962
Impulsivity-Reflectivity	Kagan, 1965
Convergent-Divergent Thinking	Hudson, 1966
Leveller-Sharpener	Holzman & Klein, 1954
Holist-serialist	Pask, 1972

A number of studies have investigated the benefits of developing an AHDSG based around the Wholist-Analytic dimension of cognitive style, with particular focus being paid to Witkin's Field Independence/Dependence model. However, relatively few studies have investigated Pask's Holist/Serialist model [2]. Research has indicated that Holists and Serialists tend to approach hypermedia in different ways, for example Ford and Chen found that Holists preferred to navigate using the sitemap and spend more time studying the high-level content [6]. On the other hand, Serialists preferred to utilise the Back/Forward buttons in order to navigate and spend more time studying the deeper levels. Table 3 outlines the differences between the Holist and Serialist interfaces implemented in the Mampadi et al. study [8].

Table 3. The differences between the Holist and Serialist interfaces implemented in the Mampadi et al. study [8].

Adaptive hypermedia	Holist interface	Serialist interface
Direct Guidance	No guidance	Next/previous buttons
Link Hiding	Rich links	Disabled links
Adaptive Layout	Hierarchical map	Alphabetic index

Mampadi et al. [8], found that an AHLS based on the Holist-Serialist cognitive model has the potential to improve the performance and perceptions of students in higher education. This study aims to investigate whether similar affects are observed among learners in KS3 (aged 11–14) when using an AHDSG. The adaptive techniques employed by Mampadi et al. could be considered as coming under the category of *adaptive navigation support* [34].

3   Hypothesis

It was the hypothesis of this case study that it would produce evidence to indicate that an AHDSG based on Pask's Holist-Serialist cognitive model might have the potential to improve the performance of learners in KS3.

In order to allow comparison, a serious game was designed and developed with three modes; ordinary, serialist and holist. The serialist and holist modes employs the following adaptive hypermedia techniques outlined by Mampadi et al. [7]:

- Direct guidance: This technique is usually implemented through the use of 'next' and 'previous' buttons. This suits the needs of Serialist learners, guiding them through the content;
- Link hiding: Serialists tend to prefer a linear navigation structure, often becoming disoriented when presented with too many navigation choices. This can be avoided by disabling the links within the body of the page;
- Adaptive layout: It has been found that Holists prefer to use a hierarchical map in order to understand the structure of the content, whereas Serialists favoured the use of the alphabetical index [8].

4   Material Preparation

4.1   Design of the Adaptive Hypermedia Driven Serious Game

The 'Discover Sutton Hoo' AHDSG was developed in order to evaluate the hypothesis. It serves as an introduction to the Anglo-Saxon period and general archaeological principles for learners in KS3. The narrative is based around Sutton Hoo, a site of great archaeological importance. An excavation carried out in 1939 uncovered an undisturbed ship burial containing a wealth of Anglo-Saxon artefacts. It is believed to be the burial of King Rædwald, the ruler of East Anglia during the 7th century.

During the development of the serious game it was decided to allow the users to take on the role of Basil Brown, the archaeologist that excavated the main ship burial during 1939. As Basil Brown the users excavate several selected representative artefacts which ensure coverage of key archaeological principles and facts regarding the Anglo Saxons. After each artefact has been selected the user is presented with a video which presents further information relating to the artefact. Knowledge and understanding are then developed and assessed using a range of interactive activities such as puzzles and quizzes.

The 'ordinary' mode of the AHDSG consists of all the features suitable for both Holist and Serialist learners. For example, it will contain both 'next' and 'previous' buttons and links within the body of the page. In the ordinary mode once the user has finished excavating the artefacts each one becomes a hyperlink which allows the user to find out more about it, this is shown in Fig. 1. In this mode the user can select each artefact in any sequence.

Fig. 1. Excavated artefacts in ordinary mode

Figure 2 shows the excavated artefacts in the serialist mode, here the user is presented with a next button which guides the user through the videos and activities in a set sequence designed to scaffold the acquisition of knowledge and understanding.

Fig. 2. Excavated artefacts in serialist mode

Finally, in the holist mode the user is presented with an index screen (as shown in Fig. 3) before uncovering the artefacts, this provides the user with an overview of all content. This enables the user to choose the sequence in which they wish to navigate through the product.

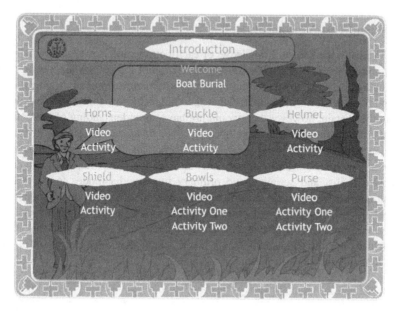

Fig. 3. Holist mode index screen

4.2   Study Preference Questionnaire

Ford (1985) developed the Study Preference Questionnaire (SPQ) for a study designed to investigate the impact of matching and mismatching holist and serialist learning materials to the cognitive styles of postgraduate students. The SPQ proved particularly effective as a cognitive style assessment tool and has therefore been utilised in several subsequent studies [3, 4, 6, 8].

In the questionnaire participants were asked to show their level of agreement with two statements. The level of agreement was measured on a five-point scale, point one indicating full agreement with the first statement and point five indicating full agreement with the second statement. In an evaluation of the questionnaire's performance Ford [5] highlighted five items, which proved particularly effective in the assessment of an individual's preferred cognitive style. For the purposes of this study these five items were adapted for use with KS3 students and presented in the form of an electronic questionnaire, which the students completed after the introduction to the topic, before using the AHDSG. The items in the questionnaire evaluate whether the learner prefers to:

- Focus on the most important parts of information or read through the information in order;

- Learn about one topic or multiple topics at the same time;
- Look at the parts of a topic that interest them the most or learn each part in a logical order;
- Wait until they fully understand a topic before moving on or not;
- Read a book in order or skip about between sections.

4.3 Pre- and Post-Assessments

In order to assess the subject knowledge of each participant prior to using the system, an electronic, multiple-choice assessment based around the Anglo-Saxons was developed using Fronter [13], the participating school's virtual learning environment (VLE). At this point in KS3 it is anticipated that the students know that Anglo-Saxon were settlers in the Britain, however they would not have an understanding of their customs. A similar assessment was also developed in order to assess the amount of progress made by each student after using the system, a sample of the questions included in the post assessment can be seen in Fig. 4. This allowed the comparative effectiveness of the adaptive (holist and serialist) and ordinary hypermedia modes to be evaluated. Some students scored above 70% in the pre assessment, although this demonstrated a high level of prior knowledge it stills shows room for development, which can be evidenced through analysis of the gain scores. Therefore, it was decided that it would be valuable to include these participants in the study. The only exception is the six students that scored 100% in the pre assessment.

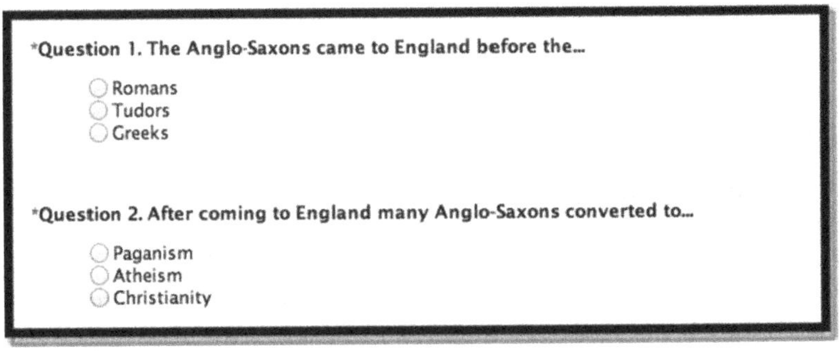

> *Question 1. The Anglo-Saxons came to England before the...
>
> ○ Romans
> ○ Tudors
> ○ Greeks
>
> *Question 2. After coming to England many Anglo-Saxons converted to...
>
> ○ Paganism
> ○ Atheism
> ○ Christianity

Fig. 4. Questions from the post assessment

5 Study

The study was conducted within a large UK secondary school. 66 Year 7 students (11–12 years old) participated in the experiment over a period of two days. The school provides all Year 7 students with one 50 min ICT lesson per week, therefore the participants already possessed the skills necessary to operate the AHDSG.

An ICT suite in the participating secondary school was chosen as the most suitable environment for this evaluation. The participants were already familiar and comfortable with this environment. The computers were laid out in a U around the edge of the room, with an interactive whiteboard (IWB) at the front for teacher demonstrations.

In order to evaluate the comparative effectiveness of the adaptive and ordinary modes the students were divided into two groups, Group A used the mode which matched their cognitive style, whereas every student in Group B used the ordinary mode. Three form groups were provided by the school for participation in the study during their normal ICT lessons, two of these forms groups formed Group A and the remaining group formed Group B. The participants from each group went through the same procedures, with the mode of the system being the only variable. Three 50 min sessions took place over the two days; each session consisted of one researcher and 20–23 students. Prior to the first session each of the research instruments were placed on the school's VLE (Fronter) in order to allow the results of each activity to be accurately recorded.

The following outlines the procedure that was followed during each session:

- The participants were informed that they were going to be using an educational program in order to learn about the Anglo-Saxons.
- The researcher used the IWB to introduce the pre-assessment. Next the participants were asked to take the pre-assessment to measure their level of knowledge before using the system. The students could only attempt each question once.
- The researcher introduced the SPQ and explained that it is designed to identify how the students prefer to use electronic learning material. The participants then completed the SPQ.
- Based on the result of the SPQ the participants in Group A were directed to use appropriate mode that have been designed for the Discover Sutton Hoo system. Students in Group B (both Holists and Serialists) were all directed to the ordinary mode. At this stage each participant was issued with a pair of headphones to facilitate full emersion within the system.
- Finally once the participants had completed all the activities in the Discover Sutton Hoo system they were directed to the post-assessment, which included questions designed to assess the current level of understanding.

6   Results and Discussion

6.1   Analysis

The results of the SPQ were used to categorise each participant as either a serialist or holist. Participants that received results of below 50% in the SPQ were categorised as holists and the participants that received results 50% or above were categorised as serialists. The gain score for each participant was calculated by subtracting the pre-assessment score from the post-assessment score, this measure was used as an indication of the progress made after using the AHDSG.

This data was split to form four tables; Holists (Adaptive Hypermedia), Serialists (Adaptive Hypermedia), Holists (Ordinary Hypermedia), and Serialists (Ordinary Hypermedia). The mean pre-assessment, post-assessment and gain scores were calculated for each of the aforementioned tables, these can be seen in Table 4 below.

Table 4. The means of pre-assessment, post-assessment and gain scores

	Holist		Serialist	
	Ordinary	Adaptive	Ordinary	Adaptive
Pre-Assessment	60%	55%	67%	66%
Post-Assessment	80%	84%	82%	89%
Gain	33%	53%	22%	34%

6.2 Impact on Learner Performance

The performance of learners in both groups was analysed using the pre-assessment, post-assessment and gain scores. The mean scores for the holists and serialists in both groups are shown in Table 4 below:

Looking at Table 4 above it can be seen that the mean post-assessment and gain scores for the Holists in the adaptive hypermedia group are higher than the mean gain scores for the ordinary hypermedia group; this relationship is also illustrated in Fig. 5 below. The mean post-assessment and gain scores for the Serialists in the adaptive hypermedia group are also higher than the mean scores for the ordinary hypermedia group. There is a 20-percentage point difference in the mean gain scores of the ordinary and adaptive groups for the Holists and a 12-percentage point difference for the Serialists. The overall mean gain score, calculated by taking the mean pre and

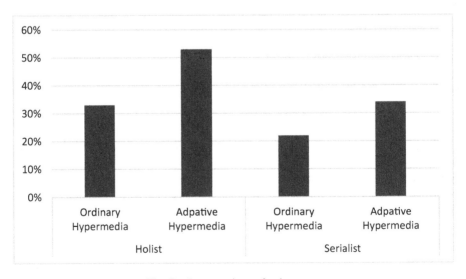

Fig. 5. A comparison of gain scores

post-assessment scores for all participants and calculating the percentage change, is 36%. A related-samples Wilcoxon Signed Rank Test demonstrated that the effect size of the results for both groups combined is significant (p < .001). An independent-samples Mann-Whitney U test was employed to test the significance of the difference in results between the two groups. This demonstrated that the difference in the results was not significant (p.071).

Although the mean gain scores give some indication that matching the navigation system to the preferred cognitive styles of learners may have a positive impact on performance, this conclusion cannot be confirmed as the difference is not significant. However, the use of either type of system does seem to produce an increase in performance that is significant. These results could potentially be explained by the fact that the learners that used the non-adaptive version of the system were able to navigate the system in any manner and may have instinctively navigated in a way that matched their preferred cognitive style.

7   Conclusions

This study set out to examine whether AHDSGs based on Pask's Holist/Serialist model of cognitive style have the capacity to improve the performance of learners in KS3. An AHDSG designed to teach KS3 students about Anglo-Saxons and basic archaeological concepts was developed in order to evaluate this hypothesis. Analysis of previous studies relating to AHDSGs and cognitive style has shown that little attention has been paid to Pask's Holist/Serialist model and the main focus been on undergraduate and postgraduate students. This study aimed to shift the focus in order to investigate the impact on younger learners.

The results of this study have demonstrated that all participants made measurable progress after using the system, regardless of whether it was adapted to their preferred cognitive style. There was not a significant difference in performance between the participants that used the system that adapted to their preferred cognitive style and those that did not. This could be potentially be explained by the way in which the 'ordinary' version of the system enabled the learners to navigate in either a liner or non-linear manner; thus, potentially resulting in them navigating in accordance with their preferred cognitive style. This area could potentially be explored further by capturing and evaluating the navigation approaches employed by holists and serialists when using the 'ordinary' version of the system.

The focus of this exploratory study was limited to performance, however there is scope to evaluate other factors that have been examined in previous studies such as perceptions and satisfaction. Therefore, it is recommended that further research is needed to investigate the possible impact of AHDSGs on a range of factors in order to fully evaluate the potential benefits of these systems for young learners.

References

1. Brusilovsky, P.: Adaptive educational hypermedia: from generation to generation. In: Proceedings of 4th Hellenic Conference on Information and Communication Technologies in Education, Athens, pp. 19–33 (2004)
2. Chewley, N., Chen, S.Y., Liu, X.: Cognitive styles and web-based instruction: field dependent/independent vs. Holist/Serialist. In: Proceedings of the 2009 IEEE International Conference on Systems, Man, and Cybernetics, San Antonio, pp. 2074–2079 (2009)
3. Clarke, J.A.: Cognitive style and computer-assisted learning: problems and a possible solution. Assoc. Learn. Technol. J. **1**(1), 47–59 (1993)
4. Ellis, D., Ford, N., Wood, F.: Hypertext and learning styles. Final report of a project funded by the Learning Technology Unit. Employment Department, Sheffield (1992)
5. Ford, N.: Learning styles and strategies of postgraduate students. Br. J. Educ. Technol. **16**(1), 65–79 (1985)
6. Ford, N., Chen, S.Y.: Individual differences, hypermedia navigation and learning: an empirical study. J. Educ. Multimedia Hypermedia **9**(4), 281–312 (2000)
7. Kwok, H., Jones, D.: Instantaneous frequency estimation using an adaptive short-time Fourier transform. In: 1995 Conference Record of the Twenty-Ninth Asilomar Conference on Signals, Systems and Computers, California, pp. 543–547 (1995)
8. Mampadi, F., Chen, S.Y., Ghinea, G., Chen, M.: Design of adaptive hypermedia learning systems: a cognitive style approach. Comput. Educ. **56**, 1003–1011 (2011)
9. Messick, S.: The nature of cognitive styles: problems and promises in educational research. Educ. Psychol. **19**, 59–74 (1984)
10. Nelson, T.: A file structure for the complex, the changing, and the indeterminate. In: Proceedings of the 1965 20th National Conference, ACM 1965, Cleveland, pp. 84–100 (1965)
11. Nelson, T.: No More Teachers' Dirty Looks. Comput. Decisions **9**(8), 16–23 (1970)
12. Pask, G.: Styles and strategies of learning. Br. J. Educ. Psychol. **46**, 128–148 (1979)
13. Fronter Learning Platform. http://uk.fronter.info. Accessed 10 Oct 14
14. Riding, R., Cheema, I.: Cognitive styles – and overview and integration. Educ. Psychol. **11**(3/4), 193–215 (1991)
15. Sadler-Smith, E.: The relationship between learning style and cognitive style. Pers. Individ. Differ. **30**, 609–616 (2001)
16. Wardrip-Fruin, N.: What hypertext is. In: Proceedings of the fifteenth ACM conference on Hypertext and Hypermedia, Santa Cruz, pp. 126–127 (2004)
17. Akbulut, Y., Cardak, C.S.: Adaptive educational hypermedia accommodating learning styles: a content analysis of publications from 2000 to 2011. Comput. Educ. **58**(2), 835–842 (2012)
18. Ulicsak, M., Wright, M.: Games in Education: Serious Games. Futurelab, Bristol (2010)
19. Dele-Ajayi, O., Sanderson, J., Strachan, R., Pickard, A.: Learning mathematics through serious games: An engagement framework. In: 2016 IEEE Frontiers in Education Conference (FIE), Eire, pp. 1–5 (2016)
20. Hendrix, M., et al.: Integrating serious games in adaptive hypermedia applications for personalised learning experiences. In: White, S. (Ed.) Proceedings of eLmL 2013, The Fifth International Conference on Mobile, Hybrid, and On-line Learning, pp. 43–48. IARIA (2013)
21. Mayo, M.J.: Games for science and engineering education. Commun. ACM **50**(7), 31–35 (2007)

22. Garris, R., Ahlers, R., Driskell, J.E.: Games, motivation, and learning: A research and practice model. Simul. Gaming 33(4), 441–447 (2002)
23. Wrzesien, M., Raya, M.A.: Learning in serious virtual worlds: evaluation of learning effectiveness and appeal to students in the E-Junior project. Comput. Educ. 55(1), 178–187 (2010)
24. Economou, D., et al.: Westminster Serious Games Platform (wmin-SGP) a tool for real-time authoring of roleplay simulations for learning. EAI Endorsed Trans. Future Intell. Educ. Environ. 16(6), e5 (2016)
25. Prensky, M.: The motivation of gameplay. Horizon 10(1), 5–11 (2002)
26. Protopsaltis, A., Pannese, L., Pappa, D., Hetzner, S.: Serious Games and Formal and Informal Learning. eLearning Papers 25, 1887–1542 (2011)
27. Pivec, P.: Game-based Learning or Game-based Teaching? Becta report (2009)
28. De Freitas, S.: Using games and simulations for supporting learning. Learn. Media Technol. Spec. Issue Gaming 31(4), 343–358 (2006)
29. De Freitas, S., Neumann, T.: The use of 'exploratory learning' for supporting immersive learning in virtual environments. Comput. Educ. 52(2), 343–352 (2009)
30. Egenfeldt-Nielsen, S.: Beyond Edutainment: Exploring the Educational Potential of Computer Games. University of Copenhagen, Copenhagen (2005)
31. Squire, K., Jenkins, H.: Harnessing the power of games in education. Insight 3, 5–33 (2003)
32. Squire, K.: Replaying history: Learning world history through playing civilization iii. Indiana University, Indiana (2004)
33. Erenli, K.: The impact of gamification: a recommendation of scenarios for education. In: 2012 15th International Conference on Interactive Collaborative Learning (ICL), pp. 1–8. IEEE (2012)
34. Papanikolaou, K.A., Grigoriadou, M., Kornilakis, H., Magoulas, G.D.: Personalizing the interaction in a web-based educational hypermedia system: the case of INSPIRE. User Model. User Adap. Inter. 13(3), 213–267 (2003)
35. Truong, H.M.: Integrating learning styles and adaptive e-learning system: current development, problems and opportunities. Comput. Hum. Behav. 55, 1185–1193 (2015)
36. Felder, R.M., Silverman, L.K.: Learning and teaching styles in engineering education. Eng. Educ. 78(7), 674–681 (1988)

A Generalized Pedagogical Framework for Creating Mixed-Mode Role-Play in Multi-User Virtual Environments

Enas Jambi[1,2(✉)], Michael Gardner[1], and Victor Callaghan[1]

[1] University of Essex, Colchester, UK
{eamjam,mgardner,vic}@essex.ac.uk
[2] University of Jeddah, Jeddah, Saudi Arabia

Abstract. Science students face considerable challenges when attempting to absorb and visualize abstract concepts presented to them in the classroom; educators use a number of methods to support their students in this regard. Our focus is on two such methods currently being used by educators: role-play and 3D simulation; these are designed to immerse the student in the learning process. Both methods attempt to make the invisible, visible. However, the literature demonstrates a lack of research, in particular, into the effectiveness of learning through structured role-play and the impact of this method on students using Multi-User Virtual Environments (MUVEs).

This paper exhibits the effects of an interactive role-play learning activity, supported within a MUVE, on the learning process. The activity is generated by a data-driven framework that acts as a template for the creation of the role-play the role-play is generated automatically from pre-defined data stored in a database. The framework is generalizable, which means that it can be used for other role-play subjects by re-configuring the data in the database. This paper aims to demonstrate the advantages of the 'immersion' that Virtual Reality (VR) can provide to its users via the means of allowing them to take on the role of an object involved in a message-passing system. This object will be one which is collaborative with other objects in a role-play activity. The role-play activity will be generated by a data-driven pedagogical framework called MMRP.

1 Introduction

1.1 Background

Most students lose focus at some point in the course of a long speech or lecture, and educators face the challenge of keeping their students' enthusiasm and attention on the subject. According to McConnell [1], it can be seen that the teacher's choice of learning activity has a huge impact on the students' understanding and engagement in the classroom. McConnell suggests minimizing the risks associated with adopting any given activity by keeping such activities short and well-structured.

There are several advantages to the use of simulation in an educational context. Firstly, it supports the learning-by-doing approach [2]. Secondly, it is a robust tool for

D. Beck et al. (Eds.): iLRN 2019, CCIS 1044, pp. 158–171, 2019.
https://doi.org/10.1007/978-3-030-23089-0_12

enhancing the engagement of the students and for giving them a sense of control over the course of their experiments [3]. Finally, it provides the students with immediate feedback [4].

Simulation can be used by educators as a method for explaining complex ideas across a range of disciplines. This leads us to a discussion of the main focus of our study - which is the use of role-play in education. Role-play is a form of simulation that can be used to encourage students to work collaboratively in order to solve issues which arise. For example, Colella [5] conducted an experiment using drama ('role-play' here indicates actual, physical actions and interactions undertaken via drama) to teach science and the use of technology. In this experiment, the students participated in a simulation, carried out in the real world, using small communication computers called Thinking Tags; these could be used to transform the students into participants in a large-scale micro-processor mediated world.

With newly available, advanced technologies, role-play can be used within Virtual Worlds (VWs); thus, students can be immersed in the learning process, and this can help them to become more engaged. There are several examples in the literature of role-play being deployed in a VW, such as those mentioned in the "Six Thinking Hats" framework description by Sue Gregory and Yvonne Masters [6] and in "Online Role Play Stories" by Mary Dracup [7]. However, generally there is a lack of research into generating role-play activities which are to take place as part of a structured learning design.

1.2   The Scope of the Paper

In light of the above, we introduce here the Mixed-Mode Role-Play (MMRP) framework [8], which is a novel data-driven pedagogical framework for generating learning role-play activities that are based on passing messages between 'actors' in a virtual environment. One of the actors becomes, effectively, an avatar controlled by a human player (this is the humanized object) and the others are automated and supported by the system – hence 'mixed-mode'. The humanized object provides the student with the impression of being in the position of embodying their actions; this is one of the 3D environment's affordances [9].

The data used for rendering and generating the virtual environment's objects and their interactions for the role-play activity are read from an attached database. The environment and the activity are populated automatically in real-time and in relation to a selected scenario. In this present study, we claim that employing a data-driven approach supports the generality of our proposed framework. The data-driven approach employed in the MMRP framework provides it with generalization qualities. Indeed, this framework, for generating role-play activities, has three levels of generalization:

- First level: humanized object generalization.
  In many of the possible, generated role-play activities, the humanized object can be changed while the played scenario remains fixed (i.e., the student can play different roles in each of the generated activities).

– Second level: learning task generalization.
This means that the scenario of a role-play can be changed in order to generate a number of different role-play activities with different learning objectives.
– Third level: subject generalization.
The database is alterable, under specific guidelines, so that it can lead to the generation of role-play simulations other than the one (prototype simulation) related to networking, described in this paper.

In addition, of course, generated role-play activities which operate in virtual environments may lead to better learning. Enabling the student to imitate an object in a role-play message-passing activity, interacting with other objects in a virtual environment, could provide better learning and understanding in a more beneficial way than conventional approaches; this would be by enhancing students':

- Learning engagement
- Association with the role of the imitated object

In order to examine the feasibility of MMRP, the claimed generalization, and its learning effectiveness, three evaluation phases, each designed to validate one level of the claimed framework generalization were used; these are presented later.

However, in the first two sections of this paper, we emphasize the affordances of drama (role-play) from a theoretical point of view and the benefits of rendering it in a virtual environment.

2 A Theoretical View of Drama in Science Education

Role-play is defined as 'behaving in accordance with a specified function' in The Concise Oxford English Dictionary (1978 edition) [10] and is believed to be a powerful tool for learning. Its use in learning is often based on learners engaging mentally and physically in a trajectory activity, acting in interchangeable roles according to a scenario-script. Braund [11], in his research, points out that there is a lack of role-play activities taking place in science lessons, generally, and introduced his theoretical model for the use of drama in science education - which is based on Brook's 'empty space' theory of drama [12]. Braund's science-learning model defines drama in science education as a process of rationalizing between two worlds of knowing: the learner's world and the scientist's. This model has two levels whereby the ways in which different activities operate across the distance between the learner's world of knowledge and the scientific world of knowledge may be viewed. The first level is that of the general model, where the empty space between the two worlds is filled with learning activities which are placed there in order to reduce the amount of cognitive dissonance present and to close the gap between the two worlds. The second level, which is the focus of our research, shows how drama helps to fill the 'empty space' between these two worlds (Fig. 1). The researcher claims that his model can better support a 'constructivist approach' to learning which improves the student's engagement and interest in the subject matter.

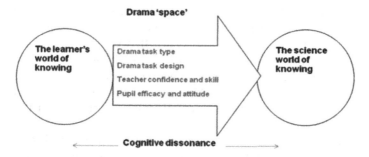

Fig. 1. A model for learning science through drama

3 Virtual Reality in Education

Virtual Reality (VR) refers to computer-created environments that simulate real environments, where the users of such an environment are represented by avatars and can interact with each other and with virtual objects [13]. Many studies and researchers have investigated the potential impacts of using VR in education. One of the affordances which has a special interest to us, is that it can foster an active environment, so increasing the students' engagement with the learning content.

However, seeing the lack of explicit guidelines concerning the use of VR as a tool in experimental learning, Jarmon et al. [14] carried out a study on 'how to utilize the 3D virtual world in an experimental project'. Using an example project, he was able to demonstrate the effectiveness of using such an environment in learning and this quite effectively encouraged educators to then use VR in experimental learning - as a 'playground' for learners.

From a theoretical point of view, Winn [15] identified that constructivist approaches often provide the best basis for creating educational applications using VR. Such an approach means that the learners will often boost their cognition and construct their learning through relating their reflections about the simulated objects in the virtual environment to previously learnt abstract concepts.

Mantovani [16] indicates that even if it is admitted that there is potential in using a virtual environment for educational experiments, it must also be recognized that there are further problems and challenges which need to be addressed. These can often be due to practical considerations such as the high cost of development, the lack of reference standards, and issues around usability and access. Educators, and designers of Multi-User Virtual Environments (MUVEs), should be aware of these challenges.

4 Role-Play in Virtual Environments

As we discussed earlier, one of the fundamental benefits of using role-play in teaching and learning is to improve the student's engagement with the learning process which can increase their understanding of the subject. The realism and engagement represented by an educational game (N.B., a structured game is another term used to refer to role-play) can have an impact on learning outcomes, according to Tashiro and Dunlap's study [14]. Winn [11] added, in his study, that realism and engagement can be increased by conducting the role-play activity in a 3D VW; this is due to the immersive nature of such an environment. A virtual world can enhance the user's feelings of immersion, allowing them to build their knowledge from direct experience resulting from being a part of the virtual world. Moreover, a virtual world provides a platform from which to observe the participants and the overall activity, with the ability to record the outcomes.

In addition, a 3D VW can offer a richer experience for the users than a simple 2D Web application, often combining many features together in a single environment. These can include instant messaging within the group, voice chat, rich user profiles, and creative collaboration via online social interactions that involve sharing various objects and services within the virtual world [4].

VR can be used to support students to reach their desired learning outcomes through constructivist and problem-based learning. Alzahrani [17] presented, in his thesis, empirical evidence based on his experience that participants' performance was improved by using a VR platform – as compared to that achieved when using a 2D web-based platform.

Another significant advantage of 3D VWs is that these environments have shown great potential for collaborative learning [9, 18], via the use of Multi-User Virtual Environments (MUVEs). The collaborative features that are provided by a MUVE can be used to support group role-play activities.

This study explores the opportunities afforded by the use of virtual worlds for group role-play activities. It demonstrates an approach which can enhance overall learning effectiveness and creativity while reducing the costs and risks typically associated with these types of activities.

5   Framework Overview

With respect to the above, a computational pedagogical framework has been designed here, called MMRP (Fig. 2), which was able to generate an effective role-play activity for use within a virtual environment. The actions dictated by this framework are divided into those concerned with human factors and those concerned with machine factors; they operate interchangeably across three main layers [8].

MMRP is proposed as a mechanism for exploring the learning affordances of humanizing a technical object in a simulated system, within a RPVE.

From a computer science point of view, MMRP is a data-driven model; the framework acts as a template which allows for the rendering of role-play activities and 3D objects within a VW automatically. It generates an interactive role-play simulation, and the processes of the simulation will change, in real-time, in a way which is dependent on the user input. The environment and its objects are created on the fly from data stored in and retrieved from the repository database.

From a learning-theoretical point of view, MMRP is designed in a similar fashion to Brook's and Braund's models [11, 12]. In order to fill the gap between the two worlds, the learner's and the science's, immersion within the VE is used; the learner

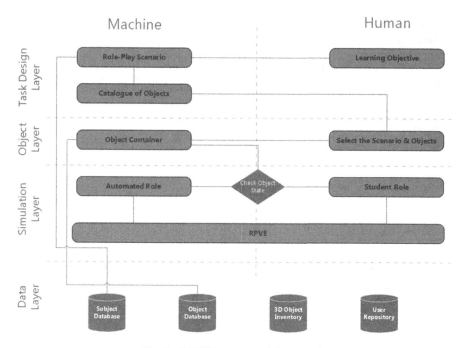

Fig. 2. MMRP conceptual framework

attempts to complete a role-play task triggered by a learning objective - collaboratively. We believe that the student enrolled in the generated role-play activity will be facilitated to fill their knowledge gap concerning the targeted subject.

With the intention of reusing the framework for other subjects which can be presented using message-passing scenarios, a standard data representation is mandatory for the structuring of the database. Moreover, CRC cards have been described by Beck and Cunningham[19] as a tool for teaching object-oriented thinking to programmers. However, Hvam and others [20] introduced a modified way of modeling a scenario with CRC cards. They added more fields to the structure of the CRC card in order to enhance the resultant role-plays. These additional fields were: aggregation, generalization, and knows/does. These additional fields help link objects which are from different classes. They are useful for tracing the roles of inheritance and 'has a' relations. This model not only enriches the environment's object population but also supports role tracking.

In our model, the data is structured as CRC cards, each of which comprises class name, responsibilities, collaborator, aggregation, and knows/does (Fig. 3). Then, the data is inserted into a database to be retrieved in order to create the OO class that will be used to render the 3D objects in the VE. The objects' names are the same as the class names used in the CRC cards. The responsibilities defined are related to the protocols which can be used and the messages which can be passed. The collaborator is retrieved from the next object field. The additional fields assist in organizing the hierarchy and the relationships which exist between the objects.

Class name	ID	Type
Application	1	Main
Responsibilities		
Serves as the window for users and application processes to access network services.		
Aggregation		
Superparts:		
Subparts: HTTP FTP SMTP		
Knows/Does:		Collaborations
Knows		Transport
Does		
• Makes sure that the other party is identified and can be reached		
• Determines protocol and data syntax rules at the application level		

Fig. 3. Application layer CRC card as an example

6   Experimental Framework

The evaluation experiment was conducted as a proof-of-concept for the purpose of validating the study claims related to the MMRP generalization levels and the learning effectiveness of Mixed-Mode Role-Play in RPVEs. Two experimental phases were designed. First, one based on the Internet Protocol Suite (TCP/IP) layers; the (TCP/IP) layered networking scenario represents a typical learning scenario for Higher Education computing and networking students [8] (Fig. 4). Another phase, the *Database phase (DB),* provided quite different activities; these were created around the topic of the acceptance of languages by *Finite State Machines (FSMs).*

Fig. 4. Participants conducting the experiment

6.1   The Evaluation Measurements

Validating the Fidelity of MMRP as a Pedagogical RPVE. MMRP generates role-play activities which act as visualization tools to assist in learning. In order to evaluate such learning tools we utilized the same evaluation technique that were used for the VirPlay3D2 evaluation [21] (a visualization tool for OO learning), with some additional criteria, as follows:

- User acceptance:
    - Does the user enjoy playing their role, interacting with the other objects?
    - Is the environment easy to use?
    - Is the access to information straightforward?
    - Does the user understand the environment's design?
    - Does the user understand the interactions between themselves and the environment's other objects, and between the other objects?
- The metaphors:
    - Does the user understand what each 3D object represents?
    - Does the interaction/message-passing between the objects give the user an idea of how the actual objects in the real world interact with each other?
- The usefulness of the information represented in the role-play scenario:
    - Are the descriptions of the role-play tasks and the environment's objects sufficient?
    - Are the system messages displayed on the screen adequate?
    - Is the message-passing represented on the screen sufficient for the understanding of the roles' processes?

Model Validation. As Sargent [22] states, the purpose of a simulation model must be referred to in order to determine its (the simulation's) validity. In the development phase, several questions were raised which were then answered in the testing of the model used here. The model's output variables provided the answers to these developmental questions. The accuracy of these outputs were in an acceptable range.

The parameters of the MMRP tests can be categorized as follows:

- Animation Validation: To validate the framework's operational behavior and the displaying of graphics while learning scenarios and tasks changed.
- Parameter Variability: To test the effectiveness of changing the input (the scenario, and the humanized object) on the outcomes while also changing the uploaded data.

Learning Gain and Student's Feedback. The participants were asked to take pre-tests and post-tests so that their learning gain could be measured. The outcomes of these tests and the collected data were analyzed and compared across the experimental groups. The post-test questions were predesigned in accordance with the module,

'Introduction to Computing', that the activity is designed around. After answering these questions, the participants were asked to analyze and comment on the roles that they had taken upon themselves in the simulation and the achievements that they had attained in relation to the tasks they had taken part in – so that they (the participants) could provide overall feedback, verbally.

Learning Engagement and Role Association Questionnaires. Wiebe [23] developed a new self-report instrument for user-engagement by extending the User Engagement Scale (UES) of O'Brien and Toms [24] to include user engagement in the context of game-based environments. Our platform implements a form of game-based simulation. Thus, we applied Wiebe's enhanced instrument in order to measure and analyse student engagement. There are four scalable factors: Focused Attention (FAz), Perceived Usability (PUz), Aesthetics (AEz), and Satisfaction (SAz). These factors were used in the construction of a questionnaire to be filled-in by every student after participation in the activity, based on their experience.

6.2   The Evaluation Phases

Network Learning Phases. The learning experiment phases took place at the University of Jeddah. This location was chosen because of the ease of access it afforded to the researcher, in terms of the required resources and the number of students available for participation in the experiment.

Thirty-six students participated in the network learning activities. All the participants were at their third level at the university, or higher. This made it almost certain that they had been introduced to the concepts of network layers and protocols. They were dived equally into groups: *Control Group (CG), Humanized Group (HG),* and *Scenario Group (SG).* After signing a confidential consent form, each participant took a pre-survey to confirm that they had the requisite knowledge concerning the subject of networks. Then, after they had completed the given learning tasks, they were required to take the post-test and respond to the evaluation measurement survey.

1. Conventional learning approach phase, CG. In this phase, the 12 participants engaged individually in the Wireshark [25] activity in order that the incoming/outgoing packets processed by their lab device could be captured. The students analyzed the captured packets messages and the protocols in each layer, based on a guide they received from the instructor (read more about Wireshark on wireshark wiki [26]).

2. MMRP Phases. *Network Virtual Environment.* In a virtual environment, the network layers populate as 3D capsules. These represent the main objects of the learning scenario which interact with each other by passing messages. Every layer capsule is surrounded by boxes representing the protocols of that layer. There are four layer-capsules and the humanized object is represented by an avatar controlled by the user (Fig. 5). The user is able to change the camera view; this brings greater fidelity to the 3D environment and results in a greater sense of presence. The views which can be referred to are the user's view, the entire environment's view, and the current object's view.

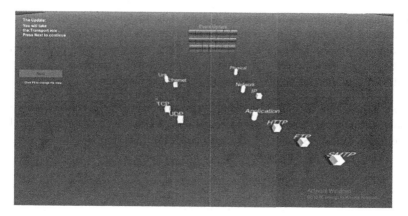

Fig. 5. The overall environment views

Network Learning Scenarios. In each scenario, the network layers interact with each other by passing messages in order to complete selected tasks (such as, to retrieve a web page from a server). The 3D environment's objects represent the network layers. The participants enrolled individually to take on the role of one of the layers (which then became the humanized object) and interact with the other layers (which remained automated by the system) to achieve a given task. The humanized object means the layer that the student is imitating. This is represented in the VE by an avatar, and the user controls this via their keyboard (Fig. 6).

Fig. 6. The humanized (Transport Layer) role

The user actions:

- Observe the other objects undertaking their roles.
- Receive the messages from the previous layer.
- Choose the correct protocol based on the received message.
- Deliver the message to the next object.

The return:

- Complete the role-play activity.
- Achieve the learning objective.

It should be emphasized, however, that the data-driven architecture of the framework dictated that data for rendering the environment's object was not stored in the world a-priori. The environment and its objects were populated on the fly, which meant that different objects appeared with different scenarios. This process is what we believe shaped the generalization term that we are concerned with here.

The Unit of Learning. To plot the learning scenarios and the objects' roles within these scenarios, the role-play activity is rendered into interoperable Units of Learning (UoLs) in accordance with IMS Learning Design (IMS-LD), [27] (Fig. 7).

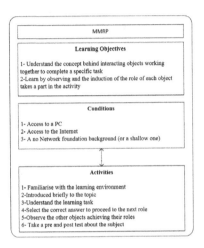

Fig. 7. Unit of learning

The Experimental Groups

– HG: Fixed Scenario, Varying Humanized Object
  Twelve undergraduate students participated, each individually, in three MMRP generated role-play activities. In addition to validating the first generalization level of MMRP, this phase purposed to evaluate the effectiveness, in terms of the student's learning, of changing the humanized object across three runs of the same scenario.
– SG: Fixed Humanized Object, Varying Learning Scenario
  The 12 students in this group each played, individually, the same humanized object role across three different scenarios; this was so that the second level of the framework generalization could be validated.

3. DB Phase, Changing the Database to Represent a New Subject. As mentioned earlier, any course targeted for the employment of MMRP should contain role play scenarios wherein the objects of the scenario interact with each other by passing messages. To validate the framework's third level of generalization, subject generalization, another set of role-play activities was generated using the MMRP framework, this time focused on finite-state machine scenarios. Finite-state machines (FSM) represent a basic concept within Computational Theory that fits the requirements for use in these experiments. A FSM is any device which stores only its own state at a given time and can receive an input which causes a change to this state and/or an action or output to take place. There are only a finite number of states which such a machine can adopt. It is the lowest level of structure used in models of computation.

"A *finite-state machine* $M = (S, I, O, g, s_0)$ consists of a finite set S of *states*, a finite *input alphabet, I,* a finite *output alphabet, O,* a *transition function, f* that assigns to each state and input pair a new state, an *output function g* that assigns to each state and input pair, an output, and an initial state s_0" [28].

A FSM-related database was\created using the CRC card data organization presented earlier. Then, the data was retrieved to generate FSM-focused activities and this resulted in a FSM virtual environment as follows:

- The FSMs' various *States* are rendered as the environment's objects.
- The *Inputs* become the scenarios or the passing of messages between these objects.
- The *transition function f* is the responsibility of each object.
- The *Outputs* become the collaboration.

7 Findings and Conclusions

The measurement factors used for the evaluation were designed mainly to measure the learning gain, the model validation, and the learner's engagement and acceptance.

Based on the pre-test results, 33.3% of the participants knew only the terminologies and the terms of the network layers and protocols and only 57% of them could give brief description about the function of each layer and its protocols. The preliminary post-tests results regarding the students' achievements across the learning groups (*CG, HG* and *SG*) revealed that the MMRP groups were at an advantage compared to the conventional learning approach group (Table 1).

Table 1. Post-test results

Group	Average assessment score
CG	37.46%
HG	74.36%
SG	55.5%

Most of the participants in the MMRP groups' activities commented positively on their experience. One said 'They were beautiful and helpful activities that would help me not to forget the presented information while enjoying learning'. However, many of the participants recommended that the display design should be improved to make it more attractive. In addition, students' answers about the system acceptance measures showed a high level of acceptance, by these learners, of the virtual environment.

Likewise, the user-engagement results demonstrated high levels of attention, perceived usability, aesthetics, and satisfaction.

The learning gain, the participants' feedback, and the questionnaire outcomes back-up the claimed affordances, in terms of learning, of rendering role-play scenarios in VR.

The FSM model is currently in the final stages of implementation. Its associated animations and its parameter variability are to be tested shortly. Although not complete as yet, the FSM model has validated that the framework can be used for subjects other than the one used for the prototype simulation.

The above are only preliminary results from the evaluation. A critical statistical analysis of the collected data will follow and be presented for publication.

In summary, the aim of the MMRP framework is to yield contributions to both the fields of pedagogy and of computer science. The experimental framework which has been presented here is designed to validate the claim that the data-driven approach – involving data streamed from a repository to create a virtual environment and roles - supports the generalization claims for the MMRP framework. Moreover, the generated Mixed-Mode Role-Play activity wherein some of the roles are played by human participants and some are operated automatically by the system serves as a novel pedagogical framework, enabling the student to be part of a virtual world simulation, so that they can become more immersed in the learning process. Replacing the network database with another subject database which has the same structure (CRC card structure) does not affect the functionality of the framework. It simply renders different objects which are related to the alternative database's subject matter.

For the computer science field, our novel framework provides an approach to the construction of an object container which acts as a template for generating the OO objects of a role-play scenario – i.e., a data driven architecture. CRC Cards used as a technique for creating Mixed-Mode Role-Play simulation for message-passing scenarios. In addition, the prototype is an adjustable and editable set-up in which the system architecture is designed as a distributed and isolated construction of subsystems.

References

1. McConnell, J.J.: Active learning and its use in computer science. ACM SIGCSE Bull. **28**(SI), 52–54 (1996)
2. Anzai, Y., Simon, H.A.: The theory of learning by doing. Psychol. Rev. **86**(2), 124 (1979)
3. Tashiro, J.S., Dunlap, D.: The impact of realism on learning engagement in educational games. In: Proceedings of the 2007 Conference on Future Play. ACM (2007)
4. Boulos, M.N.K., Hetherington, L., Wheeler, S.: Second life: an overview of the potential of 3-D virtual worlds in medical and health education. Health Inf. Libr. J. **24**(4), 233–245 (2007)
5. Colella, V.: Participatory simulations: building collaborative understanding through immersive dynamic modeling. J. Learn. Sci. **9**(4), 471–500 (2000)
6. Gregory, S., Masters, Y.: Real thinking with virtual hats: a role-playing activity for pre-service teachers in second life. Australas. J. Educ. Technol. **28**(3), 420–440 (2012)
7. Dracup, M.: Online Role Play Stories, Engagement and Learning in Higher Education. Deakin University, Victoria (2011)

8. Jambi, E., Gardner, M., Callaghan, V.: Supporting mixed-mode role-play activities in a virtual environment. In: Computer Science and Electronic Engineering (CEEC). IEEE (2017)
9. Dalgarno, B., Lee, M.J.: What are the learning affordances of 3-D virtual environments? Br. J. Educ. Technol. **41**(1), 10–32 (2010)
10. McSharry, G., Jones, S.: Role-play in science teaching and learning. Sch. Sci. Rev. **82**, 73–82 (2000)
11. Braund, M.: Drama and learning science: an empty space? Br. Educ. Res. J. **41**(1), 102–121 (2015)
12. Brook, P.: The Empty Space: A Book About the Theatre: Deadly, Holy, Rough, Immediate. Simon and Schuster, New York (1996)
13. Bainbridge, W.S.: The scientific research potential of virtual worlds. Science **317**(5837), 472–476 (2007)
14. Jarmon, L., et al.: Virtual world teaching, experiential learning, and assessment: an interdisciplinary communication course in second life. Comput. Educ. **53**(1), 169–182 (2009)
15. Winn, W.: A conceptual basis for educational applications of virtual reality. Technical Publication R-93-9, Human Interface Technology Laboratory of the Washington Technology Center, University of Washington, Seattle (1993)
16. Mantovani, F.: 12 VR learning: potential and challenges for the Use of 3D environments in education and training. In: Towards Cyberpsychology: Mind, Cognition, and Society in the Internet Age, vol. 2, no. 207 (2001)
17. Alzahrani, A.: Towards the Development and Understanding of Collaborative Mixed-Reality Learning Spaces. University of Essex, Colchester (2017)
18. Duncan, I., Miller, A., Jiang, S.: A taxonomy of virtual worlds usage in education. Br. J. Educ. Technol. **43**(6), 949–964 (2012)
19. Beck, K., Cunningham, W.: A laboratory for teaching object oriented thinking. In: ACM Sigplan Notices. ACM (1989)
20. Hvam, L., Riis, J., Hansen, B.L.: CRC cards for product modelling. Comput. Ind. **50**(1), 57–70 (2003)
21. Jimenez-Diaz, G., Gonzalez-Calero, P.A., Gomez-Albarran, M.: Role-play virtual worlds for teaching object-oriented design: the ViRPlay development experience. Softw.: Pract. Exp. **42**(2), 235–253 (2012)
22. Sargent, R.G.: Verification and validation of simulation models. In: Simulation Conference (WSC), Proceedings of the 2009 Winter. IEEE (2009)
23. Wiebe, E.N., et al.: Measuring engagement in video game-based environments: investigation of the user engagement scale. Comput. Hum. Behav. **32**, 123–132 (2014)
24. O'Brien, H.L., Toms, E.G.: Examining the generalizability of the user engagement scale (UES) in exploratory search. Inf. Process. Manag. **49**(5), 1092–1107 (2013)
25. Combs, G.: Wireshark is 2.6.2. (1998). https://www.wireshark.org/download.html
26. Wireshark Wiki. The wiki site for the Wireshark network protocol analyzer (2017). https://wiki.wireshark.org/
27. Burgos, D.: What is wrong with the IMS learning design specification? constraints and recommendations. In: LWA, Citeseer (2010)
28. Rosen, K.H.: Discrete Mathematics and its Applications. McGraw-Hill, New York (2011)

Immersive Virtual Environments and Learning Assessments

Anna Carolina Muller Queiroz[1,2(✉)],
Alexandre Moreira Nascimento[1,3], Romero Tori[1],
and Maria Isabel da Silva Leme[1]

[1] Universidade de São Paulo, São Paulo SP 05508-900, Brazil
acmq@stanford.edu
[2] Stanford University, Stanford, CA 94305, USA
[3] Lawrence Berkeley National Laboratory, Berkeley, CA 94720, USA

Abstract. The purpose of this systematic literature review is to give a state-of-the-art overview of how learning assessments have been used in studies using Immersive Virtual Environment (IVE) and its applications in education. Forty-six studies were reviewed and categorized according to: type of knowledge, technological immersion, skills learned, context, techniques, processes and methods of assessment. This review identified scarcity of studies focusing conceptual knowledge assessment, few studies using qualitative assessments as well as paucity of artificial intelligence methods applied in learning assessments. Research gaps are discussed and future studies on the use of IVE in education are suggested.

Keywords: Immersive virtual environments · Learning assessment · Education

1 Introduction

As technology advances, content presentation format has varied significantly, as well as the way people access information [1–3]. In this context, immersive virtual environments (IVE) are gaining attention and popularity [4–7]. IVEs can vary significantly depending on the equipment used, among which we can mention virtual reality, augmented reality and mixed reality environments [8].

The interest in using immersive virtual environments in education has existed for many decades. It has started with the design of virtual reality environments in the 1940s [9, 10]. Several studies point to the benefits of immersive virtual learning environments [11–18], particularly in terms of engagement and motivation to learn [12, 14, 19, 20].

In 1996, Salzman, Loftin, Dede and McGlynn [21] recommended that studies aiming to investigate how IVEs can impact learning should take into account evaluation variables of learning, technology and the nature of the task, among other elements. More than fifteen years after this publication, Jia, Bhatti and Nahavandi [22] identified that most studies focusing IVEs in education investigated IVE's interaction and usability factors (such as engagement and adverse effects of IVE), but only few ones focused on learning assessment.

© Springer Nature Switzerland AG 2019
D. Beck et al. (Eds.): iLRN 2019, CCIS 1044, pp. 172–181, 2019.
https://doi.org/10.1007/978-3-030-23089-0_13

In this sense, this study seeks to trace the state of the in how learning assessments have been used in IVEs studies. It aims to identify the current state of research, gaps and research opportunities. Finally, it aims to offer guidance for the future use of IVE in education and research.

2 Methodology

This research used the systematic literature review protocol. There is a tradition in technology research area of examining literature review on a specific topic for better understand the state of the art in such topic and to discern development patterns from it [23].

This study used a similar research methodology as that employed by Freina and Ott [24] for their literature review on the use of virtual reality's head-mounted displays in education. *Scopus* online database was chosen because of its vast amount of indexed recognized publications in the main subject areas related to the theme of this research (Computing, Engineering, Psychology and Education) and due to its analytics tools.

After an exploratory survey, the search keys for title and abstract selected were: "immersive virtual environment" AND "assessment". The 89 records returned in the search were categorized according to the kind of assessment focused in the study: "IVE evaluation", "learning assessment" or "other type of evaluation". Inclusion criterion was: studies investigating how IVEs impact learning. Studies focusing the IVE's evaluation only were excluded. Other exclusion criteria were: duplicate papers, unavailability of complete papers, and papers focusing not related topics. Figure 1 shows the search flow.

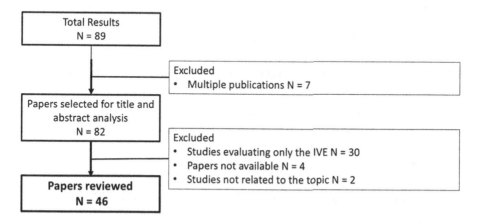

Fig. 1. Search flow

Forty-six papers were included and completely reviewed. Due to page restrictions in this paper, the list of these studies is available after request. The publication's year, authors' country of affiliation and subject area were extracted from the selected studies, using *Scopus*' analytics tools. Subject areas were grouped according to their corresponding main area.

Studies' methods and findings were categorized according to the elements described below:

2.1 Immersion (Visual, Auditory or Haptic)

These categories were based on Queiroz et al. [25]. For visual immersion it was considered as source of stimulus: single/multiple monitor, Video Wall, HMD or CAVE. For audio immersion it was considered: monophonic, stereophonic or three-dimensional sounds. As for haptic immersion, it was considered only its use or not;

2.2 Knowledge (Conceptual, Procedural or Both)

Conceptual knowledge is considered what connects more basic elements that have already been organized and explained [26]. It involves classification and categorization of principles, and, generalizations of theories, models and structures. This type of knowledge is related to the explanation of what is known and learned. On the other hand, procedural knowledge refers to the use of criteria and methods in problem solving. It encompasses the knowledge of specific techniques, skills and methods, as well as the perception of how and when to use a certain procedure [26];

2.3 Skills (Motor, Cognitive, Emotional)

Motor skill involves physical activity or motor coordination. Cognitive ability is one that depends on attention, memory, processing, and manipulation of information for its acquisition. Finally, it was classified as emotional ability those ones in which participants' emotional, feelings and physiological responses were assessed;

2.4 Context (Primary School, High School, Higher Education, Health, Corporate or Other)

The context refers to the type and/or level of education, whether formal (primary, secondary or higher education); in the corporate environment; or in another context, such as professional education. The studies were categorized according to the description presented in the papers about the participants;

2.5 Assessment Techniques (Patterns, Metrics or Artificial Intelligence)

Pattern-based techniques are based on the evaluation of behaviors, movements, decisions, speech, or some other aspect presented by the learner before, during or after the use of IVE, which allows comparisons with one or more reference standards. For metric analysis it was considered the evaluation made by obtaining numerical measures of performance, such as range of movements, number of correct answers, frequency of behaviors, among others. Artificial Intelligence (AI) encompasses the use of techniques such as data mining, machine intelligence and machine learning to obtain and analyze learning data.

2.6   Evaluation Processes (Automatic, Semi-Automatic or Manual)

The automatic assessment refers to those processed computationally, without manual processing. The semi-automatic assessment was considered in cases where part of the evaluation process was done computationally, and part was done manually. Manual assessment refers to the ones relying solely on human interaction for the collection and analysis of learning data.

2.7   Assessment Methods (Quantitative or Qualitative)

Assessment methods resulting in numerical data were considered quantitative, hence using statistical analysis to determine the performance of apprentices. The qualitative assessments referred to the evaluations based on open questions, interviews, reports and observations that were not coded into numerical data.

3   Results

Figure 2 shows the distribution of the 46 selected studies by publication's date and one trend line (linear regression). It was identified that half (23) of the studies were published from 2014 on. The trend line R^2 was 0.49, which shows that around half of the number of publications variance is explained by the variable year, indicating a potential growth trend over the years.

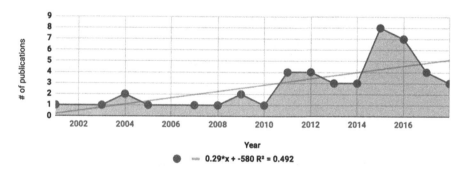

Fig. 2. Publications per year

Despite the heterogeneity of the studies' countries of origin (Fig. 3), almost half (21 studies) were developed by researchers from the United States. Also, there is a great concentration of this research topic in developed countries.

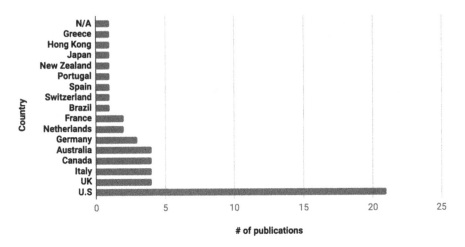

Fig. 3. Number of publications by country of authors' affiliation

Considering the subject area, studies in Agrarian and Biological Sciences, Computer Science and Medicine predominate (together they account for 51% of the studies). They are followed by studies in Social Sciences, Engineering and Psychology, as can be seen in Fig. 4.

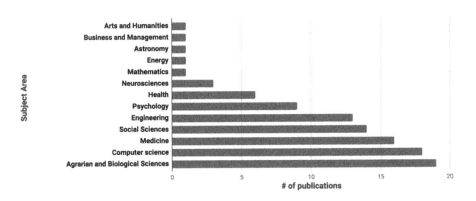

Fig. 4. Subject area

Regarding the type of knowledge, most of the studies investigated procedural knowledge (67%), followed by studies that investigated both procedural and conceptual knowledge (19%). Only 13% of the studies investigated conceptual knowledge alone. Considering the skills learned, most of the studies targeted cognitive abilities (53%), followed by emotional skills (24%) and motor skills (17%).

All studies used some type of visual immersion, being single monitor and HMD the most frequent ones (Fig. 5). The auditory immersion was used in 69% of the studies.

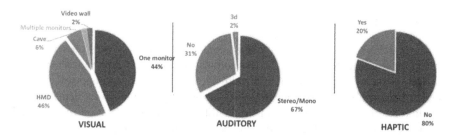

Fig. 5. Types of immersion

A monophonic or stereophonic source was used in 67% of them. Only one study (2%) used three-dimensional auditory immersion. Finally, only 20% of the studies used haptic immersion.

Participants' context was quite diverse, being composed of the general public (28%), patients or health professionals (22%), students of higher education (20%), participants from corporate settings (13%) and only 2% of them had high school students as participants.

Regarding the assessment techniques, most of the studies used metric assessments (67%), followed by the pattern-based ones (30%). Only two studies (3%) used AI techniques to support learning assessment. The automatic assessment process was the most frequent, being used in 45% of the studies, followed by manual processes, present in 40% of the studies. Most of the studies (85%) used only quantitative assessments, as shown in Fig. 6.

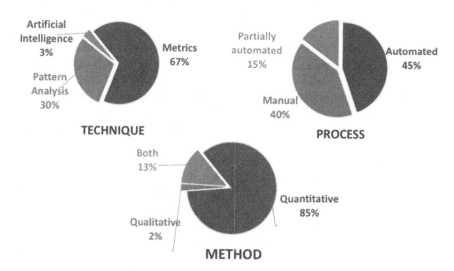

Fig. 6. Techniques, processes and methods of assessment

4 Discussion

A growth trend on the number of publications about the topic was observed. Considering the availability of immersive technologies, this delay is expected as technology has to be first developed, then it starts slowly to be diffused and applied in several research fields [27]. Although idealization and investigations of IVEs applications in education are not recent, changes in availability, costs and maturation of these technologies seem to have influenced the number of publications [5].

The concentration of research in developed countries was evidenced. This fact corroborates related work about immersive virtual environment in education [28, 29] and about countries' access to technologies [30, 31]. Thus, a delay in the publications from countries with lower research budgets is expected. In this sense, perhaps an inflection point is on the way and it can be expected an increase on the number of research in countries with less abundant resources, since these technologies have gone through a significant cost reduction and increased competition [5].

Regarding the type of knowledge targeted, there are only few studies that evaluate the use of IVE and conceptual knowledge acquisition. This corroborates Jia, Bhatti and Nahavandi [22] that highlight the need for research on the use of IVE for conceptual knowledge. This is an important point that needs to be addressed by the scientific community to support next solid steps for IVE adoption in education. Therefore, it is a fundamental topic for the future research agenda, as great amount of the primary and secondary education's curriculum relies on conceptual knowledge.

Shortage of studies that considered the qualitative learning assessment was noticed. Qualitative assessments usually require more time and specialized professionals to be carried out [32] and perhaps this is one underlying reason for publications with this focus being less frequent [33]. On the other hand, the use of IVE allows automatic registration of users' behavior, which facilitates later qualitative analysis [34]. An underuse of this tool was identified in the analyzed studies. Better use of automatic data collection can increase the number of studies and the power of analysis of qualitative assessments in future studies. Additionally, the need for longitudinal studies was identified, which corroborates several studies about IVE in education, as Queiroz, Tori, Nascimento and Leme [28], Tamaddon and Stiefs [35], Gelsomini [36] and Salzman, Loftin, Dede and McGlynn [21]. Future studies could assess the performance of students who have developed skills using IVEs over long period of time and compare it to traditional and other alternative teaching methods.

Only two studies used AI techniques to support learning assessments. Using Learning Analytics and AI techniques based on machine learning bring enormous potential for learning assessment [37]. Sophisticated machine intelligence techniques allow complex and non-linear relations between multiple variables to be identified, which makes it possible, for example, to identify causes of individuals' learning difficulties [38]. In addition, such techniques reduce the time of analysis, as well as using data mining allows the increase of the power of discovery of implicit information in the collected data in smaller intervals of analysis time [37]. Thus, the integration of these techniques is suggested in future research.

The small number of studies targeting high school students points to the need of future research targeting this population. There are many abstract concepts in high school curriculum that students need to assimilate and master [39] in order to succeed academically. Studies using IVEs to support conceptual knowledge acquisition has shown encouraging results [16, 40, 41] and significant increase in students' motivation and engagement in learning activities [14, 17, 19], suggesting an important research field to be explored.

5   Conclusions

The present study sought to outline the current state of research on learning assessment in IVEs' studies, as well as to identify gaps and future research opportunities, providing guidance for future studies targeting IVE in education.

The main limitations of the present study are related to the search strategy used in the literature review protocol. *Scopus* was the only databased used and it was chosen because it is highly regarded and considered to have enough comprehensiveness. Still, the keywords always impose limitations on this type of literature review study, which potentially left out studies, since they may have used different descriptors from those used in the present search. However, restricted use of keywords was used to avoid too much increase in the number of records returned in the search with low or no relation to the topic of interest, as identified in previous exploratory research.

Among the main findings, it is highlighted the concentration of studies in developed countries, a shortage of studies aimed at conceptual knowledge assessment and few studies using qualitative assessments or methods of artificial intelligence.

Based on the gaps identified, their relevance and their potential impact on the use of IVE in education, an agenda of future studies was proposed to investigate how learning assessment can be used in IVE's studies in populations of developing countries, as well as to apply artificial intelligence and qualitative methods of assessment.

As future works we plan to extend our research on IVE and learning assessment, performing a comprehensive analysis of the studies, including a meta-analysis of the reported studies.

Acknowledgments. Anna Carolina Muller Queiroz thanks CNPq, process n. 141876/2017-4. During this research, Romero Tori was sponsored by a grant from FAPESP (process 2016/26290-3) and received a scholarship from CNPq (process n.311991/2015-7).

References

1. Hsin, C.-T., Li, M.-C., Tsai, C.-C.: The influence of young children's use of technology on their learning: a review. Educ. Technol. Soc. **17**(4), 85–99 (2014)
2. Lévy, P., Bononno, R.: Becoming Virtual: Reality in the Digital Age. Da Capo Press, Cambridge (1998). Incorporated
3. Thompson, P.: The digital natives as learners: technology use patterns and approaches to learning. Comput. Educ. **65**, 12–33 (2013)
4. Armstrong, P.: Just How Big Is The Virtual Reality Market And Where Is It Going Next? Forbes, Jersey City (2017). https://www.forbes.com/sites/paularmstrongtech/2017/04/06/just-how-big-is-the-virtual-reality-market-and-where-is-it-going-next/

5. Burke, B., Cearley, D.W., Blau, B.: Top 10 Strategic Technology Trends for 2018: Immersive Experience. Gartner, Stamford (2018). https://www.gartner.com/en/documents/3867163

6. Cook, A.V., Jones, R., Raghavan, A., Saif, I.: Digital Reality: The Focus Shifts from Technology to Opportunity. Deloitte, New York (2017). https://www2.deloitte.com/insights/us/en/focus/tech-trends/2018/immersive-technologies-digital-reality.html

7. Rosedale, P.: Virtual reality: the next disruptor: a new kind of worldwide communication. IEEE Consum. Electron. Mag. 6(1), 48–50 (2017). https://doi.org/10.1109/MCE.2016.2614416

8. Biocca, F., Delaney, B.: Immersive virtual reality technology. Commun. Age Virtual Real 15, 57–124 (1995)

9. Dede, C.: Technological supports for acquiring 21st century skills. Int. Encycl. Educ. 3, 158–166 (2010)

10. Sutherland, I.E.: A head-mounted three dimensional display. In: Proceedings of the December 9–11, 1968, Fall Joint Computer Conference, Part I, pp. 757–764. ACM (1968). https://doi.org/10.1145/1476589.1476686

11. Bailey, J.O., Bailenson, J.N.: Immersive virtual reality and the developing child. In: Brooks, P., Blumberg, F. (eds.) Cognitive Development in Digital Contexts, pp. 181–200. Elsevier, San Diego (2018)

12. Dalgarno, B., Lee, M.J.W.: What are the learning affordances of 3-D virtual environments? Br. J. Educ. Technol. 41(1), 10–32 (2010)

13. Dawley, L., Dede, C.: Situated learning in virtual worlds and immersive simulations. In: Spector, J.M., Merrill, M.D., Elen, J., Bishop, M.J. (eds.) Handbook of Research on Educational Communications and Technology, pp. 723–734. Springer, New York (2014). https://doi.org/10.1007/978-1-4614-3185-5_58

14. Dede, C.J., Jacobson, J., Richards, J.: Introduction: virtual, augmented, and mixed realities in education. In: Liu, D., Dede, C., Huang, R., Richards, J. (eds.) Virtual, Augmented, and Mixed Realities in Education. SCI, pp. 1–16. Springer, Singapore (2017). https://doi.org/10.1007/978-981-10-5490-7_1

15. Fowler, C.: Virtual reality and learning: where is the pedagogy? Br. J. Educ. Technol. 46(2), 412–422 (2015)

16. Salzman, M.C., Dede, C., Loftin, R.B., Chen, J.: A model for understanding how virtual reality aids complex conceptual learning. Presence Teleoperators Virtual Environ. 8(3), 293–316 (1999)

17. Wickens, C.D.: Virtual reality and education. In: IEEE International Conference on Systems, Man and Cybernetics, pp. 842–847 (1992)

18. Youngblut, C.: Educational uses of virtual reality technology (No. IDA-D-2128). Institute for Defense Analyses Alexandria VA (1998). https://apps.dtic.mil/dtic/tr/fulltext/u2/a339438.pdf

19. Bailenson, J.N., Yee, N., Blascovich, J., Beall, A.C., Lundblad, N., Jin, M.: The use of immersive virtual reality in the learning sciences: digital transformations of teachers, students, and social context. J. Learn. Sci. 17(1), 102–141 (2008)

20. Dede, C.: Immersive interfaces for engagement and learning. Science (80-.) 323(5910), 66–69 (2009)

21. Salzman, M.C., Loftin, R.B., Dede, C., McGlynn, D.: ScienceSpace: lessons for designing immersive virtual realities. In: Conference Companion on Human Factors in Computing Systems, pp. 89–90 (1996)

22. Jia, D., Bhatti, A., Nahavandi, S.: The impact of self-efficacy and perceived system efficacy on effectiveness of virtual training systems. Behav. Inf. Technol. 33(1), 16–35 (2014)

23. Scornavacca, E., Barnes, S.J., Huff, S.L.: Mobile business research published in 2000-2004: emergence, current status, and future opportunities. Commun. Assoc. Inf. Syst. 17(1), 28 (2006)

24. Freina, L., Ott, M.: A literature review on immersive virtual reality in education: state of the art and perspectives. In: The International Scientific Conference eLearning and Software for Education, vol. 1, p. 133 (2015)
25. Queiroz, A.C.M., et al.: Virtual reality in marketing: technological and psychological immersion (2018)
26. Anderson, L.W., et al.: A Taxonomy for Learning, Teaching, and Assessing: A Revision of Bloom's Taxonomy of Educational Objectives, abridged edn. Longman, White Plains (2001)
27. Queiroz, A.C.M., Tori, R., Nascimento, A.M.: Realidade virtual na educação: panorama das pesquisas no Brasil. In: Anais do XXVIII Simpósio Brasileiro de Informática na Educação (SBIE 2017), pp. 203–212 (2017)
28. Queiroz, A.C.M., Tori, R., Moreira, N.A., da Silva Leme, M.I.: Using HMD-based immersive virtual environments in primary/K-12 education. Commun. Comput. Inf. Syst. 840(accepted paper), 1–14 (2018)
29. Queiroz, A.C.M., Kamarainen, A.M., Preston, N.D., da Silva Leme, M.I.: Immersive virtual environments and climate change engagement. In: Immersive Learning Research Network Proceedings, p. accepted paper (2018)
30. Das, R.C.: Handbook of Research on Global Indicators of Economic and Political Convergence. IGI Global, Hershey (2016)
31. Walsham, G., Sahay, S.: Research on information systems in developing countries: current landscape and future prospects. Inf. Technol. Dev. 12(1), 7–24 (2006)
32. Marton, F., Säaljö, R.: On qualitative differences in learning—ii outcome as a function of the learner's conception of the task. Br. J. Educ. Psychol. 46(2), 115–127 (1976)
33. Karabulut-Ilgu, A., Jaramillo Cherrez, N., Jahren, C.T.: A systematic review of research on the flipped learning method in engineering education. Br. J. Educ. Technol. 49(3), 398–411 (2018)
34. Passig, D., Tzuriel, D., Eshel-Kedmi, G.: Improving children's cognitive modifiability by dynamic assessment in 3D immersive virtual reality environments. Comput. Educ. 95, 296–308 (2016)
35. Tamaddon, K., Stiefs, D.: Embodied experiment of levitation in microgravity in a simulated virtual reality environment for science learning. In: 2017 IEEE Virtual Reality Workshop on K-12 Embodied Learning through Virtual & Augmented Reality (KELVAR), pp. 1–5 (2017)
36. Gelsomini, M.: An Affordable virtual reality learning framework for children with neuro-developmental disorder. In: Proceedings of the 18th International ACM SIGACCESS Conference on Computers and Accessibility, pp. 343–344 (2016)
37. Spector, J.M., et al.: Technology enhanced formative assessment for 21st century learning. Educ. Technol. Soc. 19(3), 58–71 (2016)
38. Cope, B., Kalantzis, M.: Big data comes to school: implications for learning, assessment, and research. AERA Open 2(2), 2332858416641907 (2016)
39. Libâneo, J.C., Alves, N.: Temas de Pedagogia: Diálogos entre didática e currículo. Cortez Editora, Sao Paulo (2017)
40. Kamarainen, A.M., Thompson, M., Metcalf, S.J., Grotzer, T.A., Tutwiler, M.S., Dede, C.: Prompting connections between content and context: blending immersive virtual environments and augmented reality for environmental science learning. Commun. Comput. Inf. Sci. 840, 36–54 (2018)
41. Ketelhut, D.J., Nelson, B.C., Schifter, C.C., Kim, Y.: Using immersive virtual environments to assess science content understanding: the impact of context. In: Proceedings of the IADIS International Conference on Cognition and Exploratory Learning in the Digital Age, CELDA 2010, pp. 227–230 (2010)

Immersion and Presence

Presence Is the Key to Understanding Immersive Learning

Andreas Dengel[1(✉)] and Jutta Mägdefrau[2]

[1] Faculty of Computer Science and Mathematics, University of Passau, Innstr. 33,
Passau, Germany
`andreas.dengel@uni-passau.de`
[2] Faculty of Arts and Humanities, University of Passau, Innstr. 41, Passau, Germany
`jutta.maegdefrau@uni-passau.de`

Abstract. Presence as the subjective feeling of 'being there' is one of
the main psychological components in immersive virtual environments.
Research shows that presence can have an effect on learning outcomes
in educational virtual environments. As presence can be considered as
an individual psychological variable, its crucial role in the process of
immersive learning is influenced by numerous subjective and objective
factors. On the basis of the Educational Framework for Immersive Learning (EFiL), we developed a research model including the factors presence,
immersion, cognitive abilities, motivation, and emotion. The hypotheses of the research model have been examined in a study with 23 students testing three different immersive educational virtual environments
for learning computer science. The results of 67 presence questionnaires
could confirm the hypotheses of the research model deriving from the
EFiL partly. The factors immersion, emotion, and cognitive abilities were
predictors for presence. An assumed, predictive effect of intrinsic motivation towards learning computer science on presence could not be verified.

Keywords: Immersive learning · Presence ·
Educational virtual environments · Virtual reality · Immersion

1 Introduction

Immersive Learning in virtual and mixed environments can be considered as
a new approach to learning in an active and engaging way. We can think of
Dewey's popular approach of learning-by-doing as learning by being there (in an
immersive and engaging environment) perceiving it as an actual reality with the
possibility of interaction, uncertainty, and choice: "We hang on the lips of the
storyteller because of the element of mental suspense. [...] When an individual is
engaged in doing or making something (the activity not being of such a mechan-
ical and habitual character that its outcome is assured), there is an analogous
situation. Something is going to come of what is present to the sense, but just
what is doubtful. The plot is unfolding toward success or failure, but just when

D. Beck et al. (Eds.): iLRN 2019, CCIS 1044, pp. 185–198, 2019.
https://doi.org/10.1007/978-3-030-23089-0_14

or how is uncertain" [6]. Therefore, the feeling of being present somewhere or of something being present in combination with engagement is crucial for an active learning process.

2   Presence Is Being There

When speaking about the feeling of 'being there', research in virtual and mixed reality usually refers to the term presence. There are ongoing discussions about terminology, especially concerning the distinction of terms presence and immersion. According to similar approaches suggested by Biocca [3] and Lee [11], the feeling of presence contains the subjective elements of physical, social, and self-presence, referring to different domains of human experience. Presence can be seen as "a psychological state in which virtual objects are experienced as actual objects in either sensory or nonsensory ways" [11]. The framework from Witmer and Singer describes immersion as a psychological state referring to the feeling of being enveloped by the environment, as well as being included in and interacting with it [26]. Jennett et al. widen this definition by describing immersion as the degree of involvement with a game, distinguishing its three levels engagement, engrossment, and total immersion (including presence) [9]. On the other side, Slater suggests that immersion should be understood simply as a quantifiable description of technology from an objective point of view which is independent of the user's perception [21].

By following Slater's definition, it is possible to separate the aspect of human experience from the technological aspect. Steuer distinguishes the technological variables influencing (tele-)presence in vividness and interactivity. Vividness refers to "the representational richness of a mediated environment as defined by its formal features" [23] in terms of how the technological setting presents information of the environment to the senses. This technological variable consists mainly of the characteristics breadth (number of sensory dimensions which are presented simultaneously) and depth (resolution of the cues within the perceptual channels). Interactivity is "the extent to which users can participate in modifying the form and content of a mediated environment in real time" [23]. The factors speed of interaction (response time), range of interactivity (number of attributes which can be manipulated including their possible variations) and mapping (connection between human actions and actions within the environment) contribute to interactivity [23]. We follow these approaches by seeing presence as the subjective feeling of 'being there' in regards to the virtual or mixed environment in its entirety, including its surroundings (physical presence), its social actors (social presence), and its representation of the user's self (self-presence). Immersion, therefore, refers to an objective description of the used technology, including the stimulus-driven variables vividness and interactivity.

Immersion is one of the main factors influencing presence. Studies comparing different immersive settings and their effects on presence show associations between differences in hard- and software and the feeling of self-reported presence: Mikropoulos examined differences between the feeling of presence in egocentric and exocentric perspectives [14]; Bailenson et al. investigated the effect

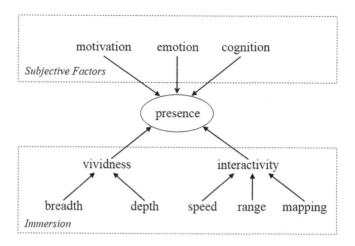

Fig. 1. Objective and subjective factors influencing presence

of field of view on presence in virtual environments [1]; Lee, Wong, and Fung investigated how Virtual Reality (VR) features like presentational fidelity and immediacy of control effect presence; they also emphasize the role of motivation for feeling present in a virtual environment [10].

Cognitive skills can also be regarded as a determinant for presence: According to Schubert, Friedmann, and Regenbrecht, the construction of a spatial-functional mental model of a virtual environment induces a sense of presence [20]. Constructing the representation of one's own bodily actions as possible actions in the virtual world while suppressing incompatible sensory input are the two cognitive processes involved for feeling present in the mediated world [23]. The idea of users willingly suppressing incompatible sensory inputs can be referred to as a "suspension of disbelief that they are in a world other than where their real bodies are located" [22]. Such an understanding of cognitive activities also corresponds with Biocca's theory of presence being a labile psychological construct oscillating between physical, imaginal, and virtual environments [3].

As the physiological measurement methods of presence show [15], emotional variables that are connected to the purpose of the virtual experience, like anxiety and fear for phobia treatments [18], also influence the user's presence. Following this idea, it can be assumed that positive emotions enhance presence in a pleasant environment. On the other hand, presence can be regarded as a crucial factor for triggering emotions in virtual and mixed realities [9,17].

An adequate model for determining the effect of motivation on presence is the self-determination theory of Deci and Ryan, distinguishing intrinsic motivation, extrinsic motivation, and amotivation [4]. Yeonhee found that intrinsic motivation and perceived interactivity as a core component of presence were moderately correlated ($r = .46$, $p < .01$) [27]. Similar effects for other internally regulated motivational constructs (i.e. identification) are expectable. A negative association between the least autonomous constructs of extrinsic motivation (external regulation/introjection) and presence could be assumed as well.

For examining presence further, we extend Steuer's model of objective techno-logical variables influencing (tele-)presence with individual subjective variables affecting presence. We can assume that the psychological feelings of physical, social, and self-presence are influenced by objective technological variables given through immersive hard- and software as well as interacting with subjective variables like motivational, emotional, and cognitive factors (Fig. 1). The level of immersion is determined through stimulus-driven characteristics of the used immersive material like vividness and interactivity. The model is not extensive and there certainly are more factors that influence presence and are influenced by presence, but the named factors have been identified to be crucial variables in terms of Immersive Learning [5] and are therefore focused on in this paper.

3   Presence Influences Immersive Learning Activities

The most interesting effects of presence to investigate in terms of Immersive Learning include the learning activities and learning outcomes. Mikropoulos notes that presence, deriving from different immersive settings, is a unique char-acteristic in educational virtual environments and influences learning outcomes [14]. Research examining such relations show diverse results. Bailey et al. inves-tigated the effect of presence on recall performance and found a negative associ-ation between presence and cued recall performance on pro-environmental prin-ciples ($r = -.45$; $p < .05$) and no significant correlation between presence and a corresponding free recall performance [2]. Another study of Mania and Chalmers found that presence was not associated with accurate memory recall [13]. Roy and Schlemminger measured language learning performance in an educational virtual environment during two weeks with three points of measurement. The results show that presence can enhance learning performance over time ($r = .365$; $p < .05$; last point of measurement) [19]. By comparing different immer-sive settings (varying fields of view between 60° and 180°), Lin et al. verified a positive effect of presence on memory structures related to the shapes, colors, relative locations, relative sizes, and event sequences of virtual environments ($r = .48$; $p < .01$) [12]. Lee et al. conducted a study on how desktop VR enhances and influences learning in the subject Biology; they found a positive correla-tion between presence and learning outcomes ($r = .64$; $p < .001$) and between presence and perceived learning effectiveness ($r = .55$; $p < .001$) [10].

On the basis of Helmke's supply-use-framework for scholastic learning [8], Dengel and Mägdefrau introduced the Educational Framework for Immersive Learning (EFiL). According to the EFiL, Immersive Learning can be seen as "learning activities initiated by a mediated or medially enriched environment that evokes a sense of presence" [5]. Learning in immersive educational virtual environments does not happen automatically but the supplied learning mate-rials have to be used actively by the learner. The perception of the didactical, immersive and content quality of the instructional materials at a certain level of presence and the interpretation of these materials may initiate learning activities. The student's (immersive) learning potential, including cognitive, emotional, and motivational factors, influences the immersive learning process interacting with and in the learning environment (context variables like school form, social composition, and cohesion of the class, etc.). Other factors affecting the process of Immersive Learning are the family and the teacher of the learner. Dengel and Mägdefrau note that the factors influencing immersive learning are interrelated; many factors influence each other mutually [5]. Presence is seen as the central factor of perceiving and interpreting the supplied immersive material: "The immersive content itself does not invoke learning activities directly as it has to be perceived by the learner first. A higher feeling of presence in terms of actually being in the immersive EVE [Educational Virtual Environment] enhances the learning activities" [5]. The learner's feeling of presence can be influenced through his or her subjective motivational, cognitive, and emotional factors, as well as through the level of immersion regarding the instructional material (Fig. 2).

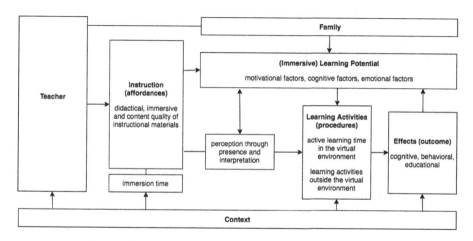

Fig. 2. The educational framework for immersive learning by Dengel and Mägdefrau [5] on the basis of Helmke's supply-use-framework [8]

The EFiL's cognitive factors "summarize all intraindividual cognitive characteristics and skills that influence learning activities, including intelligence, learning strategies, and the ability of reflective thinking" [5]. The didactical and methodical design of the immersive learning content can induce the activation of some of the cognitive factors.

We assume that the emotional factors of the learner contribute as well to the immersive learning activities as to presence. The EFiL's understanding of emotional factors follows the approach of Pekrun et al. distinguishing academic emotions into positive activating emotions (e.g. enjoyment, hope, pride), positive deactivating emotions (e.g. relief), negative activating emotions (e.g. anger, anxiety, shame), and negative deactivating emotions (e.g. hopelessness, boredom) [17]. As we want to determine the predictors for presence in educational virtual environments rather than determining the factors influencing learning activities in general, we follow the approach of distinguishing positive emotions and negative emotions as possible influences for presence while not differentiating activating and deactivating emotions.

The EFiL includes Deci and Ryan's continuum model with lesser or higher degrees of motivational regulation (amotivation external regulation, introjection, identification, intrinsic regulation) [4] with their occurrences of global, contextual and situational motivation [25]. Global and contextual motivation (e.g. academic motivation towards learning in general/in a specific subject) are considered as relatively stable individual characteristics which can only be changed slowly and partly [25]. The learner's situational motivation refers to current activity and can be influenced e.g. through the supplied immersive hardware/software, through other situational characteristics of the learner and the learning environment.

The EFiL gathers numerous studies investigating one or multiple effects of and between these variables in terms of immersive learning. Presence, as a central variable which is influenced by factors like immersion, emotion, cognition, and motivation seems to play a crucial role in immersive learning activities. However, studies which include multiple objective, situational, and stable psychological variables are rare. In order to explore the assumptions of the EFiL further, an examination on what seems to be the central key to understanding Immersive Learning is needed. Therefore, this paper focuses on extracting the subjective feeling of presence by investigating its predictors.

4   Research Model

For this pilot study investigating some of the objective and subjective variables influencing presence, we use hypotheses deriving from assumptions underlying the EFiL. For investigating the effect of immersion (IMM) on presence (PRES), different educational virtual environments have to be compared (effect of different immersive software on presence) in different immersive technologies for each environment (effect of different immersive hardware on presence). In order to assess cognitive abilities, we assume that scholastic performance (SP) can map the overall cognitive skills reasonably. Therefore, the scholastic performances in the core subjects Math (SP_MA), the students' native language (German, SP_GER), as well as in the subject of the learning content of the educational virtual environment (Computer Science, SP_CS) are assessed. Also, a composite score of the three subjects is calculated (SP_OVR) to display a simplified overall scholastic performance. In terms of the emotional factors, we assess the academic emotions suggested by the EFiL: the positive activating emotions (enjoyment, hope, and pride) and the positive deactivating emotion relief are aggregated to the factor positive emotions (EMO_PO); the negative activating emotions (shame, anger, and anxiety) and the negative deactivating emotions (hopelessness and boredom) are aggregated to the factor negative emotions (EMO_NE). Regarding the motivational factors, we assess the external regulation (MOT_EX), as well as introjected (MOT_IJ), identified (MOT_ID), and intrinsic (MOT_IN) academic motivations towards learning computer science. In this study, we focus on the variables influencing presence. Therefore, the research model does not cover all relations noted in the EFiL. In particular, we want to focus on physical presence as this manifestation of presence is relevant to all EVEs (some EVEs might not include social actors/a representation of the user's self). The hypotheses below result in the research model shown in Fig. 3.

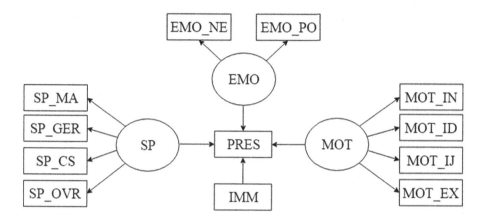

Fig. 3. Research model for the presence study

1. A higher level of immersion predicts a higher sense of presence.
2. Higher previous scholastic performance predicts a higher sense of presence (a: German, b: Math, c: Computer Science, d: Composite Scholastic Performance).
3. The student's emotional state predicts his or her sense of presence (a: positive emotions increase presence, b: negative emotions decrease presence).
4. The student's motivation towards learning Computer Science predicts his or her sense of presence (a: intrinsic motivation increases presence, b: identified motivation increases presence, c: introjected motivation decreases presence, d: external regulation decreases presence)

5   Method

5.1   Sample

23 (seven female) eighth-grade students from an Austrian school took part in the experiment. Their Computer Science teacher did not cover the topics of the virtual environments prior to the study.

5.2   Instruments

As we wanted to focus on the role of physical presence, we used the Slater-Usoh-Steed (SUS) questionnaire [22]. The questionnaire consists of six questions assessed on a 7-point Likert scale ($\alpha = .88$). Three different methods for the calculation of the presence value have been suggested: the original SUS Count method [22] counting all items with a value of 6 or higher (maximum of 6 points), the adapted method by Peck, Fuchs, and Whitton [16] counting all items with a value 5 or higher (maximum of 6 points) and the SUS Mean value [22] with a possible maximum of 7. We assessed external regulation (six items, $\alpha = .81$), introjected motivation (four items, $\alpha = .52$), identified motivation (four items, $\alpha = .79$), and intrinsic motivation (five items, $\alpha = .84$) on a 5-point Likert scale with a questionnaire evaluated by Hanfstingl et al. [7]. While the original survey measured motivation towards an unspecified subject, the questionnaire used in the study was adapted so that it assessed the students' motivation towards the subject Computer Science. The questionnaire for assessing the emotions shame, enjoyment, anger, hope, pride, hopelessness, relief, anxiety, and boredom on a 6-point Likert scale was adapted from a survey used by Titz [24]. The emotions were categorized into the scales positive emotions ($\alpha = .83$) and negative emotions ($\alpha = .35$). The introjected motivation scale and the negative emotion scale were excluded from further analysis due to their poor scale reliability scores (Fig. 4).

Fig. 4. Educational virtual environments for learning computer science (Components of a Computer, Asymmetric Encryption, Finite State Machines)

The educational virtual environments cover contents from computer science education: *Components of a Computer*, *Asymmetric Encryption*, and *Finite State Machines*. The environments have been developed with Unity and display a game-like setting for learning about the subject contents. Information was presented using texts and images. The *Components of a Computer* environment let the user enter a computer and learn about its different parts by repairing it from the inside. The *Asymmetric Encryption* environment uses magic potions as a metaphor for public and private key encryption processes. The *Finite State Machines* environment uses a treasure hunt game on varying islands as a metaphor for the states (islands) and the transition functions (boats) of an automaton. The used immersive settings are a laptop, a mobile VR and an HTC Vive. Due to their characteristics of interaction and vividness, the HTC Vive was considered to be the most and the laptop setting the least immersive setting.

5.3 Procedure

Three days prior to the study, the students completed the motivation question- naire and learning objective examinations for the three learning topics. The participants used an individual code for these pre-questionnaires which they would also use again later for the questionnaires in the study. In order to secure confidentiality, the students' teacher noted their scholastic performance in the subjects German, Math, and Computer Science on the pre-questionnaire with- out noting down the individual code. For the study itself, the class was randomly divided into three groups (two groups with eight members, one group with seven members). One student in a group of eight did not finish the study because of motion sickness after the mobile VR experience for the *Components of a Com- puter* environment. The participants of each group experienced all three soft- ware prototypes, but each group was provided a different technological setting for every program (Table 1). Within each group, the participants were handed a sheet with the task to collect stamps for all the technological settings (one stamp) and the filling out of the related questionnaires for presence and learning outcome (another stamp). The questionnaires had to be filled out immediately after the VR experience. The six stamps could be collected for the completion of the laptop experience, the mobile VR experience, the completion of the HTC Vive experience and, respectively, the related questionnaires. This resulted in 67 datasets in total (one for each presence questionnaire). Doing so, it was pos- sible to randomly mix the order of the programs among the students as well as the benefit that each student could take his or her own time in completing the VR experiences and the questionnaires without being pressured by peers who may have already finished. After the students were divided into groups and lead to their rooms, they were asked to fill out the emotion questionnaire. After all students finished their stamp cards, they took part in a short presentation explaining the metaphors used in the different games as well as the desired learn- ing objectives. As these learning outcomes cannot be considered as predictors of presence, their relation to presence was not investigated in this paper.

Table 1. Technological settings for the groups

	Group A	Group B	Group C
Components of a Computer	Mobile VR	HTC Vive	Laptop
Asymmetric Encryption	HTC Vive	Laptop	Mobile VR
Finite State Machines	Laptop	Mobile VR	HTC Vive

6 Findings

The different methods of measurement showed high correlations among each other. In order to map the students' heterogeneous manifestations of their feeling of presence as good as possible, we used the SUS Mean value for the further analyses ($r = .95$, $p < .01$ for counting method '5 and above' with mean value; $r = .88$, $p < .01$ for counting method '6 and above' with mean value). Because of the small sample of this pilot study, we decided in favor of analyzing the different factors separately rather than using structural equation modeling.

Table 2. ANOVA showing the Variation between Presence Means in the three different Technologies

	N	Mean	SD	Sum of Squares
Laptop	23	3.22	1.17	4.759
Mobile VR	23	4.54	1.39	
HTC Vive	21	5.29	1.20	

An ANOVA measuring variation between the students' presence means in the three different immersive settings (Table 2) showed significant differences between the settings laptop, mobile VR and HTC Vive [F (2, 64) $= 15.27$, $p < .01$, $\eta_p^2 = .32$]. A higher level of immersion lead to a higher sense of presence.

Table 3. Correlations between Presence and Previous Scholastic Performance

	1	2	3	4
1. German	–			
2. Math	.57**	–		
3. Computer Science	.63**	.75**	–	
4. Composite Score	.83**	.90**	.89**	–
5. Presence	.40**	.15	.12	.25

Note. **p $<.01$

The previous scholastic performance in the subjects German, Math and Computer Science showed significant correlations among the subjects (Table 3). The grades in German showed a significant correlation with the presence mean value ($r = .40$, $p < .01$). A better scholastic performance in the subject German, therefore, was associated to a higher sense of presence.

We found a significant correlation between the positive emotions and presence ($r = .26$, $p < .05$). Stronger positive emotions lead to higher presence. A possible effect of negative emotions on presence could not be examined due to a poor scale reliability value (see 5.2).

The motivational constructs intrinsic motivation and identified motivation were strongly correlated ($r = .68$, $p < .01$). There was no significant correlation between motivation (intrinsic motivation, identified motivation, external regulation) and presence. The relation between introjected motivation and presence was not investigated further due to the poor scale reliability value mentioned above.

7 Discussion

The study was designed to explore the determinants of presence. The effects of the level of immersion as well as of the learner's scholastic performance, emotional state, and motivation towards learning the subject associated with the learning environments on presence were investigated. By following Slater's definition of immersion as a quantifiable description of the used technology, it was possible to separate the supply-side of the EFiL (a teacher can choose to supply a certain immersive technology, including hardware and software) from the use-side of the framework (the learner's perception of the virtual world at a certain level of presence, his or her emotions, cognitive abilities, and motivation).

H1 (a higher level of immersion predicts a higher sense of presence) can be maintained: An ANOVA between the technologies showed significant differences with the HTC Vive inducing the highest sense of presence and the laptop setting inducing the lowest sense of presence. These results relate to the characteristics of immersion postulated by Slater [21]: The mobile VR can be seen as more immersive than the laptop setting deriving from a higher level of interactivity due to the head tracking in the mobile VR; the head-mounted-display setting can be regarded as the most immersive setting (increased speed of the interactivity and better resolution/vividness in terms of the perceptual depth) compared to the mobile VR. With regards to this hierarchy of immersive systems, the analysis of variance shows that a higher level of immersion predicts higher presence.

As for the students' previous scholastic performance, the performance in the subject German was found to be predictive for presence. This could be explained by the high amount of German texts in the VR environments which may have made feeling present dependent to a certain level of reading skills, represented through the grade in the subject German. Another possible explanation is that a higher interest in reading, especially fictional texts, could possibly lead to an increased fantasy, accompanied by an increased cognitive ability to create mental models. With the data collected, it is not possible to explore this idea further. We have to decline hypotheses $H2_b$ (Math), $H2_c$ (Computer Science), and $H2_d$ (Composite Scholastic Performance). A generalization of H2 (higher previous scholastic performance predicts a higher sense of presence) is, therefore, not possible. But, maintaining hypothesis $H2_a$ (German) indicates that cognitive abilities which are related to the manner of how knowledge is acquired in the learning environment may influence the feeling of presence. The absence of a connection between Maths/Computer Science and presence could be caused by the design of the software: The game-based learning environment used metaphors and the learning objectives were not really apparent to the user.

The positive emotions (combining positive activating emotions and positive deactivating emotions) were found to be predictive for presence. As neither the laboratory nor the programs were designed to induce or increase negative emotions, the absence of significant associations between presence and negative emotions, activating or deactivating, is not surprising. $H3_a$ (positive emotions increase presence) can be maintained: The student's sense of presence correlates with his or her emotional state regarding positive emotions. H3 (the student's emotional state predicts his or her sense of presence) cannot be generalized as an investigation of $H3_b$ (negative emotions decrease presence) was not appropriate due to poor scale reliability for the negative emotions. Further research on the effects of emotions on presence in EVEs is needed.

To the surprise of the authors, none of the motivational constructs were found to be significantly correlated to presence; H4 (the student's motivation towards learning Computer Science predicts his or her sense of presence) has to be declined. This could possibly be explained by a lacking connection between the motivation towards learning computer science and the students' engagement in the software as the programs were designed as games which did not require any previous knowledge about the topics. Thus, the students possibly did not connect the contents to the subject, encouraging them to impartially engage with the environment. As the scale reliability for introjected motivation was low, we could not test $H4_b$. This may be an indicator that the questionnaire used for the study was not fully applicable to the subject Computer Science and may have to be revised for further investigations.

8   Implications for Immersive Learning in Educational Virtual Environments

This study could contribute as well to presence research as to the research realm of immersive learning clarifying the role of technological and person-specific variables for developing a sense of presence in EVEs. Not all assumptions of the EFiL regarding presence could be verified. For some of the effects found, it is not yet clear, why and how they influence presence. In order to explore these factors further, larger studies would be needed. Also, while the EFiL hypothesizes mutual relations between the subjective factors, we focused on predictive effects of certain subjective and objective variables on presence. Long term studies with broad use of immersive educational technology would be needed in order to determine whether there are long term effects of presence on cognitive abilities, emotional states, and motivational attitudes.

Even though Jennett et al. argue that presence is only a small part of a user's gaming experience [9], the current study could verify the localization of presence as a central factor in the process of Immersive Learning: Objective variables like the level of immersion, given through the design of software components and the used technology, as well as subjective variables like cognitive abilities and emotional capability, predict presence. As the person-specific variables also influence learning processes in general, understanding the concept of presence, how presence is induced and how it influences learning is indispensable for understanding learning processes involving immersive technology. After consolidating the crucial role of presence in Immersive Learning, further research in terms of learning activities and learning outcomes is needed: While it was possible to resolve some central questions on the determinants of presence, the results differing from the theoretical framework raise even more interesting and yet unresolved questions on the details of how presence interacts with the factors involved in the process of Immersive Learning. In a next step, a design for a larger study will be developed to investigate the effects of immersion, presence, cognition, emotion, and motivation among each other as well as on learning outcomes.

Presence as the subjective feeling of being physically in an environment, actually interacting with the social actors of this environment, and connecting one's self with the avatar representation inside the environment seems to be crucial for immersive learning. Together with influences from the supply side as well as from the individual use-side of the learner, presence is connected to many subjective constructs influencing learning processes in immersive educational virtual environments; it might be the key to understanding Immersive Learning.

Acknowledgements. The SKILL project is part of the "Qualitätsoffensive Lehrerbildung", a joint initiative of the Federal Government and the Länder which aims to improve the quality of teacher training. The programme is funded by the Federal Ministry of Education and Research. The authors are responsible for the content of this publication.

References

1. Bailenson, J.N., Beall, A.C., Blascovich, J., Loomis, J., Turk, M.: Transformed social interaction, augmented gaze, and social influence in immersive virtual environments. Hum. Commun. Res. **31**, 511–537 (2005)
2. Bailey, J., Bailenson, J.N., Won, A.S., Flora, J.: Presence and memory: immersive virtual reality effects on cued recall. In: Proceedings of the International Society for Presence Research Annual Conference, 24–26 October, Philadelphia, Pennsylvania, USA (2012)
3. Biocca, F.: The Cyborg's dilemma progressive embodiment in virtual environments. In: Humane Interfaces: Questions of Method and Practice in Cognitive Technology. Human Factors in Information Technology, Amsterdam, vol. 13, pp. 113–144 (1999)
4. Deci, E.L., Ryan, R.M.: Intrinsic Motivation and Self-Determination in Human Behavior. Plenum Press, New York (1985)
5. Dengel, A., Mägdefrau, J.: Immersive learning explored: subjective and objective factors influencing learning outcomes in immersive educational virtual environments. In: 2018 IEEE International Conference on Teaching, Assessment, and Learning for Engineering (TALE), Wollongong, Australia, pp. 608–615 (2018)
6. Dewey, J.: Observation and Information. How We Think, pp. 188–200. D.C. Heath, Lexington (1910)

7. Hanfstingl, B., Andreitz, I., Thomas, A., Müller, F.H.: Evaluationsbericht Schüler-und Lehrerbefragung 2008/09. Interner Arbeitsbericht. Klagenfurt, Institut für Unterrichts-und Schulentwicklung (2010)
8. Helmke, A., Weinert, F.: Bedingungsfaktoren schulischer Leistungen. Max-Planck-Inst. für Psychologische Forschung (1997)
9. Jennett, C., et al.: Measuring and defining the experience of immersion in games. Int. J. Hum. Comput. Stud. **66**(9), 641–661 (2008)
10. Lee, E.A.-L., Wong, K.W., Fung, C.C.: How does desktop virtual reality enhance learning outcomes? A structural equation modeling approach. Comput. Educ. **55**(4), 1424–1442 (2010)
11. Lee, K.M.: Presence, explicated. Commun. Theory **14**(1), 27–50 (2006)
12. Lin, J.-W. Duh, H., Parker, D.E., Abi-Rached, H., Furness, T.A.: Effects of field of view on presence, enjoyment, memory, and simulator sickness in a virtual environment. In: Proceedings of the IEEE Virtual Reality 2002, Los Alamitos, California, USA 164 171 (2002)
13. Mania, K., Chalmers, A.: The effects of levels of immersion on memory and presence in virtual environments. A reality centered approach. Cyberpsychol. Behav. **4**(2), 247–264 (2001)
14. Mikropoulos, T.A.: Presence: a unique characteristic in educational virtual environments. Virtual Reality **10**(3–4), 197–206 (2006)
15. Nichols, S., Haldane, C., Wilson, J.R.: Measurement of presence and its consequences in virtual environments. Int. J. Hum. Comput. Stud. **52**, 471–491 (2000)
16. Peck, T.C., Fuchs, H., Whitton, M.C.: Evaluation of reorientation techniques and distractors for walking in large virtual environments. IEEE Trans. Visual. Comput. Graphics **15**(3), 383–94 (2009)
17. Pekrun, R.: A Social-Cognitive, Control-Value Theory of Achievement Emotions. Motivational Psychology of Human Development. J. Heckhausen, Ed. Oxford: Elsevier, pp. 143–163 (2000)
18. Price, M., Anderson, P.: The role of presence in virtual reality exposure therapy. J. Anxiety Disord. **21**, 742–751 (2007)
19. Roy, M., Schlemminger, G.: Immersion und Interaktion in virtuellen Realitäten: Der Faktor Präsenz zur Optimierung des geleiteten Sprachenlernens. Zeitschrift für interkulturellen Fremdsprachenunterricht. Didaktik und Methodik im Bereich Deutsch als Fremdsprache, **19**(2), 187–201 (2014)
20. Schubert, T., Friedmann, F., Regenbrecht, H.: The experience of presence: factor analytic insights. Presence **10**(3), 266–281 (2001)
21. Slater, M.: A note on presence terminology. Presence Connect **3**, 1–5 (2003)
22. Slater, M., Usoh, M.: Steed: depth of presence in virtual environments. Presence Teleoper. Virtual Environ. **3**, 130–144 (1994)
23. Steuer, J.: Defining virtual reality. Dimensions determining telepresence. J. Commun. **42**(4), 73–93 (1992)
24. Titz, W.: Emotionen von Studierenden in Lernsituationen: Explorative Analysen und Entwicklung von Selbstberichtskalen (367). Waxmann, Münster, New York, München, Berlin (2001)
25. Vallerand, R.J., Pelletier, L.G., Blais, M.R., Brière, N.M., Senécal, C., Vallières, E.F.: The academic motivation scale: a measure of intrinsic, extrinsic, and amotivation in education. Educ. Psychol. Meas. **52**, 1003–1017 (1992)
26. Witmer, B.G., Singer, M.J.: Measuring presence in virtual environments: a presence questionnaire. Presence: Teleoper. Virtual Environ. **7**(3), 225–240 (1998)
27. Yeonhee, C.: The Impact of Interaction in Virtual Reality Language Learning as Active Learning. Korean Educational Research Association, New York (2018)

Enhancing Emotional Effectiveness of Virtual-Reality Experiences with Voice Control Interfaces

Hunter Osking[(⊠)] and John A. Doucette[iD]

New College of Florida, Sarasota, FL 34234, USA
{hunter.osking14,jdoucette}@ncf.edu

Abstract. Virtual Reality (VR) systems are becoming widespread, and can create deeply immersive experiences. Although the visual component of VR systems mimics the user's presence in virtual spaces, dialogue control systems used in VR experiences are often adapted from older media. When selecting dialogue, older systems can break the illusion of presence in the virtual space, which is particularly jarring in interactive narratives. Using a voice control dialogue system may preserve this illusion and therefore enhance the emotional impact of narrative experiences. We evaluate this hypothesis on participants playing the same game that were assigned to use either a voice recognition or a more traditional point-and-click style interface. We find that the use of voice control with VR enhances the game's emotional impact and users' perceived enjoyment, as measured through a post-experiment survey instrument. We also present interesting qualitative results from interviews with participants. Our findings suggest that incorporating voice control into interactive VR narratives could improve their appeal for both consumer markets and psychological applications.

Keywords: Virtual reality · Interfaces · Video games

1 Introduction

With the advent of Virtual Reality comes a new kind of immersive experience. Never before have players been able to enter virtual worlds in such a convincing and dizzying manner. Players are now able to engage with games and applications as though they stand directly inside a virtual world. The potential of this increased engagement is immense. VR games do not just allow for more immersive experiences than traditional computer games [3,14], they also allow for more empathetic experiences [1,4,12,16].

While there has been research on how different control systems can increase immersivity in VR programs (e.g., [3,6,9]) and on the importance of stimulating users' feelings of presence to produce emotional responses in VR environments [5], there has been little research looking into the question of how the

© Springer Nature Switzerland AG 2019
D. Beck et al. (Eds.): iLRN 2019, CCIS 1044, pp. 199–209, 2019.
https://doi.org/10.1007/978-3-030-23089-0_15

choice of control systems can help to make VR applications more emotionally intense. Our hope is to uncover ways for developers to maximize the emotional intensity of VR applications, increasing VR's usefulness as a tool for both scientific and artistic applications.

This study also introduces *Flowers for Dan dan* as a research tool. *Flowers for Dan dan* is a VR video game in which the player progresses through an interactive story by choosing between prewritten dialogue options. The game places the player in the role of a character who is dealing with both the death of his dog and the emotional toll that the death is taking on his family. Since the game deals with themes of grief and loss in such a personal way, emotional intensity is essential to its effectiveness as a work of art. Because of this, the technological aspects of *Flowers for Dan dan* were designed with a single question in mind, "How can we maximize this game's emotional effectiveness in regards to its user interface"? To address this question, we compare a novel control system for choosing dialogue against a more traditional one. In particular, we assess voice recognition as a means of choosing between branching dialogue options in a VR context, versus a system where players point at their desired option and select it by clicking a button. Participants were asked to play one of the two versions of the game and to complete two sets of interview questions afterwards, the first being a questionnaire used for quantitative analysis and the second being a conversational interview used for qualitative analysis.

The results of the study point toward voice recognition as a mechanic that can increase both the player's enjoyment of a virtual reality program and the intensity of their emotional response to it. Interestingly, the quantitative results suggest that players who used voice recognition found the game to be more enjoyable, and more emotionally effective. The qualitative interviews that followed provide us with interesting comments to augment these findings and supplement the quantitative results. Players who used the voice recognition mechanic were more likely to comment that they felt a strong sense of connection with the character they played, and were more likely to say that they felt as if the conversations they had in the game were their own. This suggests that the physical action of saying sentences aloud within a VR environment increases the connection between the player and the meaning of the words spoken aloud.

2   Background

In this paper we analyze how the implementation of a voice recognition control system might affect a players' experiences in a dialogue driven VR application. This paper's novelty springs from the way in which it utilizes voice recognition as a means of selecting prewritten branching dialogue options alongside an immersive virtual reality system. By "prewritten dialogue" we mean that the dialogue options that the player can choose from have all been written in advance. By "branching" we mean that the player can select from among several dialogue options at different points in an interactive story, and that different dialogue options can produce different future states. This is what creates the sense of player autonomy, as the branches allow the player to steer the conversation down the track of their choosing. When we say that the game uses voice recognition we are referring to one version of the game that requires the player to read their preferred dialogue option aloud to select it, in contrast to another version of the game in which dialogue is selected using more conventional controls. It is through this combination of prewritten branching dialogue and voice recognition that the game reaches its novelty - at times the game feels less like a game and more like participating in a theater piece. This theatrical quality results in a fresh experience that feels simultaneously personal and performative.

This paper is fundamentally a study on control systems for interactive narratives. Perhaps the best example of a preexisting interactive narrative being used to evaluate different ways of interacting with virtual worlds is the game *Façade*. *Façade* was made in response to a perceived lack of emotional video games in 2005 [10]. The game places the player in the middle of a dinner party with their friends Trip and Grace. As the night progresses, the illusion of Trip and Grace's happy marriage deteriorates, and it is up to the player to calm them down (or help guide them into a vicious fight). *Façade* attempts to find a middle ground between a procedural simulation of drama and a predetermined simulation of drama. In other words, the plot is simultaneously generated on the spot while still being confined to a strict set of narrative moments. This allows for the game to have an open ended feeling, while still granting the author the narrative leeway to direct the story. *Façade* has been used in a multitude of studies as a tool to help researchers evaluate open questions in human-computer interaction. These studies span a wide array of topics ranging from researchers using modified versions of Façade as a way to test the immersive elements of Augmented Reality (AR) [6] and dialogue systems [15], to using it as way to qualitatively assess the experience of interactive storytelling [7,13].

Papers on *Façade* include Dow et al.'s *Presence and Engagement in an Interactive Drama* [6], which is the study that is most closely related to ours. In it, researchers tested three different modes of play for the game *Façade* and then used qualitative tests to measure the effectiveness of each method. The first method involves the player using the original *Façade*'s interface (mouse and keyboard controls on the PC), the second method involves the player choosing their options by saying them aloud while viewing the scene through a regular computer screen (this is different from *Flowers for Dan dan* in that the player could say anything they wanted, whereas *Flowers for Dan dan* requires that the player only read the prewritten options out loud), and the third method places the player in an interactive "Augmented Reality" (AR) environment where the apartment in *Façade* was entirely modelled, and where the player interacts with the characters using voice controls. This last environment contrasts with the VR system of *Flowers for Dan dan*, because in the AR system the player is present in a physical recreation of the game world into which the characters are projected, whereas in VR, the player feels projected into a fully virtual world. Afterwards, players were asked to compare and contrast their opinions on each user interface. The results are slightly counterintuitive suggesting that the increased immersion users experienced in the AR version of *Façade* actually decreased their engagement with the game. Some players became so deeply immersed that they could not comfortably engage with the narrative events.

Dow et al.'s work [6] heavily influenced our study's methodology, specifically relating to how it used qualitative questioning to extract its subjects' more abstract feelings on the game's user interface. The methodology of our study differs in a few major ways. The first and most significant difference is that our study uses a between-subjects design and divides its players into one of two treatments - meaning that each subject only got to play one version of the game, rather than using Dow et al.'s within-subjects design. Our reasoning for this methodological change stemmed from the fact that the *Flowers for Dan dan* had fewer possibilities for the player to explore than *Façade*, making it likely that the player might follow similar paths on a repeat playthroughs. To combat this issue, we employed a larger number of subjects than Dow et al.'s study, and augmented our interview process with a quantitative section so that we could compare and contrast the differences in answers between treatments in both concrete and abstract ways.

Another key difference between our study and Dow et al.'s [6] is in its general focus. Their study was primarily interested in examining the impact of different control interfaces on presence and engagement, while our study examines how different control interfaces (specifically voice recognition and more traditional motion controls) can affect a game's emotional effectiveness. A few other studies have asked similar questions, examining how different interfaces may affect emotional engagement. Fang et al.'s work [8] compared digital games to board games and discovered that board games remain popular and relevant in part because players are more emotionally effected by them than they are by digital games.

3 System

Study participants were asked to play a short dialogue-based video game using either a standard control system (two hand-held controllers) or a mocked-up voice-control system. After playing the game, participants completed a questionnaire and a semi-structured interview. In this section, we describe the equipment, the control interfaces, and the selected game in detail. In the next section, we describe the experimental design and recruitment of subjects (Fig. 1).

3.1 Equipment

Our study utilized an Oculus Rift Headset [11] and a standard commodity desktop computer for running VR applications. The computer we used exceeded the required performance specifications for the Oculus Rift, ensuring a seamless experience for users. The game that we developed for our experiments was created using Unreal Engine 4, a popular game engine optimized for interactive 3d visual processing and for use with the Oculus Rift headset [11]. The game's branching dialogue system was controlled using the Articy editor, a tool for organizing video game media assets and written content [2].

Fig. 1. (a) Player talks to Dad at his door. (b) Player grabs Dandy's hand to see if he is in pain.

3.2   Control Interfaces

Two versions of the game we used in our experiments, *Flowers for Dan dan*, were created. The versions were identical except for the method in which the player's dialogue responses were chosen. The first version of the game utilized Voice Recognition Controls (which will henceforth be abbreviated to VRC), and the second version utilized Point and Click Motion Controls (which will henceforth be abbreviated to PCMC). In both schemes, dialogue options appear as floating text in the player's field of view when the plot demands a spoken response from the player. The only difference is the manner in which the player indicates which of the several dialogue options they would like to say.

Players using PCMC were required to point at their desired response with the left motion controller. Upon pointing, their desired selection would be highlighted, and they would press the thumbstick down on the controller to choose the options. These controls mirrored those for selecting dialogue options in other popular Virtual Reality games, including *From Other Suns*, *Fallout 4 VR*, and *Skyrim VR*.

Players using VRC chose their desired dialogue option by simply reading it out loud. Upon reading their desired option, the text box would slowly fill up with a blue bar highlighting the text in the option they chose. This was implemented so that the players would have some sort of feedback telling them that their voice was actually being recognized.

Despite the fact that the commercial version of *Flowers for Dan dan* has had working voice recognition controls since July 2017, we utilized a "Wizard of Oz"-style system to facilitate the selection of dialogue options, similar to Dow et al.'s approach with *Façade* [6]. This prevented imperfections in the system's implementation from ruining the experience for the player and allowed experiments to proceed without spending time tuning the system to each participant's voice. While the player interacted with the game, the experimenter sat at a nearby computer ostensibly monitoring the game. The experimenter was able to see the player's perspective and manually selected whichever dialogue option the player spoke by silently pressing a key as soon as the player had spoken enough to clearly differentiate between the various options.

3.3   *Flowers for Dan dan* Summary

Flowers for Dan dan starts the player in a wooded area. Beneath them stands a gravestone and a prompt that reads "Pull Weed to Start Game." The game starts once the weed is pulled, and the player is transported to a space cloaked by darkness. A voice can be heard booming from a spot behind the player - the voice is of the protagonist's father praying for the improvement of the health of the family dog, Dandy. While praying, he is interrupted by a phone call, and he asks the player if they would be willing to finish the prayer by themselves. The scene continues with the player solitarily praying for the improvement of Dandy's health. As the player reads the remainder of the prayer, Dad can be faintly heard off in the distance having a conversation with his friend, the family doctor, about the seriousness of Dandy's sickness. The prayer ends with the player petting Dandy's tummy while Dad gets mad at his friend for suggesting that it is inhumane to keep Dandy alive.

Once the prayer is finished, the darkness surrounding the player lifts, and the player discovers they are standing in the living room of the protagonist's house. Just as this happens, Dad angrily exits the living room and enters his bedroom. Dandy lies at the players feet, exactly where he could be seen during the prayer, but he is no longer getting his tummy rubbed. Instead, he is lying on his side making pained moans. Behind the bedroom door, Dad can be heard arguing with his friend about the nature of Dandy's health - he sounds convinced that Dandy is not seriously ill and that there is no need for anyone to act "humanely." In the midst of the argument, Dad opens an eye slot on his door and calls at the player to squeeze Dandy's paw, at the direction of the doctor. Upon doing so, Dandy makes a horrible screeching yelp, which Dad responds to in horror. Dad yells at his friend and hangs up the phone. Behind his door, Dad can be heard sadly mumbling to himself.

At this point, the player is prompted to knock on Dad's door to find out what is going on. What follows is a long conversation with Dad, held through the door, where Dad shifts between being angry at the doctor for suggesting that Dandy should be put down and being bitterly depressed about Dandy's declining health and inevitable death. The conversation ends with the protagonist telling their Dad that they love him. In return the father reassures the player that he loves them too. The player is then prompted to "Walk Around and Think about Hard Stuff." A sad song plays for a minute while they move around the house and reflect on the events of the game. The game then fades to black.

4   Experiment

We assessed the usefulness of VRC and PCMC controls for the game through a between-subjects experiment in which players played the game with one of the two possible control systems and then completed a questionnaire and interview. Participants were undergraduate students from a small residential college, recruited through flyers and email advertisements. Every student who responded to the advertisements was invited to play the game. The students were all adults between the ages of 18 and 23. A total of 23 participants were recruited and 22 of them completed the study activities (Fig. 2).

Fig. 2. A participant talks to the Dad at his bedroom door. (Images used with permission.)

After being assigned a control system via a coin flip, players were asked to put on the virtual reality headset. Since the game lacks a tutorial section in which the controls are explained, the experimenter would briefly explain the controls to the player. If players ever got confused by the controls during their playthrough (as did many players who had not used VR systems before), the experimenter would re-explain any of the controls that they seemed to be misunderstanding.

Upon completing the demo, the experimenter would ask the player to place the headset and the controllers on the floor. Participants were then asked to complete a short five question questionnaire in which they quantitatively ranked their feelings about different aspects of the game using a 7-point Likert Scale. The experimenter left the room while participants filled out the questionnaire. Once finished with the questionnaire, the participant would notify the experimenter, who would then re-enter the room. The experimenter would then ask participants open ended questions that could be used to gauge their feelings about the game on several separate axes. While they spoke, the experimenter took detailed notes of their answers, which were turned into paraphrased quotations (each of the participants consented to this paraphrasing of their answers verbally).

5   Results and Discussion

In this section, we present the results we gathered from the experiment described in the previous section. Our results are organized into related findings.

5.1 Emotional Response

Our main result is related to the degree of emotional response experienced by participants. When asked to rank their emotional response to the demo on a 7-point Likert scale, players who used voice recognition controls (VRC) reported a higher score on average than those who played using point and click motion controls (PCMC), as summarized in Table 1. Participants who used VRC reported a mean score of 5.8 on the Likert scale, compared with a score of just 4.7 for participants who used PCMC. This difference was statistically significant ($p = 0.02$, t-test, $n = 22$, H_0 = identical means). These results indicate that the game is more emotionally effective with VRC than with PCMC and suggest that VR systems that wish to achieve greater emotional impact should incorporate support for VRC. Responses from the qualitative interviews support these results.

Table 1 shows the average scores given by participants to each of the questions listed in the leftmost column, on a 7-point Likert scale. Standard deviations are also listed. The rightmost column shows the p-value of a 2-sided 2 sample t-test with a null hypothesis that the mean scores of the subjects did not depend on their control scheme. Bolded values are statistically significant.

Table 1. Results

Question	Voice recognition controls	Point and click motion controls	P-value
On a Scale of 1–7, how realistic did you find the game?	$4.92 \pm .5$	$4.9 \pm .9$	.96
On a Scale of 1–7, how immersive did you find the game?	6.1 ± 1.5	5.3 ± 1.1	.18
On a Scale of 1–7, how emotionally affected were you by the game?	5.8 ± 1.0	4.7 ± 1.1	**.02**
On a Scale of 1–7, how difficult did you find it to use the interface for selecting dialogue options?	2.3 ± 1.2	2.8 ± 1.6	.44
On a Scale of 1–7, how much did you enjoy using the game's dialogue interface?	6.3 ± 1.1	4.8 ± 1.5	**.01**

Players who used VRC frequently reported feeling that the game's emotional impact was improved by the control system. One player commented that without VRC they "would have been less attached [to the game]." One subject found that the talking component of the game forced them to pay attention to what they were saying because it forced them "to identify with [the dialogue]."

Players also made frequent comments on how the voice recognition forced them to engage with the dialogue options in visceral and uncomfortable ways. Most players were enthusiastic about this aspect of the game, finding that it successfully aided the game's emotional ambitions. One player complimented this aspect of the game saying:

> *When I said "I love you Dad" it made me say something that in the past has felt weird [for me to say]. It looks at masculinity in a really interesting way. It's not something I would have said if I were not forced too, and that shows potential in the design.*   - (P4 of VRC)

While a majority of players seemed to appreciate this aspect of the game, some thought that the increased emotional effects of VRC hindered their enjoyment of the game.

> *There were times where it was hard to say [the dialogue options]. I wish I could have just not used my words and just made a choice. It was like being a boss and having to fire your employee. It was like I was firing someone and I had to say it to their face. I wish I could have just clicked on it so I could be cold and dark.*   - (P1 of VRC)

When asked more specifically how the game made them feel, the responses from the participants who used VRC were more rich in their usage of emotional language. For example:

> *I definitely felt a moment of genuine sadness when the music came on and I started walking to the bedroom, but then I realized "No I need to go see Dandy [the dying dog]." It was a genuine compulsion. And then I went into the room, but then I remembered what Dad said about the sleeping pills, and then [went] to go check on [the pills] so I could contemplate the reality [of the pending euthanasia].*   - (P3 of VRC)

Participants who used VRC also became more engaged with the game. It was very common for players to start the game speaking in their normal voice without any inflection, but to then adapt their tone to better fit the dialogue options once they became more emotionally invested. One player even commented that they adopted "a partial southern accent to read the options," mirroring the accent of the protagonist's father in the game.

5.2 Difficulty

Our data suggests that participants did not find one control system to be more difficult to use than the other ($p = 0.44$, $n = 22$, two-sided t-test, $H_0 = $ identical means). These results are interesting considering that voice recognition controls were new to every participant who used them.

6   Conclusions and Future Work

This study showed that voice recognition can make VR video games and applications more enjoyable and more emotionally impactful. Our qualitative results also support the idea that VRC enhanced participants' embodiment of the game's protagonist, as demonstrated by their adoption of accents, use of gestures, and the increased emotional impact of the dialogue. Our findings suggest that VR device manufactures could benefit from the incorporation of VRC directly into their devices, and that game designers and others interested in using VR to create emotionally impactful experiences should consider the use of VRC.

Other future studies could explore the immersive effects of VRC and its relation to the phenomenon of player-character embodiment in a more quantitative way than we did in this study. Measuring the ratio of playtime for which users adopt the intended accent, emotional affect, or gestures of the protagonist when using VRC could be an effective approach. There was a moment in almost every playthrough using VRC in this study where the player would shed their own voice and adapt the voice of the character in the game, but a more detailed analysis could formalize this finding.

References

1. Ahn, S.J., Bostick, J., Ogle, E., Nowak, K.L., McGillicuddy, K.T., Bailenson, J.N.: Experiencing nature: embodying animals in immersive virtual environments increases inclusion of nature in self and involvement with nature. J. Comput. Mediat. Commun. **21**(6), 399–419 (2016)
2. Articy Software GmbH & Co.: Articy: draft the professional game design solution. https://www.nevigo.com/en/articydraft/overview/. Accessed 15 April 2019
3. Bowman, D.A., McMahan, R.P.: Virtual reality: how much immersion is enough? Computer **40**(7), 36–43 (2007)
4. Carey, K., Saltz, E., Rosenbloom, J., Micheli, M., Choi, J.O., Hammer, J.: Toward measuring empathy in virtual reality. In: Extended Abstracts Publication of the Annual Symposium on Computer-Human Interaction in Play, pp. 551–559. ACM (2017)
5. Diemer, J., Alpers, G.W., Peperkorn, H.M., Shiban, Y., Mühlberger, A.: The impact of perception and presence on emotional reactions: a review of research in virtual reality. Front. Psychol. **6**, 26 (2015)
6. Dow, S., Mehta, M., Harmon, E., MacIntyre, B., Mateas, M.: Presence and engagement in an interactive drama. In: Proceedings of the SIGCHI Conference on Human Factors in Computing Systems, pp. 1475–1484. ACM (2007)
7. El-Nasr, M.S., Milam, D., Maygoli, T.: Experiencing interactive narrative: a qualitative analysis of façade. Entertain. Comput. **4**(1), 39–52 (2013)
8. Fang, Y.M., Chen, K.M., Huang, Y.J.: Emotional reactions of different interface formats: comparing digital and traditional board games. Adv. Mech. Eng. **8**(3), 1687814016641902 (2016)
9. Lee, J., Kim, M., Kim, J.: A study on immersion and VR sickness in walking interaction for immersive virtual reality applications. Symmetry **9**(5), 78 (2017)
10. Mateas, M., Stern, A.: Façade: an experiment in building a fully-realized interactive drama. In: Game Developers Conference, vol. 2, pp. 4–8 (2003)

11. Oculus VR Inc.: Oculus rift overview. https://www.oculus.com/rift/. Accesses 15 April 2019
12. Riva, G.: Affective interactions using virtual reality: the link between presence and emotions. CyberPsychol. Behav. **10**(1), 45–56 (2007)
13. Roth, C., Klimmt, C., Vermeulen, I.E., Vorderer, P.: The experience of interactive storytelling: comparing "Fahrenheit" with "Façade". In: Anacleto, J.C., Fels, S., Graham, N., Kapralos, B., Saif El-Nasr, M., Stanley, K. (eds.) ICEC 2011. LNCS, vol. 6972, pp. 13–21. Springer, Heidelberg (2011). https://doi.org/10.1007/978-3-642-24500-8_2
14. Ryan, M.L.: Narrative as Virtual Reality: Immersion and Interactivity in Literature and Electronic Media. Johns Hopkins University Press, Baltimore (2001)
15. Sali, S., et al.: Playing with words: from intuition to evaluation of game dialogue interfaces. In: Proceedings of the Fifth International Conference on the Foundations of Digital Games, pp. 179–186. ACM (2010)
16. Seinfeld, S., et al.: Offenders become the victim in virtual reality: impact of changing perspective in domestic violence. Sci. Rep. **8**(1), 2692 (2018)

Hyper/Actual Immersiveness Scale to Evaluate Experiences in Mixed Reality Using Design Thinking

Fadi Chehimi[(⊠)]

Accenture, London EC3M 3BD, UK
fadi.chehimi@accenture.com

Abstract. Mixed Reality (MR) has steadily proliferated to become one of the most trending technologies now. In order to maintain this progressive momentum, delivering highest degrees of immersion is key. Continuous experimentation helps get there but it must be accompanied by an effective evaluation process. Many researchers have developed subjective and objective methods to measure immersion and presence in MR, but most use fixed analysis criteria. In this paper we introduce a new method that is user-driven, not researcher-driven, that adapts to the varying cognitive and physical states people go through in MR. It utilizes Empathy Maps to capture feelings, thoughts, actions and verbal expressions from a first-person perspective. We also introduce an experience continuum to score those states based on how artificial or realistic they felt.

Keywords: Augmented Reality · Design Thinking · Evaluation method · Mixed Reality · Virtual Reality

1 Introduction

In the past few years, Mixed Reality has become one of the most trending technologies, "recapturing" the attention of both industry and academia. MR is not new, Milgram and Kishino introduced it in their 1994 paper along with the Reality-Virtuality Continuum which "relates to the mixture of classes of objects presented in any particular display situation" [19]. The continuum exhibits one class that is fully synthesized on one pole, Virtual Reality (VR), and on the other a class that has the physical world enhanced by computer generated objects, Augmented Reality (AR). We use the term "MR" and the combined "AR & VR" interchangeable in this paper.

Both AR and VR have steadily progressed since Milgram's work. They travelled through Gartner's technology Hype Cycle from the "Innovation Trigger" phase with unproven promises in 2010 [7], to the "Slope of Enlightenment" where their benefits are being realized now [8]. Breakthroughs in displays, optics, tracking, sensors etc. have made this happen. However, user experience (UX) in AR and VR has been often overlooked in the midst of this technological evolution. Researchers agree that it has not reached its potential to evoke the senses yet [1, 6, 17, 22]. Dünser et al. argues that this is caused largely by the lack of knowledge on how to conduct UX evaluations and

© Springer Nature Switzerland AG 2019
D. Beck et al. (Eds.): iLRN 2019, CCIS 1044, pp. 210–221, 2019.
https://doi.org/10.1007/978-3-030-23089-0_16

what metrics to use [5]. It is therefore paramount to establish efficient frameworks that could identify degrading experience factors and promote the sense of immersion.

Measuring immersion, or "presence" [30], has been studied extensively by researchers from HCI, psychology and design fields. Some proposed objective physiological methods to track bodily metrics as sign of presence, e.g. heart rate, skin temperature and muscle tension [26, 27]. Many others created subjective questionnaires and rating systems which users had to provide answers for during or after experiments [2, 10, 24, 31]. Notably, the literature still lacks proper user-centered evaluation methodologies as highlighted by [6, 13].

By inspecting survey-based methods, we found researchers have developed distinct sets of questions that related to specific problems or contexts. We argue that this approach is limited as it fails to tackle the following research questions:

- Would the predefined set of questions be transferable and executable across different MR application contexts?
- Could they reliably adapt to the deviation in users' previous experiences and expectations of MR [23]?
- What criteria makes one set superior to another? What kind of method and metric are used [5]?
- Are they relevant to current technical state-of-the-art?

This paper is an attempt to address those open-ended questions. We introduce the Hyper/Actual Immersiveness Scale, a novel user-driven method that is questionnaire free. It can apply to any situation and adapt to attitudes and actions. It is user-driven because it gives participants full control over describing the emotional, cognitive and physical states they go through to measure immersion in MR. No ties to predefined set of questions. These dimensions flex based on the context and user engagement. The method also allows participants to score their experience along the Hyper-Actual Experience Continuum which stretches between two extremes: *Hyper Reality* and *Actual Reality*.

The agility of our scale is made possible through using Empathy Maps from the Design Thinking framework, which companies and enterprises are adopting to innovatively solve problems [20]. Empathy Map is a collaborative user research tool used by designers and developers to get closer to the actual needs of the end-user they are creating an application or service for. It is generally made of four quadrants that collate data about what the user Thinks, Feels, Does and Says. Experts and end-users participate in creating this data to form conceptual cognitive, emotional, attitudal, behavioral and physical model that reflect actual states.

We have applied Design Thinking and created Empathy Maps for clients in a multitude of industry domains. We have witnessed first-hand how they help consultants and user researchers resolve ambiguity and gain deep empathetic understanding (and set aside own assumptions) of the needs, desires and hurdles of conceptual personas.

Also, we have previous experience building AR and VR systems. We understand the challenges that may impact the sense of immersion in such systems (e.g. navigation, pose tracking, interaction models, agency, visuals quality, motion-sickness, multisensory feedback, etc.). Hence, it was logical for us to explore assessing such challenges by applying the principles and values from the Design Thinking.

In the next section, we review the relevant research concerned with evaluating presence in MR. This is followed by an introduction to (1) our new Hyper-Actual Experience Continuum, (2) details on the Hyper/Actual Immersiveness Scale and how Empathy Maps are utilized, and (3) an explanation of the convergence process of the three, before concluding with what we see as potential future work.

2 Related Work

Prominent research contribution has been made in the area of evaluating UX and presence in MR [4, 12, 26, 27, 29, 33]. Authors of those comprehensive surveys cumulatively reviewed hundreds of previous research papers to categorize the effort and highlight gaps. They unanimously agree that for MR systems to reap their value, research should shift focus from studying it as a "technology-centric medium" to explore more of the benefits, drawbacks and impact on the user. According to [4], the available user-centric studies of human perception and cognition in AR are limited to examining issues like effects of alterative rendering techniques, depth-perception and effects of display specifications. Analyzing general experience, behavior and attitude is still lacking.

Gabbard et al. [9] for example argued that user-based experiments are critical for driving better design activities, usability studies and experience discovery in VR. They proposed a cost-effective progressive method that leveraged a set of heuristic guidelines to evaluate usability. It revolved around (1) defining the intended user tasks, (2) analyzing their potential usability problems, (3) comparing them to established interaction design principles, (4) applying formative user-centered evaluations, and finally (5) performing comparative empirical assessments with maturing interactions designed to elicit similar user tasks.

Similarly Ristos and colleagues [26] have developed another foundational assessment framework for UX in AR that can be expanded on a case-by-case basis. They created conceptual core groups that feed input to their system from several sources (visual, auditory, haptic, kinesthetic and sensory fusion), and produce multi-form output. It takes into account the underlying correlation of the use-case, context, health and safety, and integrity, privacy and security. All these contribute to measuring immersion but they rely on human observation, user surveys and using tracking sensors (e.g. cameras, touchscreens, accelerometers, heart rate, etc.) to capture their data.

Although each of Ristos' grouping of notions and Gabbard's progressive stages adapt to their specific requirements, the frameworks remain largely dependent on fixed sets of assessment questions and dimensions defined by the researchers (not considering the variable user situation).

On the other hand, Dünser et al. [5] proposed applying common HCI principles such as affordance, reducing cognitive overhead, and low physical effort to design productive AR applications. Although their approach is for heuristic evaluation and usability inspection, not for measuring presence, it is still valid to consider here. If an AR interface is not designed well to perform its intended task easily, it becomes a distraction and degrades the overall performance, defeating the meaning of presence.

Another approach utilized creating scenarios in an online survey to evaluate AR service concepts in early development phases [23]. The scenarios Olsoon and collogues evaluated were materialized as language-based descriptions of the assumed use of AR. They aimed at eliciting a metaphorical experience of the envisioned application. This study however focused more on the experiential aspects of AR and user acceptance issues, not perceptual or usability issues.

It is worth noting that Kalawsky [15] questioned the validity of using presence at all to evaluate performance in immersive environments. He argued that in order to properly measure presence, researchers need to consider inter-sensory interactions to resolve perceptual conflicts. He suggests that even if that is done, the user will experience fewer sensory cues in virtual environments than in the real world which would result in incorrect sensory simulation and as a result distorted presence. Kalawsky's point remains valid until today. The current technical state-of-the art has not reached a point where it could simulate realistic perceptions simultaneously across several sensory modalities. This is however the envisioned future denoted as "Actual Reality" in this paper.

3   Hyper and Actual Experience Continuum

Milgram et al. introduced his Reality-Virtuality Continuum in [19] and explained that it aimed at classifying MR visual displays and the nature of scenes presented on them, virtual or real. They accounted for the mixture of computer-generated elements and real objects to work out their classification criteria. The Hyper-Actual Experience Continuum we introduce here focusses more on classifying the "human experience" factors delivered by those displays. It presents an evaluation spectrum with two ends: Hyper Reality and Actual Reality.

Hyper Reality is a provocative concept coined by the designer Matsuda [18]. It presents a vision of a future where the physical and virtual realities merge and it produces a city experience that is saturated with media, contextual information and call to-action triggers as shown in Fig. 1.

a. gestural driven AR search   b. ambient city AR info   c. in-store AR virtual assistant

Fig. 1. Screenshots from the Hyper Reality concept video by Matsuda [18]

The word "saturated" is key here as it emphasizes the negative implications that too many superimposed virtual artifacts would bring to the experience with the augmented real world. The user (almost) gets blocked away from their surroundings by the overwhelming virtual stimuli. The noisy and superficial visuals form perceptually conflicting cues that reinforce user presence in a contradicting environment [15].

This is the anti-pattern of immersion in AR. It forms the first extreme experience in the Hyper-Actual Experience Continuum which is made of 5 levels, with 1 = Hyper Reality (center) and 5 = Actual Reality (outside), Fig. 2. MR applications should aim to radiate away from Hyper Reality and have their virtual content to serve its purpose of immersing and improving the ergonomics with its container environment in more realistic fashion, not to conflict with the senses.

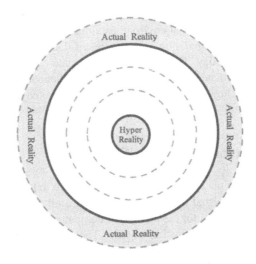

Fig. 2. Hyper-Actual Experience Continuum

On the other end of the spectrum sits *Actual Reality*, a wishful level of 100% realistic experience that delivers true presence. Theoretically, it would synchronize all sensory modalities including tactile, visual, auditory and proprioception with photo-realistic visuals. It is assumed to teleport users to the reality it endorses (augmented or virtual).

Y&R, a digital agency, created the Actual Reality term for a VR campaign for Jaguar F-TYPE Sports Car [32]. They had a real car exhibit in one motor show where attendees sat in the passenger seat and were given fake VR headsets through which they were told could experience "exactly what it is like on the track", Fig. 3. This pre-empted perceptual beliefs that it was a VR experience, whilst in reality it wasn't.

The headset was nothing but a VR pass-through device showing a feed from a foward facing camera. What users assumed to be VR simulation on the headset screen was a live video of an actual stunt ride on a real race course they were taken on behind the exhibit stage, performed by an experienced precision driver sat next to them. The excessive acceleration, engine roars, body rolling, and action turns all were real, contrary to the preconceptions participants were made to believe, and the mental model they were set into.

a. real car on hydraulic axes   b. camera feed in fake headset   c. user on actual stunt ride

Fig. 3. Screenshots from Jaguar F-Type Actual Reality VR campaign video [32]

Delivering an experience that makes the user question their senses is the ultimate target of immersion in MR. Actual Reality advocates this and forms the other extreme experience in our continuum, the outside of the continuum as shown in Fig. 2. It represents plausible illusions with inter-sensory intersection [15] that makes people really feel as if they were there, when "there" does not really exist.

The above two concepts emerged to us as a result of continuously observing and analyzing the development of AR and VR in the industry. They form the metric to benchmark MR applications against with the following two guidelines:

- Hyper Reality corresponds to how immersion should not be convoluted by computer generated artifacts that lead to obtrusive experiences
- Actual Reality shows the degree of complemented realism that MR experiences should be designed to match

4   The Hyper/Actual Immersiveness Scale

Much like any user-centered application, AR and VR offer personal experiences with multifarious first-person perspectives. Impressions and psychological modes are influenced variably. What could relate to one user may not for another, and that changes fundamentally with the environment it is applied in or the nature of application used. For example, the ergonomic requirements and immersion level that one would experience in IKEA Place AR, a furniture placement mobile app, from the comfort of their sofa [14] is far more different from that of a Thyssenkrupp field engineer looking at an AR manual to fix a faulty elevator hanging in the air [25].

Additionally, presence is a subjective sensation, much like mental workload. It is a mental manifestation that is not so amenable to objective physiological definition and measurement [28]. This said, we believe that any measurement method used to assess the sense of immersion in AR and VR must adhere to those contextual variances and constraints, and consider the people involved in them.

Hyper/Actual Immersiveness Scale is a subjective evaluation method that is adaptive and user-driven, not predefined by researchers' fixed set of questions. It permits test subjects to intrinsically create the "dimensions" to assess immersiveness against as they engage with the test MR application. We refer to those dimensions as *evaluation points.* These points are equivalent to questions on traditional question-naires, but they do not exhibit the same instructiveness and interference questioning would often introduce [30]. They emerge naturally from the flow of conversation between "authoring" users and the experiment coordinators though Empathy Mapping.

An Empathy Map is a poster-size graphic that is broken into four quadrants as Fig. 4 illustrates: Thinks, Feels, Does and Says. Those form the core "human factors" we elicit in our scale [21]. It allows for building a holistic, hypothetical picture of all cognitive and physical modes of an assumed persona. Traditionally, UX specialists, Design Thinking practitioners, client representatives and sponsor users, i.e. actual users, work together in discovery workshops to prescribe those modes. They explore what and how the persona says, does, thinks and feels when using that application [11]. Each participant writes down their individual thoughts on sticky notes and sticks them on the corresponding quadrant on the Empathy Map as Fig. 4 shows. The group then analyzes the collateral, validates it and concludes a common "perceived" understanding of that persona's position and mindset.

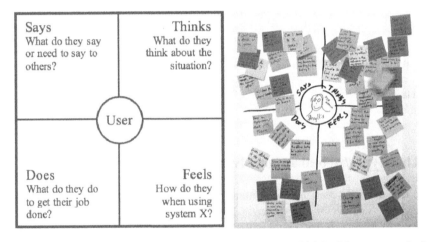

Fig. 4. (left) Empathy Map of the cognitive and physical states; (right) sticky notes on the four human zones of an Empathy Map

We have adopted Empathy Maps as the core of our Hyper/Actual Immersiveness Scale to measure the influence an AR or VR application has on the four human factors. One major difference we have introduced though to its traditional application is that we require running the discovery workshop with real users of the application being studied, not experts who try to empathize with a persona and think like them.

We want qualitative behavioral data in each of the four quadrants that feeds back actual feelings, thoughts, actions and verbal expressions of *real users* (not fictional). In other words, the documented evaluation points on sticky notes would reflect first-person impressions. This is required since, as discussed earlier, opinions vary from one to another depending on the depth of their emotional arousal, perception of the graphical illusions, and prior experiences with MR [23]. Those experts though can still participate as test subject in the evaluation.

The other variation to standard Empathy Maps is its augmentation with the Hyper/Actual Reality Continuum as in Fig. 5. This produces an artifact that allows participants themselves to quantitatively evaluate their thoughts and feelings on the sticky notes. Each note gets assessed against how "actual" or "hyper" it felt, looked and sounded, and gets placed on the correct scale circle within its quadrants (out of 5 levels).

The final result is a chart with all evaluation points sorted by their realistic/natural characteristics and acceptance by all participants, on the four human factors and with a scale value. These cumulatively generate a total immersion score as detailed next.

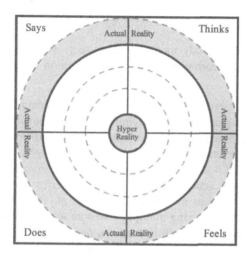

Fig. 5. Empathy Map combined with Hyper-Actual Experience Continuum

5 Using the Scale and Getting a Score

Using the Hyper/Actual Immersiveness Scale for evaluating MR applications is like the rest of the Design Thinking framework tools. It simply requires understanding of the process flow, basic preparation for the discovery workshop, some practice and organization, and a lot of sticky notes. Below are the steps for the complete process:

Step 1: Find a quiet and reasonably sized room with no obstacles to run the MR experiment in. It must have enough wall space to hang the Empathy Map poster (Fig. 4) on and floor space for participants to gather around and discuss.

Step 2: Recruit enough test subjects from various experience backgrounds to get balanced scalar variance that does not make the mean score misleading [3]. According to Ritch et al. [17], there is no one-size-fits-all for determining the optimal size of test participants in usability studies. It varies based on the nature of the experiment and intended outcome. The research suggests that 3 to 20 participants can provide valid results. Based on our past experience running Design Thinking workshops (not within MR context), we recommend having around 10 users. The amount of sticky notes that would be generated from 10 participants during a 10 min Empathy Mapping session (as detailed in step 6 below) would produce enough thoughts and experience reflections for the evaluation metric.

Step 3: At the beginning of the session, introduce the experiment and your AR or VR application to participants, without exposing too much detail that could distort their raw cognitive mode or create preconceptions. This could lead to biased evaluation points on the quadrants and skew final results.

Step 4: Collect the following information from each participant before experiment (short profiling questionnaire to assess deviations in the results or for analytics):

- Age category
- Level of any prior experience with AR, VR or both, using Likert rating scale [16] with 0 being "no previous experiences" and 6 being "used 10 + applications on several device form-factors"
- Any vision, hearing or body motor disorders (e.g. wearing glasses, having poor sight but no glasses, hearing aids, slow bodily reaction time, biomechanical limitation, etc.)

Step 5: Run the MR experiment with each participant separately. Depending on the type of application being assessed, a time limit for the experiment could be introduced, or it could be tracked based on task(s) completion. Ask participants to think aloud if they can without exaggeration (so assessor can capture thoughts and feelings). If there is a group (maximum of 4 at one time), run parallel experiments in isolated rooms so that verbal expressions or actions do not susceptibly interfere with others' judgement. Capture as many observations of their cognitive and physical states around the four human factors as possible. Having multiple assessors would make this more efficient where one could watch the physical interactions outside the MR application, and the other track engagement within (through an external monitor). Those expert observations would be useful for cross checking at a later stage during the evaluation process.

Step 6: Once the experiment is complete, ask participants (individuals or groups) to gather around the Empathy Map poster on the wall. Explain what that artefact is for and how to use it. Then, let them spend 10 min jotting down their feelings, thoughts, sayings and doings that they expressed during the MR experiment on sticky notes and stick them on the corresponding quadrants (as described previously). Encourage group discussions as that validates common beliefs and drives more realistic input into the process.

Step 7: When time runs out, go through the collateral of sticky notes with the group and discuss their thinking process and opinions. Try to cluster similar notes together, this will be handy when calculating the score. Compare what is on the map with your captured observations in Step 5 and validate your impressions with the groups'. If any not covered, elicit a provocative discussion to analyze whether it applies or not.

Step 8: Explain the process of evaluating the sticky notes using the Hyper-Actual Experience Continuum to the whole group at once. Briefly define what Hyper and Actual experiences mean and play Matsuda's Hyper Reality video [18] and Jaguar's F-Type fake VR campaign video [32] to illustrate the two extremes of the continuum. Advise participants to think about the positive and negative vibes demonstrated in the videos and use that as their benchmark. When done, present the second version of the empathy map with the continuum augmented on it, Fig. 5. Put it on the wall next to the basic Empathy Map already used.

Step 9: Ask participants to retrospectively move the sticky notes from the first map to the correct scale circle that defines its Hyper or Actual level on the second. Group communication and discussion is key here to reach a common and reliable consensus. This is where the power of the Hyper/Actual Immersiveness Scale lays (user-driven analysis). The group self-directs and decides collectively the relevance and effect that the documented evaluation points had on the experiment and their sense of immersion. They adjust the score on the continuum-augmented Empathy Map according to the overall feedback. If some evaluation points have been clustered, i.e. same note documented by multiple participants in the same group, then this becomes its default score.

Step 10: Finally, calculate a final score. Because participants are left to their freedom to document their attitude, emotions and actions (yet guided throughout the process), the evaluation points captured on the Empathy Map tend to differ from one user to another or from experiment to experiment. The way we balance this deviation is by calculating the total for the different evaluation points on each of the four quadrants, regardless of what those points were. If they relate to one human factor and have been quantified by the group then they valuably contribute to the overall experience on that quadrant. The total points score for each human factor gets averaged and a final immersiveness score is calculated from the average of all, presented in the following format:

$$I_{s|f|t|d}$$

where s, f, t and d are the average of evaluation points for each human factor: Says, Feels, Thinks and Does respectively, and I is the total immersiveness average. The higher the I the more Actual the experience has been deemed by the group. However, the variation in the evaluation would point values is the actual indication of where the experience needs be improved. For example, if s, f and t are high and d is low it means that the user is likely to be more immersed visually and audially but less engaged physically, they are exposed to more of a passive experience. Allowing navigation or interactions could increase immersion more.

6 Conclusion and Next Steps

The Hyper/Actual Immersiveness Scale we present in this paper is non-instrumental. It is not a script or a fixed researcher questionnaire like the conventional presence evaluation methods discussed by the research community. Rather, it is a process driven by real users that adapts to their feedback and perceptions. They collaboratively and democratically describe the cognitive and physical states they experience in MR. The framework guides them through to reach a quantitative scientific result that use at its core qualitative behavioral data sourced by the wisdom of the crowd.

Although this data may sound variable and inconsistent across users, experiments and environments, all input parameters funnel through the four paramount mind and body states to generate abstract, yet normalized picture of the true immersion degree.

It removes "confusion of" or "misunderstanding" survey questions that could be caused by language skills barriers. Participants do express their experiences with their own language, associate it to a known human factor, and simply give it a weight.

The score we get from applying the scale gives indication as to what human factor angles need be improved to bring immersion in MR closer to the sought-after Actual Reality. Having natural experiences mediated through immersive technologies such as AR and VR is the ultimate goal, and having a flexible natural measurement paradigm that helps quantifying that more accurately is the purpose of this work.

We have created a continuum to use for assessing immersion in AR and VR. We have also defined a process to evaluate and score it. Our next step is to use this method to evaluate actual MR applications in lab and non-lab environments and report our findings. We have introduced the theory and we need to evaluate its effectiveness in real situations. We hope the research community would evaluate it too with their own work, or compare it against existing immersion/presence analysis frameworks. The constitutes of the method are agile and flexible, and so the method itself. The more it gets applied, that more it will adapt and incrementally improve.

References

1. Arifina, Y., Sastria, T., Barlian, E.: User experience metric for augmented reality application: a review. Procedia Comput. Sci. **135**, 648–656 (2018)
2. Avery, B., Piekarski, W., Warren J., Thomas, B.: Evaluation of user satisfaction and learnability for outdoor augmented reality gaming. In: 7th Australasian User interface conference, pp. 17–24 (2006)
3. Bustamante, E., Spain, R.: Measurement invariance of the Nasa TLX. In: Proceedings of the Human Factors and Ergonomics Society Annual Meeting, vol. 52, pp. 1522–1526 (2008)
4. Dönser, D., Grasset, R., Seichter, H., Billinghurst, M.: A survey of evaluation techniques used in augmented reality studies. Technical report, HIT Lab NZ, University of Canterbury (2008)
5. Dönser, D., Grasset, R., Seichter, H., Billinghurst, M.: Applying HCI principles to AR systems design. In: 2nd International Workshop at the IEEE Virtual Reality Conference (2017)
6. Dirin, A., Laine, T.: User experience in mobile augmented reality: emotions, challenges, opportunities and best practices. Computers **7**, 33 (2018)
7. Fenn, J. Raskino, M.: Emerging technologies hype cycle is here. Gartner (2010). https://blogs.gartner.com/hypecyclebook/2010/09/07/2010-emerging-technologies-hypecycle-is-here/. Accessed 04 Aug 2018
8. Forni, A.: Gartner identifies three megatrends that will drive digital business into the next decade. Gartner. https://www.gartner.com/en/newsroom/press-releases/2017–08–15-gartner-identifies-three-megatrends-that-will-drive-digital-business-into-the-next-decade. Accessed 04 Aug 2018
9. Gabbard, J., Hix, D., Swan, J.: User-centered design and evaluation of virtual environments. IEEE Comput. Graph. Appl. **19**, 51–59 (1999)
10. Gabbard, J., Swan, J., Hix, D., Kim, S., Fitch, G.: Active text drawing styles for outdoor augmented reality: a user-based study and design implications. In: IEEE Virtual Reality Conference, pp. 5–42 (2007)

11. Gibbons, S.: Empathy mapping: the first step in design thinking. Nielsen Norman Group. https://www.nngroup.com/articles/empathy-mapping/. Accessed 29 Jul 2018
12. Irshad, S., Rohaya, D., Rambli, A.: Advances in mobile augmented reality from user experience perspective: a review of studies. In: International Visual Informatics Conference, pp. 466–477 (2017)
13. Irshad, S., Rohaya, D., Rambli, A., Adhani, N., Shukri, S., Omar, Y.: Measuring user experience of mobile augmented reality systems through non-instrumental quality attributes. In: 5th International Conference on User Science and Engineering (2018)
14. IKEA place app website. https://highlights.ikea.com/2017/ikea-place/. Accessed 31 Aug 2018
15. Kalawsky, R.: The validity of presence as a reliable human performance metric in immersive environments. In: 3rd International Workshop on Presence (2000)
16. Likert, R.: A technique for the measurement of attitudes. Arch. Psychol. **22**(140), 1–55 (1932)
17. Macefiel, R.: How to specify the participant group size for usability studies: a practitioner's guide. J. Usability Stud. **5**(1), 34–45 (2009)
18. Matsuda, K.: Hyper reality website. http://hyper-reality.co/. Accessed 05 Aug 2018
19. Milgram, P., Kishino, F.: Taxonomy of mixed reality visual displays. Trans. Inf. Syst. **12**(12), 1321–1329 (1994)
20. Mootee, I.: Design Thinking for Strategic Innovation. Wiley, New Jersey (2013)
21. Moray, N.: Ergonomics. Taylor & Francis, London (2005)
22. Olsson, T., Ihamäki, P., Lagerstam, E., Ventä-Olkkonen, L., Väänänen-Vainio-Mattila, K.: User expectations for mobile mixed reality services: an initial user study. In: European Conference on Cognitive Ergonomics (2009)
23. Olsson, T., Kärkkäinen, T., Lagerstam, E., V-Olkkonen, L.: User evaluation of mobile augmented reality scenarios. J. Ambient Intell. Smart Environ **4**(1), 29–47 (2012)
24. Pesudovs, K.: The development of a symptom questionnaire for assessing virtual reality viewing using a head-mounted display. Optom. Vis. Sci. **82**, 571 (2005)
25. Ridder, M.: Thyssenkrupp unveils latest technology to transform the global elevator service industry: Microsoft HoloLens, for enhancing interventions. Thyssenkrupp. https://www.thyssenkrupp.com/en/newsroom/press-releases/press-release-114208.html. Accessed 29 Jul 2018
26. Ritsos, P., Ritsos, D., Gougoulis, A.: Standards in augmented reality: a user experience perspective. In: 2nd International Workshop on AR Standards (2011)
27. Riva, G., Davide, F., IJsselsteijn, W.: Being There. IOS Press, Amsterdam (2003)
28. Sheridan, T.: Musings on telepresence and virtual presence. Presence Teleoperators Virtual Environ. **1**, 120–126 (1992)
29. Skarbez, R., Brooks Jr., F., Whitton, M.: A survey of presence and related concepts. ACM Comput. Surv. **50**, 1–39 (2017)
30. Slater, M.: Presence and the sixth sense. Presence Teleoperators Virtual Environ. **11**, 435–439 (2002)
31. Siegel, J., Bauer, M.: A field usability evaluation of a wearable system. In: 1st IEEE International Symposium on Wearable Computers (1997)
32. Stuff website: Jaguar blurs the lines between 'Virtual' and 'Reality' in driving prank. https://www.stuff.co.nz/motoring/shows/73553944/jaguar-blurs-the-lines-between-virtualand-reality-in-driving-prank. Accessed 28 July 2018
33. Swan, E., Gabbard, J.: Survey of user-based experimentation in augmented reality. In: 1st International Conference on Virtual Reality, pp. 1–9 (2005)

Investigating Children's Immersion in a High-Embodied Versus Low-Embodied Digital Learning Game in an Authentic Educational Setting

Yiannis Georgiou[1,2(✉)], Andri Ioannou[1,2], and Marianna Ioannou[2]

[1] Research Center on Interactive Media, Smart Systems and Emerging Technologies (RISE), Nicosia, Cyprus
[2] Cyprus Interaction Lab, Cyprus University of Technology, Limassol, Cyprus
ioannis.georgiou@cut.ac.cy

Abstract. Prior research has supported that game-based learning is dependent on the degree of immersion achieved, namely the degree to which children become cognitively and emotionally engaged with a given educational digital game. With the emergence of embodied digital educational games, researchers have assumed that the affordances of these games for movement-based interaction may heighten even more experienced immersion. However, there is lack of empirical research on the investigation of children's immersive experiences in embodied educational games, warranting this claim. Existing research on immersion is still restricted in highly-controlled laboratory settings and focuses on non-educational embodied games played by mostly young adult populations. Extending prior research in the educational context, this study has investigated children's immersion in a high-embodied digital learning game integrated in an authentic school classroom (Group1 = 24), in comparison to a low-embodied digital version of the game (Group2 = 20). Our findings did not support previous hypotheses regarding experienced immersion in high-embodied digital games; post-interventional surveys indicated that there was no difference in most dimensions of experienced immersion. Interviews with a subset of the children (n = 8 per condition) resulted in the identification of various (a) media form, (b) media content and (c) context-related factors, which provided plausible explanations about children's experienced immersion in the two conditions. Implications are discussed for supporting immersion in high-embodied educational digital games implemented in authentic educational settings.

Keywords: Embodied digital games · Children · Immersion · Educational settings

1 Introduction and Theoretical Framing

Immersion, as a gradated and multi-level process of cognitive and emotional involvement in digital educational games is often argued as one of the main driving forces behind children's engagement and learning [1–3]. Importantly, an increasing corpus of empirical studies has supported that heightened levels of immersion in digital

© Springer Nature Switzerland AG 2019
D. Beck et al. (Eds.): iLRN 2019, CCIS 1044, pp. 222–233, 2019.
https://doi.org/10.1007/978-3-030-23089-0_17

educational games can increase students' performance and subsequent learning [4–7]. The emergence of embodied digital educational games, which are grounded in motion-based technologies (e.g., Wii, Xbox Kinect, Leap Motion) and integrate gestures or even full-body movement into the act of learning [8] has renewed the interest in the investigation of immersive experiences. In particular, researchers have argued that the motion-based affordances of high-embodied digital games may heighten experienced immersion in comparison to prior digital games, as they allow more natural interactions closer to the task to be achieved, reduce the gamers' physical passivity, and provide an additional channel to the gamers for feeling challenged [9, 10].

Despite these arguments, there is lack of empirical research with a clear focus on the investigation of children's experienced immersion in high-embodied educational games, warranting these claims. Learning via embodied educational games is still a nascent field. Existing studies have mostly adopted experimental research for investigating whether embodied educational games may have a positive impact on students' learning or not, or design-based research to guide the principled development of embodied educational games [11, 12]. According to Karakostas, Palaigeorgiou and Kompatsiaris [13] research on high-embodied digital educational games is still fragmented, driven by specific technological innovations, and often lacking a clear focus on investigating their affordances and limitations within real classroom settings.

Acknowledging the vital role of immersion in relation to students' learning, it seems crucial to obtain a better understanding of whether and under what circumstances embodied digital educational games can have a positive impact on students' experienced immersion, when integrated in authentic educational settings. Despite this realization, relevant empirical studies on the investigation of experienced immersion is limited to the use of non-educational embodied games with young adults' populations in highly-controlled laboratory settings [14, 15]. Considering that experienced immersion depends not only on the media form (high-embodied versus low-embodied interfaces), but also on media content factors, user and context-related factors [16–18], in this study we have extended prior research in the educational context.

This study has investigated children's immersion in a high-embodied version (Kinect-based version) of the "Alien Health" digital game when integrated in an authentic school classroom, in comparison to the low-embodied version (Desktop-based version) of the same game. While prior studies, have investigated the learning affordances of the "Alien Health" game and have provided empirical substantiation supporting its learning efficacy [8, 20, 27], the present study is focused on investigating children's immersive experiences around this game. In particular, although the game was designed to instruct about nutrition, as part of this study, we were interested in investigating other aspects of this digital game focusing on the following research questions:

(a) Is there a difference in children's experienced immersion between the low- and high-embodied digital educational game conditions? and

(b) What were the main factors contributing to experienced immersion in the two conditions, as perceived by the children?

2 Methods

2.1 Participants

Forty-four 4th graders (aged 8–9 years old), who were enrolled in a public primary school participated in this study. Children were randomly assigned to the two conditions. Group1 (Kinect-based gaming condition) had 24 children (12 boys, 50%) and Group2 (Desktop-based gaming condition) had 20 children (11 boys, 55%). Before the intervention consent forms were obtained by the students' legal guardians.

2.2 Research Design

This study was grounded in an explanatory sequential design, composed of two sequential phases [19]. During the first phase, we adopted a two-group experimental design for investigating children's learning and immersion per condition. Next, we proceeded with qualitative data collection phase to deepen our understanding of the factors contributing to the children's immersion in each condition.

2.3 The Digital Game

As part of the teaching intervention we have employed the "Alien Health" digital game, which was designed to teach 4th–12th grades about nutrition [8, 20]. According to the backstory of the game children are asked to help an Alien, who is in charge of stopping the collision of an asteroid with the Earth; however, the alien is hungry, and he cannot communicate. Children's mission is to make the right nutritional choices for the alien to make him feel better. To achieve this goal, during the gameplay, children are presented with combinations of food, and are requested to make a choice, within a predefined timeframe, considering a constellation of five nutrients per food.

The specific digital learning game was chosen for two reasons. First, the digital game was available in both a low-embodied (desktop-based) and in a high-embodied (Kinect-based) version. According to the four-level taxonomy of embodiment suggested by Johnson-Glenberg, Birchfield, Tolentino, and Koziupa [21] desktop-based games are included in the two lowest levels of the taxonomy as they provide no opportunities for sensorimotor engagement. In contrast, Kinect-based games, which allow hand gestures or body movements closely mapped to the educational content that must be learned, are included in the upper levels of the taxonomy. Second, the digital game was subject to a feasibility study and findings indicated its acceptability by the children as well as its affordances to improve within-group content knowledge [6, 20]. However, although the game was designed to instruct about nutrition, as part of this study, we were interested in investigating other aspects of this digital game, focusing on children's immersive experiences.

2.4 The Interventions

Considering the research goals of this study, an 80-min intervention was developed and implemented in an authentic school classroom for each condition. Children in the low-embodied (desktop) condition were divided into pairs and used the desktop-based version of the digital game; in this version children used the mouse and the keyboard for making a choice and feeding the alien (see Fig. 1). On the other hand, in the Kinect-based condition, the children worked in groups of four as, due to the limited space of the classroom, we could only host up to six Kinect stations; yet the projection screen was large enough to allow access to all the members of the group (see Fig. 2). It should also be noted that although the game was based on a single player mode, some collaborative educational elements were included to the test conditions. In particular, the children in each group took turns in playing; the child(ren) in the rest of the group was/were asked to provide feedback to the player and after each round all the players were gathered together for reporting their food choices on a structured worksheet, discussing the selections made.

Fig. 1. A group in the low-embodied condition   **Fig. 2.** A group in the high-embodied condition

2.5   Data Collection and Analysis

2.5.1   Baseline Data

We collected baseline data using a survey, aiming at creating a profile for the children and establishing the equivalency of the two conditions. The survey had two main parts: *Gaming attitudes* and *Attitudes towards computers*. *Gaming attitudes* was measured using a Likert scale with 11 items, using a five-point Likert scale, derived from the survey of Bonanno and Kommers [22], as this was adapted and validated in the study of Bressler and Bodzin [23]. The Cronbach's alpha for the adapted instrument was $\alpha = 0.73$. Children's attitudes towards computers was assessed using the *Computer Attitude Measure for Young Students* (CAMYS) [24], which was composed of 12 items, using a five-point Likert scale. The CAMYS is considered a valid instrument and has a documented reliability alpha coefficient of $\alpha = 0.85$.

2.5.2   Immersion Survey

After the implementation, children completed the Game Immersion Questionnaire (GIQ) which measured their experienced immersion [2]. In particular children were asked to complete

(a) the *Engagement* scale, which is comprised of three subscales with a total of 9 items (Cronbach's $\alpha = 0.86$): *Attraction* (4 items, Cronbach's $\alpha = 0.81$), *Usability* (2 items, Cronbach's $\alpha = 0.73$), and *Time investment* (3 items, Cronbach's $\alpha = 0.70$),

(b) the *Engrossment* scale, which is comprised of two subscales with a total of 7 items (Cronbach's $\alpha = 0.86$): *Decreased perceptions* (4 items, Cronbach's $\alpha = 0.79$) and *Emotional attachment* (3 items, Cronbach's $\alpha = 0.79$), and

(c) the *Total Immersion* scale, which is comprised of two subscales with a total of 8 items (Cronbach's $\alpha = 0.92$): *Presence* (4 items, Cronbach's $\alpha = 0.88$) and *Empathy* (4 items, Cronbach's $\alpha = 0.87$)

2.5.3   Post-activity Interviews.

Eight children from each condition participated in semi-structured individual interviews, which took place after the intervention. Children were initially asked to report their feelings as these were related to their experienced immersion during the game-based activity (e.g. To what extent did you feel as being within the digital game rather than in the real environment? To what degree did the gaming activity capture all your senses?), and then they were probed to discuss the factors which contributed to their experienced immersion positively or negatively (e.g., What were the main factors contributing to your sense of being [or not] in the digital game? How did these factors contribute [or not] in your gaming experience?).

3   Data Analysis and Findings

3.1   Setting the Baseline

Potential differences in students' gaming attitudes and attitudes towards computers use between the groups were identified using a Mann-Whitney U test, given that the collected data did not follow a normal distribution. Results showed that there were no statistical differences in the children's gaming attitudes ($U_{(42)} = 217$, $z = -.54$, $p > .05$) and attitudes towards computers ($U_{(42)} = 203$, $z = -.87$, $p > .05$) between the groups.

3.2   Experienced Immersion

Potential differences in children's experienced immersion (three immersive levels and their dimensions) between the groups were identified using a Mann-Whitney U test, given that the collected data did not follow a normal distribution. Results showed that there were no statistical differences between the children's *Engagement* ($U_{(42)} = 171$, $z = -1.63$, $p > .05$), *Engrossment* ($U_{(42)} = 233.5$, $z = -.153$, $p > .05$) and *Total immersion* ($U_{(42)} = 218$, $z = -.519$, $p > .05$) in both conditions. Also, there were no statistically significant differences in the dimensions of the three immersive levels, with one exception. In particular, children in the low-embodied condition perceived the gaming activity as more user-friendly compared to the children in the high-embodied condition, and this difference was statistically significant ($U_{(42)} = 153$, $z = -2.09$, $p < .05$).

3.3   Factors Affecting Immersion

All interviews were transcribed and analyzed qualitatively using a top-down thematic analysis approach [25]. The factors identified as having contributed to the children's experienced immersion were classified in two basic themes (Table 1): (a) Media related factors including media form related factors (referring to the affordances of the gaming platform) and media content related factors (referring to the features of the gaming content) and, (b) Context related factors (referring to the characteristics of the physical environment and the pedagogical setting in which the game was contextualized).

These factors are discussed in the following subsections in relation to the two gaming conditions.

Table 1. The factors affecting experienced immersion per condition as reported by the children

		Condition 1 Kinect-based game*	Condition 2 Desktop-based game*
Media-related factors [Media form]	Projection	√	x
	Interface	√	x
	Controls	x	√
	Bodily movement	√	n/a
	Embodiment	√	n/a
	Single-player mode	x	x
	Synchronization	x	n/a
	Technical bugs	x	n/a
Media-related factors [Media content]	Narrative plot	√	√
	Gaming	√	√
	Learning nature	√	√
	Scaffolding	√	√
	Unrealistic items	x	x
	Time pressure	x	x
	Task difficulty	x	x
	Navigation	x	x
Context-related factors	Peer feedback	√	√
	Collaboration	√	√
	Waiting time	x	n/a
	Classroom arrangement	x	n/a
	Classroom noise	x	x

*(√) indicates the positively evaluated factors, (x) indicates the negatively evaluated factors and (n/a) indicates any factors that were not reported by the children per condition

3.3.1   Media Form Related Factors

According to the children using the high-embodied version of the game, the *large projection* (bigger screen providing more heightened sensory stimuli), the *interface* (with the use of novel technologies), the affordances of the gaming platform for promoting *bodily movement* (via the players' kinesthetic activity) and *embodiment* (via the gesture-based interactions) contributed to their experienced immersion. However, the children reported that the *controls* of the game were rather different from traditional gaming controls (e.g., keyboard, mouse). According to the children, moving the game screens forward with a hand closing action was clunky and tiresome, thus having a negative effect on their experienced immersion. In addition, the children reported that the *single-player mode* of the game, which transformed more of the group members as spectators, some *synchronization* issues often presented between player's movements and their belated projection on the screen, as well as some *technical bugs* (provoked by children's proximity to the Kinect), affected their experienced immersion negatively. On the other hand, the children of the low-embodied condition evaluated negatively most of the media form related factors. In particular, consistent with the children of the high-embodied condition they disliked the *single-player mode* of the game. In addition, they reported that the small projection (limited desktop screen) and the *interface* (traditional desktop-based computer with low graphics) had a negative effect on their experienced immersion. Yet, in contrast to the high-embodied condition, children in the low-embodied condition explained that the familiar desktop computer kept them engaged in the activity.

3.3.2 Media Content Related Factors

Given that the gaming content was similar in both conditions, it is not surprising that children in the high- and low-embodied setting evaluated the media content similarly, in relation to their experienced immersion. In particular, children in both conditions, highlighted the positive impact of the *narrative plot*, the *gaming features* (e.g., points and rewards), the integrated *scaffolding* (available hints on the nutritional value of each food), as well as the *learning nature* of the game (i.e. its innovative educational approach). On the other hand, children in both conditions highlighted that the *unrealistic items* (alien creature and, in some cases, alien food), the *task difficulty* (due to their lack of prior knowledge on the topic), the *navigation* within the game, and the *time pressure* (given that the game-based tasks which had to be accomplished in a limited timeframe) had often a negative effect on their experienced immersion.

3.3.3 Context Related Factors

Focusing on the context related factors, the low-embodied condition appears to be positively linked to the children's experienced immersion. More specifically, the children highlighted that the collaborative activity which framed the gaming activity, allowed a *productive collaboration* in their pairs (e.g., dialogue, exchange of views and ideas), while also promoted *peer feedback*. The only negative evaluated factor was classroom noise, which in some cases could even distract children's attention from the game. In contrast, according to the children in the high-embodied condition, it seems that most of the reported context-related factors were linked to the children's experienced immersion in a negative way. In particular, although children in this condition reported positively with respect to *peer feedback*, they negatively elaborated on the gaming activity as being framed by an *unstructured collaboration* with children often fighting over turn-taking and roles in the members of the group. In addition, they explained how the *waiting time* between turns, often resulted in off-task discussions and behaviors amongst the members of the group. The *classroom arrangement* which unintentionally allowed access to the projection screens of the other groups served as a distracting factor, as children could borrow solutions or intervene in the discussions and gameplay of other groups. All of these characteristics seemed to result in high levels of *classroom noise*, which was the most frequently reported factor negatively linked to children's experienced immersion in the high-embodied condition.

4 Discussion

With the emergence of embodied digital educational games, researchers have assumed that the affordances of these games for movement-based interaction may heighten experienced immersion [21]. However, there is lack of empirical research on the investigation of children's immersive experiences in embodied educational games, warranting this claim. Existing research on immersion is still restricted in highly-controlled laboratory settings and focuses on non-educational embodied games played by mostly young adult populations. Extending prior research in the educational context, this study has investigated children's immersion in a high-embodied digital learning game integrated in an authentic school classroom, in comparison to a low-embodied digital version of the game. Our findings are opposed to the findings of existing research in laboratory settings, which have previously supported the prevalence of high-embodied versus low-embodied games in young adults' experienced immersion [14, 15]. The analysis of post-interventional surveys indicated that there was no difference in most dimensions of experienced immersion with one exception. The children in the low-embodied condition deemed their gaming setting as a more user-friendly one, in comparison to the high-embodied condition.

Subsequent analysis of children's interviews regarding the factors affecting immersion between the two groups, shed more light on our findings about the children's immersive experience per condition. In particular, a set of factors related to the media form characteristics, indicated that despite the affordances of a larger projection, locomotion and embodiment, children in the high-embodied condition also reported on synchronization problems, difficulties in using the Kinect, and subsequent technical bugs. These usability issues seem to have had a detrimental effect on children's experienced immersion and could provide a plausible explanation for the difference in children's perceived usability between the two conditions. Additionally, aligned with the theoretical conceptualization of immersion as a multi-level process of cognitive and emotional involvement, such usability issues could serve as major barriers in children's successful transit via the immersive progression [1–3].

On the other hand, it is not a surprise that we have identified no difference on the media content factors when comparing the high- and low-embodied educational conditions, given that the gaming content was the same in both settings. In this context, while many content characteristics (e.g., narrative, gaming, scaffolding) were positively evaluated by the children, what seemed to have a negative influence on children's experienced immersion were the perceived tasks' difficulty in combination with time pressure and navigation difficulties within the game. Finally, what seemed to differentiate at a major degree children's experienced immersion, were a set of factors related to the context characteristics. In alignment with the study of Anderson and Wall [26], who investigated the integration of a high-embodied digital educational game in an authentic school classroom, we too found, for instance, that collaboration in the high-embodied condition was limited and quite unstructured. The detrimental effect on children's experienced immersion was also reinforced by the classroom arrangement in groups of 4 children, which increased the waiting time between players' turns, and resulted in children's off-tasks behaviors and classroom noise. In contrast, children in the low-embodied condition highlighted that the classroom arrangement in pairs, resulted in a productive collaboration and peer feedback, while also keeping in lower levels the classroom noise.

5   Limitations and Future Studies

Even though the findings of this study contribute to a better understanding of experienced immersion in high- and low-embodied digital games contextualized in authentic educational settings, some limitations of this work are also important to note. First, a set of study design challenges already discussed, such as the difference in the student group sizes per condition and therefore the students' different amount of time allocated on the gaming activity, might have affected students' immersive experiences. Future research could replicate this study trying to address these design challenges. Second, the sample of the study was small and drawn from two classrooms in a public primary school. Future research could replicate this study with a larger sample of classrooms, ideally drawn from randomly-selected schools (clustered sampling) to increase external validity (e.g., population validity). Third, this study mostly relied on self-reported and retrospective measures which may be regarded as a limitation. Future studies could use in-situ and objective measurements (e.g., eye gaze measurement via eye-trackers, EEGs, etc.) for investigating how the immersive process unfolds during the intervention. Finally, our findings are most relevant to the "Alien Health" as a specific desktop-based (low-embodied version) and Kinect-based (high-embodied version) digital game. However, this is only one example of an embodied digital educational game. Future studies could focus on different embodied digital educational games and their impact on children's immersion to examine the consistency of the reported findings in other contexts and settings (i.e., ecological validity).

6   Conclusions and Implications

Despite the limitations, the present study provides some first empirical evidence supporting that children's heightened levels of immersion during the implementation of high-embodied digital games in authentic educational contexts, should not be taken as a given. In addition, grounded in our findings we could state a set of guidelines for supporting children's immersion in high-embodied digital games implemented in real classroom settings:

1. Develop embodied games that integrate intuitive movements, that resemble movements in real life and are aligned to the users' skills and expectations.
2. Organize a training/demonstration session before the gaming activity to allow the children to familiarize themselves with the gaming controls.

3. Introduce and discuss with the children the learning topic before the gaming activity, as this could reduce the tasks' difficulty embedded in the game.
4. Plan for a smart classroom set-up and arrange for up to four Kinect-based stations (one per classroom side), splitting children's groups among the four sides of the classroom and avoiding inter-group interventions and subsequent distractions.
5. Work with smaller cohorts of children (up to 12 children) and divide them in groups of 2–3 members per Kinect station, rather than bigger groups.
6. Contextualize the game in a scripted collaborative setting, where clear roles, responsibilities, and even turn taking will be clear to all members of the group.
7. Proceed with the development of build-in collaboration features in high-embodied learning games, for involving simultaneously all the group members.
8. Develop high-embodied games with improved audio-visual characteristics for overpowering the sensory information derived from the physical world.
9. Develop high-embodied learning games combining the use of headsets and card-board glasses to improve the audio-visual sensory stimuli provided by the game.

The guidelines require the contribution of people from different disciplines: designers, programmers, educators and researchers, working together with a common goal – the design and enactment of more immersive high-embodied educational games in authentic classroom settings for advancing children's engagement.

Acknowledgements. This work is part of the project that has received funding from the European Union's Horizon 2020 research and innovation programme under grant agreement No 739578 (RISE-Call:H2020-WIDESPREAD-01-2016-2017-TeamingPhase2) and the government of the Republic of Cyprus through the Directorate General for European Programmes, Coordination and Development.

References

1. Brown, E., Cairns, P.: A grounded investigation of game immersion. In: CHI 2004 Extended Abstracts on Human Factors in Computing Systems, pp. 1297–1300. ACM (2004)
2. Cheng, M.-T., She, H.-C., Annetta, L.A.: Game immersion experience: its hierarchical structure and impact on game-based science learning. J. Comput. Assist. Learn. **31**(3), 232–253 (2015)
3. Georgiou, Y., Kyza, E.A.: The development and validation of the ARI questionnaire: an instrument for measuring immersion in location-based augmented reality settings. Int. J. Hum. Comput. Studies **98**, 24–37 (2017)
4. Cheng, M.-T., Linm, Y.-W., She, H.-C., Kuo, P.-C.: Is immersion of any value? Whether, and to what extent, game immersion experience during serious gaming affects science learning. Br. J. Edu. Technol. **48**, 246–263 (2016)
5. Georgiou, Y., Kyza, E.A.: Relations between student motivation, immersion and learning outcomes in location-based augmented reality settings. Comput. Hum. Behav. **89**, 173–181 (2018)

6. Georgiou, Y., Kyza, E.A.: A design-based approach to augmented reality location-based activities: investigating immersion in relation to student learning. In: Loizides, F., Papadopoulos, G., Souleles, N. (eds.) 16th World Conference on Mobile and Contextual Learning 2017, mLearn, vol. 1, International Association for Mobile Learning (IAmLearn), Larnaka (2017)

7. Rowe, J.P., Shores, L.R., Mott, B.W., Lester, J.C.: Integrating learning, problem solving, and engagement in narrative-centered learning environments. Int. J. Artif. Intell. Educ. **21**(1–2), 115–133 (2011)

8. Johnson-Glenberg, M.C., Savio-Ramos, C., Henry, H.: "Alien Health": a nutrition instruction exergame using the Kinect sensor. Games Health J. **3**(4), 241–251 (2014)

9. Pasch, M., Bianchi-Berthouze, N., van Dijk, B., Nijholt, A.: Immersion in movement-based interaction. In: Nijholt, A., Reidsma, D., Hondorp, H. (eds.) INTETAIN 2009. LNICST, vol. 9, pp. 169–180. Springer, Heidelberg (2009). https://doi.org/10.1007/978-3-642-02315-6_16

10. Bianchi-Berthouze, N.: Understanding the role of body movement in player engagement. Hum.-Comput. Interact. **28**(1), 40–75 (2013)

11. Georgiou, Y., Ioannou, A.: Embodied learning in a digital world: a systematic review of empirical research in K-12 education. In: Díaz, P., Ioannou, A., Spector, M., Bhagat K.-K. (eds.) Learning in a digital world: a multidisciplinary perspective on interactive technologies for formal and informal education. Springer series: Smart Computing and Intelligence. Springer (In press)

12. Sheu, F.R., Chen, N.S.: Taking a signal: a review of gesture-based computing research in education. Comput. Educ. **78**, 268–277 (2014)

13. Karakostas, A., Palaigeorgiou, G., Kompatsiaris, Y.: WeMake: a framework for letting students create tangible, embedded and embodied environments for their own STEAM learning. In: Kompatsiaris, I., et al. (eds.) INSCI 2017. LNCS, vol. 10673, pp. 3–18. Springer, Cham (2017). https://doi.org/10.1007/978-3-319-70284-1_1

14. Coppi, A.E., Lessiter, J., Freeman, J.: Get in the game: the influence of embodied play on presence and flow in videogames. In: Proceedings of the Interactive Technologies and Games Conference (ITAG), Nottingham (2014)

15. Lindley, S., Couteur, J.L., Bianchi-Berthouze, N: Stirring up experience through movement in game play: effects on engagement and social behaviour. In: Proceedings of the SIGCHI Conference on Human Factors in Computing Systems, pp. 511–514. ACM (2008)

16. Baños, R.M., Botella, C., Alcañiz, M., Liaño, V., Guerrero, B., Rey, B.: Immersion and emotion: their impact on the sense of presence. Cyberpsychol. Behav. **7**(6), 734–741 (2004)

17. Bleumers, L., Van Lier, T., Jacobs, A.: Presence and mediated interaction: a means to an end? In: Networked Television Adjunct proceedings of Euro ITV 2009, pp. 104–106 (2009)

18. Chung, J., Gardner, H.J.: Temporal presence variation in immersive computer games. Int. J. Hum.-Comput. Int. **28**(8), 511–529 (2012)

19. Creswell, J.W., Plano Clark, V.L.: Designing and Conducting Mixed Methods Research. Sage Publications, California (2011)

20. Johnson-Glenberg, M.C., Hekler, E.B.L.: "Alien Health Game": an embodied exergame to instruct in nutrition and MyPlate. Games Health J. **2**(6), 354–361 (2013)

21. Johnson-Glenberg, M.C., Birchfield, D.A., Tolentino, L., Koziupa, T.: Collaborative embodied learning in mixed reality motion-capture environments: two science studies. J. Educ. Psychol. **106**(1), 86–104 (2014)

22. Bonanno, P., Kommers, P.A.M.: Exploring the influence of gender and gaming competence on attitudes towards using instructional games. Br. J. Edu. Technol. **39**(1), 97–109 (2008)

23. Bressler, D.M., Bodzin, A.M.: A mixed methods assessment of students' flow experiences during a mobile augmented reality science game. J. Comput. Assist. Learn. **29**(6), 505–517 (2013)

24. Teo, T., Noyes, J.: Development and validation of a computer attitude measure for young students (CAMYS). Comput. Hum. Behav. **24**(6), 2659–2667 (2008)

25. Braun, V., Clarke, V.: Using thematic analysis in psychology. Qual. Res. Psychol. **3**(2), 77–101 (2006)

26. Anderson, J.L., Wall, S.D.: Kinecting physics: conceptualization of motion through visualization and embodiment. J. Sci. Educ. Technol. **25**(2), 161–173 (2016)

27. Ioannou, M., Georgiou, Y., Ioannou, A., Johnson-Glenberg, M.: On the understanding of students' learning and perceptions of technology integration in low- and high-embodied group learning. In: Proceedings of the 13th International Conference on Computer Supported Collaborative Learning (2019)

Using Cognitive Walkthrough and Hybrid Prototyping to Gather User Requirements in Early Design Virtual Reality Prototypes

Ioannis Doumanis[1](✉) and Daphne Economou[2]

[1] University of Central Lancashire, Preston, UK
idoumanis@uclan.ac.uk
[2] University of Westminster, London, UK
d.economou@westminster.ac.uk

Abstract. To evaluate Virtual Reality (VR) prototypes usability involves a variety of single-perspective or Hybrid methods. The latter has being suggested by literature as offering a more complete sets of requirements highlighting both 'in-world' and user interface problems. This paper describes our experiences in using a single-perspective method for gathering user requirements in the REVERIE (Real and Virtual Engagement In Realistic Immersive Environment) project. The study reports results involving nine evaluators who reviewed two hybrid VR prototypes with educational context. It was found that this approach was effective in highlighting a plethora of usability problems covering all aspects of the two VR prototypes. The performance of our approach was similar to the literature. Although additional validation work is required, we can conclude that our approach may provide a viable option to evaluate early design VR prototypes when required (e.g., when the expertise needed to use a hybrid method is not available). Future work aims to compare the performance of our approach with two-stage and multiple stage hybrid methods.

Keywords: Usability methods · Cognitive walkthrough · Virtual worlds · User interface · Interaction

1 Introduction

With the advent of virtual reality platforms (e.g., Oculus VR[1] and Steam VR[2]), it was not long before the medium was overrun with a plethora of applications. In the creation of such applications, designers typically collect and define user requirements by investigating the usability of VR prototypes [1]. This user-centered development process [2] uses either single-perspective or hybrid methods. A single-perspective method is an adapted Human-Computer Interaction (HCI) method [3, 4] to the requirements of the specific domain. A hybrid method applies more than one traditional HCI approach in the usability evaluation of VR prototypes (e.g., an extended cognitive

---

[1] https://www.oculus.com/

[2] http://store.steampowered.com/steamvr

D. Beck et al. (Eds.): iLRN 2019, CCIS 1044, pp. 234–246, 2019.
https://doi.org/10.1007/978-3-030-23089-0_18

walkthrough and virtual world heuristics [5]). As opposed to the former, hybrid methods can accommodate a greater range of usability problems by capturing domain-specific and user experience related issues (e.g., spatial navigation, orientation, UI, etc.). Thus, many researchers argue that using hybrid methods for usability evaluation may be more effective than using single-perspective methods [5].

Using a hybrid method may be well suited when experienced, and trained usability evaluators are available to review a VR prototype. However, in the absence of such expertise applying a hybrid method may be troublesome. In the study reported in this paper, we use a modified version of the cognitive walkthrough method [6]. This is an expert evaluation method used to examine the usability of a product. It requires one or more evaluators to walk through a series of tasks and ask a set of questions from the user perspective. We applied a modified method to two hybrid versions of the REVERIE prototypes [7, 8] (both REVERIES and the prototypes are described in Sect. 3.1). Those prototypes immersed users in two virtual environments (EU parliament in Brussels and a Virtual Gallery filled with cultural artefacts from various historical eras) where they had to participate in various educational activities. As the software was still in the early-design stage, we augmented the prototypes with storyboards and videos which provided evaluators with a step-by-step illustration of the missing user tasks (we dubbed this a hybrid prototype).

We found that our approach, single-perspective method and hybrid prototyping (see Sect. 3.2), identified a plethora of usability problems covering all aspects of the VR prototypes. We translated the usability problems into a high-quality set of user requirements to guide the future design of the prototypes. Another important deliverable of the study was a new method for effectively prioritising requirements. As opposed to existing methods, it captures input from multiple stakeholders in the requirements prioritisation process.

Our analysis shows that the proposed approach was effective in eliciting requirements for the REVERIE project. Relevant literature suggests that our approach generates comparable results to hybrid methods in usability evaluation. The remaining of the paper is organized as follows: Sect. 2 presents a review of the related work in the area; Sect. 3 gives a detailed account of the two VR applications developed using the REVERIE framework and discusses the procedure followed during the cognitive walkthrough process; Sect. 4 presents and discusses the results of the study, and the paper ends in Sect. 5 with the conclusions.

2 Related Work

Sawyerr et al., [5] suggest a two-stage hybrid method to evaluate the usability of VR prototypes. In the first stage, it uses an extended version of the Cognitive Walkthrough (CW) method [9] developed for 3D virtual environment systems. The goal of this stage is to identify usability problems related to 'in-world' interactions using a task-based approach. This method is composed of three cycles of interaction: task action; navigation; and system initiative. Within a given scenario, a user navigates around the VE to complete a given task. The system may interrupt task completion to provide guidance or help. The user may decline or accept the system initiative and resume navigation. In the second stage, the method uses a set of heuristics specifically developed for VEs [10, 11]. The set includes 16 usability heuristics and an associated usability checklist of 53 items that are grouped into three categories (i.e. Design and Aesthetics, Control and Navigation, and Errors and Help). The goal of this stage is to enhance the findings of the first stage by identifying usability problems in the user interface (UI). The researchers applied the method to a study designed to evaluate the usability of a VR application in the context of health and safety education. The cognitive walkthrough captured problems (3 problems) related to navigation. It also captured some problems (2 problems) related to task action. The system initiative did not occur within the selected scenario, and therefore it was not used. The heuristics found 36 problems mostly related to the design and aesthetics of the user interface (UI). The researchers conclude that using a hybrid method in usability evaluation may be more effective than using a single-perspective method.

This conclusion was further reiterated in the Alencar et al. study [12]. The researchers performed a usability evaluation in a technologically mature VR application (an oil platform visualisation) using a multiple-stage hybrid method consisting of several usability evaluation methods. The researchers applied heuristic evaluation [13], usage observation sessions [14], questionnaires and interviews [15] as well as the communicability evaluation method (CEM) [16] and compared the results. The combined methods identified 82 HCI issues with the VR prototype. The issues related to 'in-world' interactions and the user interface (UI) (e.g., speed of navigation and size of icons). The number of usability problems is significantly higher than the previous study which demonstrates the strength of hybrid methods in usability evaluation. However, the application of additional evaluation methods has several problems:

- it is an open question whether using a multiple-stage hybrid method is more effective than using a single-perspective or a two-stage hybrid method in early-design VR prototypes;
- it tends to increase the overall cost of the evaluation;
- some methods are complex to use even for HCI experts, for example to apply successfully the Communicability Evaluation Method (CEM) method requires evaluators to go through a list of complex steps [16].

For the evaluation of the hybrid REVERIE prototypes a simplified approach compared to the aforementioned studies was adopted. This approach consists of a modified cognitive walkthrough method. Although, utilising a fusion of methods might have extracted more usability problems our reviewers used it successfully to obtain useful results.

3   Materials and Methods

The evaluation of the hybrid REVERIE prototypes was conducted with evaluators using a modified version of the cognitive walkthrough method. The evaluators identified a range of usability problems with the two prototypes that led to the development of a series of design recommendations. These design recommendations define both the "what" and "how" to meet the physical and cognitive needs of the two VR prototypes target audience. We have prioritised the requirements (the "what" part of the design recommendations) based on the MoSCoW prioritisation method [23]. The method includes three items indicating different prioritisation levels. The "must-have" item refers to the requirements which were considered as essential for the prototypes to become ready for user testing and were all expected to be met by the next software release. The "should-have" item refers to requirements which are beneficial or useful to have in the next release of the prototypes. The "could have" item refers to requirements which could be met in a future version of the prototypes.

3.1   The REVERIE VR Prototypes

REVERIE's educational scenarios integrate a wide range of technologies and features (e.g., social networking services; tools to create personalised lookalike avatars; navigation support services; spatial adaptation techniques, AI techniques for responding to a user's emotional status) [7, 8] to create a realist and responsive learning experience for students and teachers online. In the first scenario, a group of students registered on the REVERIE social network are invited to a virtual educational trip to the EU Parliament in Brussels. The students can access an avatar authoring tool [17] which they can use to build custom avatars utilising their appearance (e.g., by mapping their face on the avatar). Once users are online, an Embodied Conversational Agent (ECA) invites them to an exploratory tour of the parliament VE. The participants' semi-autonomous avatars can automatically follow the autonomous agent through the tour. The destination is automatically given to each of the participants' avatars. The semi-autonomous avatars can also reflect each participant's facial expressions using a standard webcam. The ECA constantly analyses the user's attention and emotional status and responds accordingly much as a teacher would in a real world (e.g., try to get a student's attention if it was lost). The agent can demonstrate a range of pre-scripted behaviours (e.g., clapping, waving, happy and angry expressions, etc.) in response to the user's status. After the tour is over, the autonomous agent walks to the side of the parliament for the online debate session to start [18]. In the virtual debate session, each student presents a topic of their choice to their fellow students. Teachers can further engage and enthuse students by streaming video clips from TrueTube[3] in the virtual world. Finally, after the completion of each presentation students can vote for their preferred presentations and capture screenshots to share on their favourite social media channels. The second scenario maintains all these realistic and responsive functionalities, but immerses users in a different virtual world. Users enter a Virtual Gallery environment filled with 3D models of historical artefacts from various historical eras. There is no ECA in this scenario and users can start an educational activity as soon as they enter the world. In groups, they can observe and discuss the 3D models in a naturalistic way much as they would do in a real-world gallery.

---

[3] https://www.truetube.co.uk/

3.2   Hybrid Prototyping

At the time of running the study, the REVERIE prototypes were still on an early beta stage. To enable evaluators to review the prototypes, we augmented them with storyboards and videos to simulate the missing tasks. We call this approach hybrid prototyping (i.e., software prototype augmented with storyboards and videos). For example, the storyboard in Fig. 1, shows the required steps students have to take to capture a screenshot in the first VR prototype and share it on Facebook.

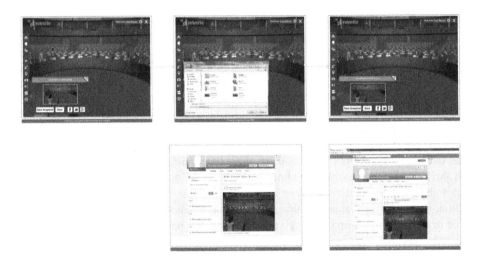

Fig. 1. One of the storyboards used to simulate the missing tasks in the EU parliament scenario.

The video prototype was used to demonstrate the behaviour of the ECA. A series of videos using Living Actor Presenter[4] have been created, featuring an ECA following the same script the autonomous guide agent would use in the VE. The videos were then assembled into an interactive video application using Articulate Storyline [19] and were displayed on the lab's main TV. The experimenter played the videos as required by the relevant tasks. A particularly challenging behaviour of the autonomous agent was its attention-grabbing capabilities. A video where the Living Actor agent displayed a similar to REVERIE agent attention-grabbing behaviour was included in the video application. The video was played as required by the experimenter when he thought that one or more of the evaluators were not paying attention to the guided tour.

3.3   The Evaluators

In total, nine evaluators reviewed the prototypes for both educational scenarios. Three of the evaluators participated in a pilot review of the prototypes to validate the design of the study. Those reviewers completed the same tasks as the rest of the users but spent

---

[4] https://www.livingactor.com/Presenter/

more time in the laboratory. They provided valuable feedback on the process and identified a range of bugs with the REVERIE prototypes that were logged and corrected prior to the main study. The remaining six evaluators were divided into two groups of three and had a variety of technical and media backgrounds. None of the evaluators had a HCI or cognitive science background. Finally, the evaluators had no previous experience using VR prototypes (Table 1).

Table 1. The group of evaluators who reviewed the two educational scenarios

Evaluators	Profile	Role	REVERIE prototype
Evaluator 1	Media producer	Teacher	Social networking & Virtual gallery
Evaluator 2	Media producer	Student	Social networking & Virtual gallery
Evaluator 3	Media producer	Student	Social networking & Virtual gallery
Evaluator 4	PSHE teacher	Teacher	EU parliament
Evaluator 5	Office assistant	Student	EU parliament
Evaluator 6	Marketing/Research assistant	Student	EU Parliament

3.4   The Modified Cognitive Walkthrough Method

The modified cognitive walkthrough method [6] starts with an analysis of the required tasks, where the experimenter specifies a sequence of actions required by the user to complete the task and the system response(s) to those actions. The evaluators' walk through the steps, asking themselves the four questions below. Evaluators were required to answer the questions for each step of the assigned tasks. Answers to the questions have a binary (Yes/No) format, but evaluators are also required to comment on their preferred answer. Finally, the method required evaluators to indicate on a scale (0% to 100%) the likelihood users will have problems doing the right thing according to the requirements of each of the following question:

1. Will the user realistically trying to do this action?

   This question finds problems with interfaces that make unrealistic assumptions about the level of knowledge or experience that users have).

2. Is the control or the action visible?

   This question identifies problems with hidden controls (e.g., buried too deep within the navigation system) and controls that are not standard and unintuitive).

3. Is there a strong link between the control and the action?

   This question highlights problems with ambiguous or jargon terms, or with other controls that look like a better choice. It also finds problems with actions that are physically difficult to execute.

4. Is feedback appropriate?

   This question helps you find problems when feedback is missing, or easy to miss, or too brief, poorly worded, inappropriate or ambiguous.

We adapted the method by:

- providing additional text explanations under each question to guide evaluators on the kind of input expected (see above);
- providing evaluators with personas representing different users of the VR prototypes;
- integrating tasks into use cases reflecting the requirements of each educational scenario.

We designed the personas based on the initial user requirements gathered during the early stages of the REVERIE project [20]. We gathered quantitative data from 277 users using an online survey with questions about various aspects of the REVERIE system (e.g., avatar types, rendering style, the social network supported etc.). We also collected qualitative data from potential users from two informal usability inspections. The first inspection took place at the Education Innovation Conference & Exhibition in Manchester, UK, in February 2014 [21]. We asked teachers and students to review videos showing the REVERIE prototypes in action and to provide feedback on the camera. The second inspection took place internally with two of the REVERIE partners. We invited various evaluators (e.g., teachers and IT specialists) to use a preliminary version of the VR prototypes and to provide feedback about their usability and usefulness in education.

3.5   The Evaluation Sessions

In each group, two evaluators reviewed the tasks from a student perspective, while one expert from a teacher perspective. We provided evaluators a standard cognitive walkthrough form to use. The form listed the tasks evaluators had to review and for each task the tools they had to use to review the tasks (e.g., software prototype, storyboards or Internet browser). At the beginning of each session, we provided training on the use of the CW method. The training session lasted 10 min (instructions and Q&A) and it was deemed necessary as no evaluator had prior experience in evaluating VR prototypes. In total evaluators analysed 36 tasks grouped into four categories:

1. user authentication and social networking tasks (11 tasks);
   The tasks included in this category, 4 tasks for teachers and 7 for students are related to the way users authenticate their credentials on the system as well as its social networking functionalities.
2. REVERIE Avatar Authoring Tool (RAAT) (6 tasks);
   The tasks included in this category referrer to REVERIE's integrated tool (RAAT) [17] for customising avatars, such as modifying the avatar's body features and mapping the user's face on an avatar.
3. EU parliament scenario (20 tasks);
   This category includes 9 tasks for teachers and 11 tasks for students, and it refers to what users (teachers and students) can do in the virtual parliament scenario.
4. Virtual 3D gallery (4 tasks);

This category includes 2 tasks for teachers and 2 for students and it refers to what users (teachers and students) can do in the Virtual Gallery scenario. It includes tasks such as exploring the Virtual Gallery to find a given object. Other tasks include rating the performance of a presenter using the system's voting features.

We asked the first group of evaluators to review the first two tasks using the virtual 3D gallery scenario. The second group of evaluators reviewed the EU Parliament scenario. The set-up of the study was the same for both groups. Each expert conducted the walkthrough of the VR prototypes individually. This was done to ensure an independent and unbiased evaluation from each evaluator for the prototypes.

4   Results and Discussion

After the walkthrough was completed, evaluators were asked to participate in a debriefing session to have their findings aggregated. The session was moderated by an external group moderator. We identified 47 usability problems with the VR prototypes. Most problems refer to the virtual parliament rather than the Virtual Gallery. This was to be expected as the Virtual Gallery scenario is much simpler to use. The user requirements were grouped into six macro-topics as appear in Table 2 below.

Table 2. User requirements classification

Topic	Requirements	Explanation
User authentication services and Social Networking integration	14	Requirements in this section refer to how users log-in to the VR prototypes and its social networking functionalities
Design of the Graphical User Interface (GUI)	12	Requirements in this section refer to the UI design of the VR prototypes & the RAAT tool
Media content	3	Requirements in this section refer to media content (external video links and 3D graphical assets) used in by the VR prototypes
Avatars	1	Requirements in this section refer to the appearance of the avatars and the way they interact in the virtual environment
Characteristics and functionality of REVERIE's virtual environments	7	Requirements in this section refer to the appearance and usability of the VR prototypes
User-user and user-agent virtual interaction features	10	Requirements in this section refer to how the VR prototypes enable and facilitate interactions among users and with the autonomous agent

44% of the generated requirements were considered as essential, while 28% as useful improvements and 28% as future improvements to the VR prototypes. In addition, none of the problems discovered were discharged, or considered to have a cosmetic nature.

Table 3. Distribution of usability problems identified by each method by a number of problems

Type of problems	Our approach	Two-stage hybrid	Multiple stage hybrid
User interface	26	36	38
In-world	21	5	44

Although referring to different systems, it is possible to draw some conclusions about the performance of our approach compared to the literature (see Table 3). Specifically, the performance of our approach is comparable to a two-stage hybrid method [5], but not the multiple stage hybrid method [12]. It also captures a similar type of usability problems covering both 'in-world' interactions and in the user interface of the two VR prototypes. Future work aims to validate these findings by comparing the performance of the three methods using the REVERIE prototypes.

4.1 Likelihood of Usability Problems

Evaluators rated on a scale (0%–100%) the likelihood a user would have a problem conducting an action in every step of the process. Below we present the average scores of the four questions of the modified cognitive walkthrough method (see Sect. 3.5) per task for the second group of evaluators. These were the evaluators who reviewed the EU parliament scenario. Table 4, shows the average scores of the teachers, while Table 5 the average scores of the students. Students had two more tasks to complete with the assistance of their teachers (see task 10 and task 11 in Table 5).

Table 4. Average scores assigned to each task by the teacher of the second group

No.	Tasks	Average scores	Std. deviation
1	Login to REVERIE using your TrueTube credentials	12.5%	25
2	Select the first educational scenario	12.5%	25
3	Select one of REVERIE's standard avatars	12.5%	14.4
4	Adjust the camera viewpoint to your preferred angle	50%	57.7
5	Explore the 3D environment	62.5%	43.3
6	Participate in the guided tour of the parliament	37.5%	14.4
7	Start a debate on the topic "Multicultural London" with students	25%	0
8	Debate on the topic "Multicultural London" with students	43.75%	37.5
9	Ask students to rate the debate	6.25%	12.5

It is evident that the teacher thought that users would most likely have problems with the majority of the tasks in the virtual EU Parliament. However, he scored some tasks lower than others which shows that he considered the importance of addressing specific usability problems more urgently than others. A particularly concerning task was number five ("Explore the 3D environment"). The teacher thought that there is a 62.5% likelihood that users will have problems with this task. Examples of usability problems teachers identified in this task were:

- the difficulty to accurately navigate the avatar in the environment using the navigation support tool;
- the difficulty to recognise the keyboard shortcut key ("M") for activating the on-screen menu.

Table 5. Average scores assigned to each task by the students of the second group

No.	Tasks	Student one	Std. deviation	Student two	Std. deviation
1	Login to REVERIE using your TrueTube credentials	44%	12.5	31%	24
2	Select the first educational scenario	63%	14.4	25%	35.3
3	Select one of REVERIE's standard avatars	56%	12.5	31%	37.5
4	Adjust the camera viewpoint to your preferred angle	44%	37.5	69%	47.3
5	Explore the 3D environment	62%	47.8	62%	48
6	Participate in the guided tour of the parliament	50%	20.4	31%	12.5
7	Test the autonomous agent's attention-grabbing features	12.5%	25	31%	12.5
8	Take a seat in the front row of the parliament	62%	25	25%	20.4
9	Debate on the topic "Multicultural London"	37%	14.4	44%	24
10	Rate the debate on "Multicultural London"	44%	12.5	12.5%	25
11	Share a snapshot of the 3D world on Facebook	37.5%	25	50%	41

As opposed to the teacher, students scored all tasks higher, which show that they considered the usability problems found in all tasks as equally important. Students agreed with the teacher on task five ("Explore the 3D environment"). They thought that there is a 62% likelihood that users will have problems with this task. Examples of usability problems students identified in this task were:

- the fact that the users cannot view 360° around their avatar (e.g., behind you or left/right);

- it is standard in games to use WASD keys instead of a map to navigate in the environment;
- there is a need for system support (on screen information) on how to find the navigation system.

Students disagreed with the teacher in the first three tasks. They thought that there is a 42% probability that users will have problems with these tasks. Examples of problems students identified with these tasks were:

- no system response upon successful login to the system;
- the difference between "Avatar Library" and "Avatar Authoring Tool" is not clear;
- there is no description of what each scenario (entertainment and education) is about.

The teacher also highlighted several problems with these tasks. However, they thought that the likelihood of users having problems with these tasks is low (12.5%). Nevertheless, fixing navigation and UI problems in the VR prototype were given a priority in the next design iteration of the prototypes. Finally, we measured the agreement between students and teacher scores (only for the same tasks) by computing the intra-class correlation coefficient (ICC). The ICC score was 0.367 with 95% CI (−.461, 0.823) indicating poor agreement. This shows that the groups did not assess the likelihood of users having problems with each task consistently. A review of the data reveals that this is due to the number of problems each expert identified for each task. The use of personas also had an impact on the type and number of usability problems evaluators identified. Although we expect evaluators to identify different usability problems, poor disagreement reveals that they may not had the same level of understanding in the use of the method. Finally, the likelihood scores can significantly inform the process of requirements prioritisation. We recommend a method consisting of the following steps:

1. assign a weight for the importance of teacher and students likelihood scores, provided that both of the REVERIE prototypes were designed to be teacher-driven experiences, this weight should be 60/40;
2. recalculate the likelihood scores based on the assigned weights;
3. convert the likelihood score to a custom nine-point scale (0 = not important, 8 = extremely important) inspired by the planning poker agile method [22];
4. assign as the score to each requirement the average of the group.

For example, for Task 1 (see Table 4) the teacher will be assigned a score of 7%. Each student will be assigned 18% and 12% respectively. This gives an average score for the group of 2 on the 9-point scale. Any requirements matching the particular task should be assigned a score of 3 indicating moderate importance. This score can be further adjusted by the project partners to account for time and budget constraints. In the REVERIE project, we considered feedback only from the project partners and prioritised requirements according to the MoSCoW prioritisation [23] method. Our proposed method is better as it takes into consideration input from multiple stakeholders.

5   Conclusion

The main goal of this study was to test the effectiveness of the modified cognitive walkthrough method and hybrid VR prototypes approach in eliciting requirements for the design of VR prototypes of the REVERIE project. The approach was found to be highly useful predominantly due to its ability to capture a high-quality set of requirements in a cost-effective manner. The modified cognitive walkthrough captured several usability problems covering all aspects of the VR prototypes. The identified problems were into six clusters covering both 'in-world' interactions and UI (e.g., the design of the UI, navigation in the VE). Despite early design, the hybrid prototypes enabled evaluators to review the usability of the VR prototypes holistically. A comparison of the performance of our approach with the literature shows that it is slightly better than the two-stage hybrid method, but worse than the multiple-stage hybrid method. However, additional work is needed to compare the performance of the three methods using the REVERIE prototypes. We therefore conclude that our approach may provide a viable alternative to use in the evaluation of early-design VR prototypes when it is required (e.g., when the expertise needed to use a hybrid or a multiple-stage method is not available).

The first avenue for future work is to compare the performance of our approach to the two-stage hybrid and multiple stage hybrid methods using the REVERIE prototypes. We hope to validate that the performance of our approach is better or comparable to two-stage hybrid methods and to strengthen the conclusion above. Then, we plan to review the training we provide to evaluators on the use of the method. An instructional video at the beginning of each session holds the potential to significantly strengthen the evaluation consistency among evaluators. We would also like to explore increasing the participating stakeholders (e.g., developers) to the evaluation process to realise a more pluralistic walkthrough [24]. This is particularly important for R&D prototypes like REVERIE where the focus is on technological innovation, as it may teach technical people (e.g., developers, managers) to be more open to user experience requirements. Finally, we would like to apply our proposed requirement prioritisation method to real-world projects and gather feedback on its usefulness from stakeholders.

Acknowledgements. The research that led to this paper was supported in part by the European Commission under the Contract FP7-ICT-287723 REVERIE.

References

1. Bellwood, P., Neuhaus, P., Juhra, C.: Adapting usability testing techniques to gather user requirements: an illustrative proposal. Stud. Health Technol. Inf. **164**, 213–218 (2011)
2. Standardization, I.O.f.: Ergonomics of human-system interaction, Part 210: Human-Centred Design for Interactive Systems, ed, ISO 9241-210
3. Bowman, D.A., Gabbard, J.L., Hix, D.: A survey of usability evaluation in virtual environments: classification and comparison of methods, presence: teleoper. Virtual Environ. **11**, 404–424 (2002)
4. Kaur, D.: A Usability Evaluation Method for Virtual Reality User Interfaces (2018)

5. Sawyerr, W., Brown, E., Hobbs, M.: Using a hybrid method to evaluate the usability of a 3D virtual world user interface. In: 2nd International Conference on Human Computer Interaction & Learning Technologies (ICHCILT 2013) Proceedings, Abu Dhabi (2013). https://goo.gl/TTSbzC. last accessed 14 May 2019

6. Bremin, S.: Rapid evaluation of TV interaction devices using a Cognitive Walkthrough method (2011)

7. Fechteler, P., Hilsmann, A., Eisert, P., Broeck, S.V., Stevens, C., Wall, J.: A framework for realistic 3D tele-immersion. In: 6th International Conference on Computer Vision/Computer Graphics Collaboration Techniques and Applications Proceedings, Berlin, Germany (2013)

8. Wall, J., Izquierdo, E., Argyriou, L., Monaghan, D.S., Connor, N.E.O., Poulakos, S.: REVERIE: Natural human interaction in virtual immersive environments. In: 2014 IEEE International Conference on Image Processing (ICIP), pp. 2165–2167 (2014)

9. Sutcliffe, A., Kaur, D.K.: Evaluating the usability of virtual reality user interfaces, vol. 19 (2000)

10. Rusu, C., Muñoz, R., Roncagliolo, S., Rudloff, S., Rusu, V., Figueroa, A.: Usability Heuristics for Virtual Worlds (2011)

11. Muñoz, R., Barcelos, T., Chalegre, V.: Defining and Validating Virtual Worlds Usability Heuristics. In: 30th International Conference of the Chilean Computer Science Society, pp. 171–178 (2011)

12. Alencar, M.F.C., Raposo, A.B., Barbosa, S.D.J.: Composition of HCI evaluation methods for hybrid virtual environments. In: 2011 ACM Symposium on Applied Computing, TaiChung, Taiwan (2011)

13. Gabbard, J., Hix, D.: A Taxonomy of Usability Characteristics in Virtual Environments, PhD thesis (1999)

14. Anders Ericsson, K., Herber, A.S.: Protocol Analysis: Verbal Reports as Data. MIT Press, Cambridge (2018)

15. Goodman, E., Kuniavsky, M., Moed, A.: Observing the user experience: a practitioner's guide to user research (Second Edition). IEEE Trans. Prof. Commun. 56, 260–261 (2013)

16. deSouza, C.S.: The Semiotic Engineering of Human-Computer Interaction (Acting with Technology). MIT Press, Cambridge (2005)

17. Apostolakis K.C., Daras, P.: RAAT - The reverie avatar authoring tool. In: 18th International Conference on Digital Signal Processing (DSP), 1–6 (2013)

18. Kuijk, F., Apostolakis, K.C., Daras, P., Ravenet, B., Wei, H., Monaghan, D.S.: Autonomous agents and avatars in REVERIE's virtual environment. In: Proceedings of the 20th International Conference on 3D Web Technology, Heraklion, Crete, Greece (2015)

19. Articulate 360, ed: Articulate Global Inc. (2017)

20. Vet, J.d., Alfonso, D.: D2.1 Initial version of User Requirements Specification, European Commision (2012)

21. CTVC, REVERIE Informal Usability Inspection. In: Education Innovation Conference and Exhibition (2014)

22. Calefato, F., Lanubile, F.: A Planning Poker Tool for Supporting Collaborative Estimation in Distributed Agile Development (2011)

23. Clegg, D., Barker, R.: Case Method Fast-Track: A Rad Approach. Addison-Wesley Longman Publishing Co., Inc., Boston (1994)

24. Hollingsed, T., Novick, D.G.: Usability inspection methods after 15 years of research and practice. In: the 25th Annual ACM International Conference on Design of Communication Proceedings, El Paso, Texas, USA (2007)

Author Index

Printed in the United States
By Bookmasters